Mental Disorders, Mental Illness and the Family Court

A Reference Guide for Non-Medical Professionals

Mental Disorders, Mental Illness and the Family Court

A Reference Guide for Non-Medical Professionals

Dr Joan Rutherford FRCPsych

Jennifer Cross JP CQSW

Dr Stephanie Tolan MRCPCH

Dr Andy Cohen MRCPsych

Bloomsbury Professional

LONDON • DUBLIN • EDINBURGH • NEW YORK • NEW DELHI • SYDNEY

BLOOMSBURY PROFESSIONAL
Bloomsbury Publishing Plc
50 Bedford Square, London, WC1B 3DP, UK
1385 Broadway, New York, NY 10018, USA
29 Earlsfort Terrace, Dublin 2, Ireland

British Library Cataloguing-in-Publication Data

A catalogue record for this book is available from the British Library.

ISBN: PB: 978 1 52652 189 7
Epdf: 978 1 52652 190 3
Epub: 978 1 52652 191 0

Typeset by Evolution Design & Digital Ltd (Kent)

Foreword

The publication of *Mental Disorders, Mental Illness and the Family Court* should be welcomed by all those who work in the field of Family Law. It is, sadly, commonplace for one or more of the family members in family proceedings, or for a child who is the subject of proceedings, to be suffering from mental ill health. Over the course of a career professionals and the judiciary are likely to gather a good working knowledge of a range of mental health conditions, but, by its nature, such insight is likely to be patchy and may well be out of date. Those starting out in their professional practice, whether in social work or the law, are unlikely to have a readily accessible knowledge base and may only pick up information on a case-by-case basis. This less than satisfactory way of accumulating essential professional understanding in relation to mental health should now be a thing of the past. The publication of this book provides what is literally an 'off the shelf' comprehensive resource, in which all of the commonly encountered mental health conditions which may affect adults or children are described in clear, non-medical, terms and in an intelligently ordered format.

In addition to readily understandable descriptions, the authors offer 'Advice to the Family Court' with respect to each condition. This, in addition to the 'Ten Tips for the Family Court' with respect to adult mental health, and the library of illustrative case studies in the Appendices, demonstrates that the focus throughout is on helping the reader, not only to understand all relevant aspects of mental illness, but also to understand how that knowledge may impact upon any particular court case.

Now that this book is available, it is easy to see that it fills a gap in the resources available to Family Justice professionals that has existed for many years. Its publication is therefore most welcome and I predict that it will soon become a recognisable presence on the bookshelves of many.

The Rt Hon Sir Andrew McFarlane
President of the Family Division
27 September 2021

Preface

Mental Disorders and the Family Court will provide a useful guide for everyone working in the family law jurisdiction. The book examines the prevalence, causes, symptoms, treatment and outcomes of a wide range of mental disorders in children, young people and adults, and provides practical advice relevant to both public and private Family Court cases in England and Wales. It also covers issues of vital importance to the court's work – from the nature of bonding and attachment, to the parenting of children who present risks, to the interplay between different disorders and the impact of mental disorders on family dynamics.

The authors bring unique perspectives on child and adult mental disorders. In compiling this guide, they have drawn on their wealth of experience and their extensive professional backgrounds in psychiatry, paediatric medicine, social work and the Family Court. As well as covering potential treatments for mental disorders, they consider the legal aspects of treatment in relation to the Mental Health Act 1983 and the Children Act 1989. Anonymised sample case studies show the impact of different disorders in real-life situations and provide a useful training resource. The guide includes hyperlinks to further helpful information.

Mental Disorders and the Family Court is presented in comprehensible language and an easy-to-navigate layout. It has been compiled to assist family court judges and magistrates, Cafcass officers, family justices' clerks, family court barristers and solicitors, children and family social workers, family mediation professionals, CAMHS teams members, independent social workers, expert witnesses, and the general reader with an interest in mental disorders and the family court jurisdiction.

This book should be read in conjunction with the Equal Treatment Bench Book (Appendix B Disability Glossary, particularly 'Impairments and Reasonable adjustments'). https://www.judiciary.uk/announcements/equal-treatment-bench-book-new-edition/

Although the publication covers the main mental disorders in children, young people and adults, it is not intended to be exhaustive.

Dr Joan Rutherford FRCPsych
Jennifer Cross JP CQSW
Dr Stephanie Tolan MRCPCH
Dr Andy Cohen MRCPsych
October 2021

Acknowledgements

Thanks to the following for contributions:

Jacob Horner BSc, intern with First-tier Tribunal, Mental Health, Dr David Rhinds, Dr Mary Mitchell, Professor Louis Appleby, Dr Henrietta Bowden-Jones, Professor Mary Robertson, Dr Joan Brunton, Mr Peter Freeman and Dr Maria McLauchlan

And special thanks to Derek Cross of Cross Publishing Services for conceiving the idea and for his contribution in developing the contents of the book so that it was ready for publication, and also thanks to Elyssa Campbell-Barr for copyediting the manuscript.

Author biographies

Dr Joan Rutherford FRCPsych
Joan became Chief Medical Member, First Tier Tribunal (Mental Health) in 2010, and is also an honorary consultant at South London and Maudsley NHS Foundation Trust. Her post combines the position of doctor at the Mental Health Tribunal with a management and training role and she is a member of the tribunal's child and adolescent mental health services panel (CAMHS). Previously, she was a consultant psychiatrist at Surrey and Borders Partnership NHS Foundation Trust from 1992–99, then at South West London and St George's Mental Health NHS Trust from 1999–2010. Joan co-authored the eBook *Mental Disorders – Information for Mental Health Tribunal Members,* which was made available to all judicial members of HM Courts and Tribunals Service in August 2019.

Jennifer Cross JP CQSW
Jenny worked for many years as a social worker/manager and approved mental health professional (AMHP) for an Inner London borough. She has professional experience in a variety of services including children and families, fostering and adoption, and adult services encompassing mental health. She has also been an academic tutor and practice assessor in the education and training of social workers and AMHPs. Jenny is a longstanding member of the Mental Health Tribunal and a member of the tribunal's CAMHS panel, the Care Standards Tribunal and the Upper Administrative Tribunal. She sat as a magistrate for 25 years, including in the Family Court, and has been a trustee of several mental health charities.

Dr Stephanie Tolan MRCPCH
Stephanie is a paediatric registrar in the North Central and East London Foundation School training scheme. She obtained an MA in Medical Ethics and Law from Kings College London in 2020, and is now a trainee member of the Ethics Committee at North Middlesex University Hospital NHS Trust. An active member of the London School of Paediatrics trainees' committee, Stephanie has a key role in their mentor system – The Paediatric Family – to support trainees throughout their training in London.

Dr Andy Cohen MRCPsych
Andy is a consultant child and adolescent psychiatrist at South West London and St George's Mental Health NHS Trust. He has worked in the field of child and adolescent mental health for over 20 years, the last 15 based in a busy community team in South West London. Andy has an interest in medical education and is the Programme Director for higher specialist training in child and adolescent psychiatry on the St George's training scheme.

Mental disorders and illness in children and young people

References are to page numbers

Mental disorders and illness in adults

References are to page numbers

Contents

Part I

The development of family relationships

Chapter 1

Bonding and attachment

1.01 The terms bonding and attachment are used to describe the initial connections between parents and their babies. These start whilst the baby is in the mother's womb.

When children and adults behave in ways that are damaging to themselves or others, consideration should be given as to why, before narrowing the cause to a mental disorder. It's important to understand how children develop physically, emotionally and socially, and how problems in these areas affect how they behave in childhood, and then as adults.

Bonding is the establishment of a close relationship between the parent or carer and the baby.

Attachment follows as a mutual connection between the baby and their parent(s).

Both are important as established by research undertaken by John Bowlby and Harry Harlow.

WHAT ARE BONDING AND ATTACHMENT, AND WHY ARE THEY IMPORTANT?

1.02 Disruptions in bonding and attachment can continue into adult life, leading to impulsive behaviour, problems trusting others and forming relationships and difficulties in problem-solving.

Research undertaken by the British child psychologist John Bowlby in the 1940s provided evidence that attachment is vital in a child's development. He studied orphaned and abandoned children living in institutions. He was the first to highlight the harmful effects of psycho-social deprivation, which he found led to (in his words) 'affectionless and delinquent children'. Bowlby's 1951 report for the World Health Organization was hugely influential in making institutional care for infants and children homelier and encouraging visits by parents when infants and small children were in hospital.

1.03 *Bonding and attachment*

Harry Harlow was an American psychologist who carried out experiments on baby rhesus monkeys in the 1950s and 1960s. Monkeys were used for both physiological and psychological experiments at that time as their body systems are close to those of humans. Rhesus monkeys had already been used to determine human blood groups earlier in the century.

In Harlow's experiment, the baby monkeys were separated from their mothers 6 to 12 hours after birth and placed with a model substitute. The substitutes were of two types: a wire mother or a cloth mother. The monkeys were bottle-fed. Although both groups were given sufficient milk, only the monkeys who had a soft mother, that they could cuddle, thrived.

There have been other animal experiments undertaken on rats (90 per cent of animal research is done on mice and rats). This showed that the stress response system in the brain of a young rat develops early. If the vital brain structures (the amygdala, prefrontal cortex, and hippocampus) don't connect early with the nervous system, the rat isn't able to manage stress.

DO FAILURES IN BONDING AND ATTACHMENT LEAD TO MENTAL DISORDERS?

1.03 On occasion, babies are taken into care immediately after birth, which may seem an authoritarian intervention by local authority children's services. However, it is clear that lack of bonding, deprivation and neglect can have consequences for the developing brain of the baby that cannot subsequently be undone, as demonstrated by Harlow's work with rhesus monkeys. Monkeys deprived of a mother from birth exhibited symptoms recognised by animal psychologists as anxiety and depression and displayed no interest in new things. When these monkeys were placed in a group together, they were either aggressive towards each other or avoided each other, rather than playing or play-fighting.

These behaviours observed in monkeys are recognisable and translatable to the behaviours of young children. Children who have been neglected tend to be anxious, impulsive, late-to-develop (for instance with toilet training), do poorly at school, and have difficult-to-manage behaviours. The failure of attachment can lead to an anxious-avoidant child. Typically, neglected children have a mental disorder described as a conduct disorder. Many show behaviours diagnosed later in adulthood as personality disorders.

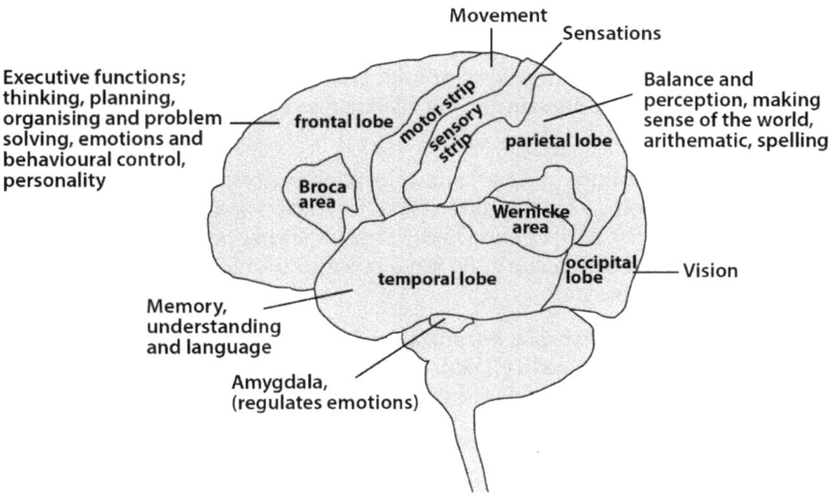

Neuroimaging in humans, which examines the brain's functioning by scanning, shows the areas affected when there are attachment problems. The brain has two hemispheres: right and left. Each hemisphere is divided into lobes. Each lobe has specific functions, and lobes on the left- and right-hand sides of the brain are different. The area of the brain that controls language is on the left in the temporal lobe and also in the parietal lobe. That is why strokes or cerebrovascular accidents in this area impair people's speech. It is the right side of the brain that is crucial to attachment.

The frontal lobe is the largest part of the brain and the last to develop and mature. The frontal lobe has many complex functions; it governs how our personality, behaviour and emotions are expressed. It is the part of the brain that controls judgement, planning and problem-solving as well as concentration and self-awareness.

The brain function of an adult or child who has not had good enough parenting differs from someone who has experienced secure attachment. The amygdala is essential for the ability to feel certain emotions and to perceive them in others. Neuroimaging studies show that a lack of connection between the frontal part of the brain and the amygdala (the area of the brain that regulates emotions) means children without a secure attachment are less able to manage their emotions, anticipate or predict consequences of their behaviour, and learn from experience.

In considering how the brain works, there are links between the areas of the brain that perceive threats and the areas that solve problems; these are called neural pathways. Neural pathways develop early – we see them form when a two- or three-year-old child learns to be able to soothe themselves when separated from their parent or carer. Neglect, abuse and inconsistent caring lead to impaired development of these links. The child cannot soothe themselves and may alternate rapidly between states of hyperarousal (fear) and withdrawal (freezing). This disorganises their ability to express or control emotions.

In adults, such emotions and behaviour result in various types of personality disorders. Terminology for the different types of personality disorders varies between the ICD-10, ICD-11 and DSM-5 classification codes. People with the types below, for instance, typically have emotions which are too intense or lack emotional response:

- **Emotionally Unstable Personality Disorder –** previously known as **Borderline Personality Disorder**, which is characterised by chaotic moods, self-harm and over-intense relationships
- **Histrionic Personality Disorder** – which manifests in constant excitement-seeking and (like emotionally unstable personality disorder) is evidence of too much emotion or poorly controlled emotion
- **Antisocial Personality Disorder** – people with this disorder tend to blame others and have little or no regard for the feelings of others, as they lacked support in learning to identify their feelings as children.

Toxins can easily damage the developing brain. Alcohol is neurotoxic, which means it damages brain cells. A mother who consumes alcohol in pregnancy risks having a baby with foetal alcohol syndrome, which means the baby has features of learning disability as well as hyperactivity and a disregard for social cues. Alcohol also affects the developing adolescent brain, so people who drink alcohol at an early age are reducing their brain's ability to mature.

When neuroimaging demonstrates the areas of the brain affected by stimulant drugs, particularly cocaine, the same areas that show attachment problems are highlighted. People with insecure attachments in childhood are more likely than those with secure attachments to become dependent on recreational (psychoactive) drugs as they grow up.

A parent or carer's ability to bond with and nurture their baby is impaired further if they have two or more mental health disorders, such as depression and personality disorder. In addition, substance abuse increases impulsive behaviour and is emotionally unavailable to the needs of others.

Note: Clearly, some parents have considerable difficulties, such as mental and physical health issues, bereavement and other caring roles (for their own parents or disabled siblings, for example) but still manage to bond successfully with their children.

Case study – Early attachment difficulties – Sara's story (see Appendix: Case studies, p 311.)

Further information

Bowlby's attachment theory

https://www.hindawi.com/journals/np/2019/1676285/

How Early Experience Shapes Human Development: The Case of Psychosocial Deprivation' by Charles A Nelson, III, Charles H Zeanah and Nathan A Fox. Neural Plasticity. 2019

https://www.ncbi.nlm.nih.gov/pmc/articles/PMC6350537/

Harlow's rhesus monkey experiments

'Affectional responses in the infant monkey' by H F Harlow and R R Zimmermann. Science. 1959. https://psycnet.apa.org/record/1960-04110-001

Brain function

https://mayfieldclinic.com/pe-anatbrain.htm

Chapter 2

Family dynamics

2.01 According to recent divorce statistics, 42 per cent of marriages in England and Wales end in divorce. Often parents come before the family law jurisdiction because they are unable to resolve an issue despite having participated in mediation.

Some parents manage a transition from living together to living apart and can be 'good enough' parents for their children, whilst others find this difficult to achieve. Parents don't have to be brilliant or perfect. According to Donald Winnicott, the British paediatrician and child analyst, parents need to be 'good enough' for a child's healthy cognitive development.

Even parents who are working together for the child's best interests may find that a child with special needs and challenges can bring them to crisis points, where they feel unable to cope.

Alternatively, there are situations of such discord or domestic abuse, where to separate the child from the family is the only solution. This chapter considers situations where the family dynamics are not helpful for the child, and what interventions can improve the experience for the child.

WHAT KIND OF FAMILY DYNAMICS MAY CAUSE PROBLEMS FOR THE CHILD?

Role reversal

2.02 This occurs when the child takes over a parental role. There may be practical reasons, such as in a migrant family where the child is the only person who speaks English well enough to communicate with authorities or in some ethnic groups in which mothers remain at home or within their own community. The same dynamic can occur when the parent is disabled, and the child becomes a carer or helper.

In these circumstances, there is a practical reason for the child's role to change. However, the child retains their identity in other settings, such as at school, in their wider family and when socialising with their peers.

Chaotic family

2.03 The term 'feral family' isn't a recognised family therapy term but was originally coined by the media to describe families without rules. Examples include: children not being educated; children spending most of their time on electronic devices; lacking self-care; eating an unhealthy diet; or having no set bedtimes.

In families that set poor boundaries, the children may appear to be out of control and meet the criteria for the diagnosis for conduct disorder. Their behaviour resembles that described by Harlow among rhesus monkeys reared without mothers when we discussed bonding and attachment in Chapter 1.

The likely explanation for such a chaotic family is that the parents themselves were not parented adequately and did not learn boundary setting; this can be a contributory factor in the development of a personality disorder. The use of alcohol and drugs increases the impulsivity and chaos of such parents. An over-liberal family may also try to parent without rules, which can again lead to the same chaos.

Certain minority groups may have cultural practices that don't adhere to UK societal norms, such as those from some Traveller communities, who allow their children to leave school at an early age, typically 11 to 13 years old. The label 'chaotic family' may be misplaced here, as the work ethic in these families is often that the girls are expected to do domestic chores in the same way as their mothers, following strict cultural rules around hygiene and the boys take on the breadwinning role with their fathers.

Enmeshed family

2.04 Family therapist, Salvador Munuchin introduced the concept of enmeshment in the 1970s. Enmeshment describes family relationships that lack boundaries such that roles and expectations are confused. The parents are overly and inappropriately reliant on their children for support and children are not allowed to become emotionally independent or separate from their parents and family members. They are emotionally fused together in an unhealthy way.

Most often, enmeshment occurs between a child and parent and may include the following signs:

- lack of appropriate privacy between parent and child;
- a child being 'best friends' with a parent;
- a parent confiding secrets to a child;
- a parent telling one child that they are the favourite;
- one child receiving special privileges from a parent;
- a parent being overly involved in their child's activities or achievements.

These circumstances may pose children with the choice of either remaining in the family and being subject to these pressures, or else – consciously or unconsciously – taking dramatic steps to free themselves from the situation.

Over-intense bonding

2.05 A close, friendly parent-child relationship is a good thing. However, when the child becomes the parent's sole emotional support and confidant, this can lead to over-intense bonding. The child is then subject to inappropriate emotional burdens. Some children cope by becoming equally dependent on the parent. The two are trapped and unable to separate, so the child cannot develop emotionally and move on to other relationships.

This dynamic is more common between mothers and daughters. It reflects a societal shift where some seem to have abandoned the traditional hierarchy of parent and child for a relationship of equals, identifying with each other more as 'BFF' (Best Friends Forever) on social media. When the boundaries of the mother-child relationship become blurred, it is unclear what behaviours are acceptable within the context of the relationship. This confusion may, in turn, lead to behaviour unrestricted by any limits on the part of either mother or child. Much conflict can arise if, for instance, the mother finds a new partner and wishes to be in the mother role again and set new rules.

Spousification

2.06 'Spousification' – also termed 'parentification' – refers to a dynamic in which parents turn to children for emotional support while ignoring the child's developmental needs. The difference between this and over-intense bonding is that it occurs mainly in mother-son relationships.

A son playing the role of a surrogate partner to his mother can feel engulfed, enmeshed, intruded upon and smothered. As a man, he may lose his sense of self, have difficulty forming romantic relationships and fail to become independent or have a family of his own.

WHAT INTERVENTIONS CAN CHANGE FAMILY DYNAMICS?

2.07 An intervention often used is family therapy. This is a form of psychotherapy that works towards reducing distress and conflict by improving interactions between family members. This approach views problems as patterns or systems that need adjusting, as opposed to viewing problems as belonging to one person. It is often referred to as a 'strength-based treatment'.

Family therapy is a talking therapy and takes place over several sessions, usually some weeks apart. The family are normally given tasks to practise between sessions. The therapy can range from counselling and advice to a more in-depth exploration of each family member's function individually and within the family.

Family therapists are trained in counselling, or specific psychological or psychoanalytical therapies. Individual family members' problems, such as depression or substance abuse, are dealt with through separate treatments, but the consequence of these issues on the family dynamics is explored.

Case study – Enmeshed family – Bea's story (see Appendix: Case studies, p 313.)

Further information

Office of National Statistics – Divorce

www.ons.gov.uk/peoplepopulationandcommunity/birthsdeathsandmarriages/divorce

Good therapy – Enmeshment

www.goodtherapy.org/blog/psychpedia/enmeshment

Relate – Understanding family dynamics

https://www.relate.org.uk/relationship-help/help-family-life-and-parenting/parenting-together/understanding-family-dynamics

Chapter 3

Overview of mental disorders in children

PREVALENCE

3.01 According to an NHS study of over 9,000 children carried out in 2017, one in eight (around 13 per cent) of 5- to 19-year-olds in the UK has at least one mental disorder. The proportion of young people reported to be affected by mental disorder varies, depending on how surveys are conducted.

A survey asking schoolchildren taking their GCSEs about anxiety had these responses:

> 'I get very anxious about exams.'
>
> 'My parents nag at me about spending time on social media, especially at night, but I need to check what other people are doing and get really good photos up...'
>
> 'I hate it when Mum and Dad argue, it makes me feel shaky, sick and anxious.'

Which of the above remarks express 'normal worries'? Do any indicate an issue of concern, bordering on 'clinical' anxiety?

THE CATEGORIES OF MENTAL DISORDERS IN CHILDREN

3.02

- **Behavioural disorders**, eg conduct disorder, attention deficit hyperactivity disorder, disinhibited attachment disorder.
- **Emotional disorders**, eg anxiety disorders, depression.

- **Development disorders**, eg autism spectrum disorders, learning disabilities.
- **Psychotic disorders**, eg schizophrenia.

BEHAVIOURAL DISORDERS

3.03 Behavioural disorders are the most common reason for referral of children and young people to Child and Adolescent Mental Health Services (CAMHS). Children diagnosed with a conduct disorder at age seven are ten times more likely to have a criminal record in adulthood. Behaviours such as conduct disorders can be displayed by children or young people because of their early experiences and are common reasons for them to be taken into care.

Children or young people can display challenging behaviours, such as conduct disorder, because of their early experiences. These behaviours can be reasons for them to be taken into care, and therefore be subject to care proceedings.

The link between conduct disorders and anxiety is interesting; the child may deal with anxiety by projecting it outwards into problem behaviour. In attention deficit hyperactivity disorder, the child often encounters difficulties due to impulsive behaviour and may become isolated from peers as they miss social cues.

Tourette's syndrome, a disorder with tics in which the child makes sudden involuntary movements or noises, may cause anxiety as the child can be isolated and bullied. When told to suppress the tics, the child's anxiety peaks.

Some childhood disorders require such support that they place an extra burden on parents, sometimes leading to a relationship breakup. These conditions can include learning disabilities, autism spectrum disorders and attention deficit hyperactivity disorder. Parental separation may cause additional mental disorders in the child, or worsen pre-existing disorders that were not as apparent before the split. But as the divorce rate in the UK is 42 per cent, clearly not every divorce produces mental disorder in the children.

EMOTIONAL DISORDERS

3.04 These are the second-most widespread group of disorders, with anxiety being the most typical presenting symptom. Around 39,000 children aged 5 to 16 in England are thought to be affected.

Their anxiety symptoms can vary depending on their situation:

- **Generalised anxiety** – Present in all situations.
- **Phobias** – Anxiety peaks with a specific situation or object, or even the thought of it.
- **Depression** – Foreboding that something terrible may happen.
- **Obsessive compulsive disorders** (OCD) – Especially when the child is stopped from their compulsive actions, as these actions reduce anxiety in the short term.
- **Eating disorders** – Especially when the child is confronted with food or prevented from vomiting or exercising.
- **Post-traumatic stress disorder** (PTSD) – Anxiety increases when the original stressor occurs or is thought to occur by the child.
- **Severe depression** – The child may experience delusions, such as being convinced of their death, or the death of family members.
- **Epilepsy** – Severe anxiety can signal a fit is imminent.

DEVELOPMENTAL DISORDERS

3.05

- **Autism spectrum disorder** (ASD) – New situations and changes to routine can cause such anxiety that the child has a 'meltdown'.
- **Gender dysphoria** (GD) – The child suffers severe distress and anxiety as they are forced to behave in an allocated birth gender role which does not feel right to them.
- **Learning disability** (LD) – For children with a learning disability, new situations can be difficult. Comorbidity (having more than one mental disorder) is high.

PSYCHOTIC DISORDERS

3.06

- **Psychosis** – Hallucinations or delusions cause severe anxiety.
- **Schizophrenia** – Paranoia and hearing voices are very distressing experiences.
- **Bipolar affective disorder** – The child may have unusual shifts in mood, energy and activity levels. Anxiety may be absent in a manic phase, but severe in a depressed state.

HOW MENTAL DISORDERS IN CHILDREN ARE DIAGNOSED

3.07 Disorders are diagnosed by clinicians referring to one of two diagnostic manuals: either the International Classification of Disease (ICD), which is mainly used in Europe; or the Diagnostic and Statistical Manual (DSM), which is mainly used in America. The 11th version of the ICD (ICD-11) is in operation from January 2022. The current edition of DSM is version five, known as DSM-5.

In both manuals each disorder is given a specific code. This classification by code is useful as a way of consistently linking symptoms to a specific disorder and matching the disorder to a specific evidenced-based treatment. For example, schizophrenia is coded as 6A20 in ICD-11 and as 295.90 in DSM-5.

SEVERE MENTAL DISORDERS IN CHILDREN

3.08 The following are the most severe mental disorders in children and adolescents that require specialist input, including inpatient psychiatric treatment, from Child and Adolescent Mental Health Services (CAMHS). These disorders are not common; fewer than one in 200 children are admitted during their childhood for treatment of a mental disorder.

The disorders in this group are:

- **Psychosis**
- **Pervasive arousal withdrawal syndrome**

  (PAWS – formerly known as pervasive refusal syndrome)

Psychosis is more common in boys, while adjustment disorders, anorexia nervosa and PAWS are commonest in girls. All disorders are complicated further by drug abuse.

12 points about mental disorders in children and adolescents

1 Symptoms of mental disorder are not always as apparent as in adults. Depression in young people often presents as anger, as well as the more usual signs, such as poor or excessive sleep or appetite, weight loss, and or reduced contact with friends.

2 Unclear symptoms can delay help being sought by the young person, and by their family and friends. Delay in seeking advice may also be an issue in some ethnic groups which attach a greater stigma to mental illness.

3 There can be long waiting times for outpatient assessment by Child and Adolescent Mental Health Services (CAMHS). There are also long waits for psychological treatment in many areas of the UK.

4 Many specialist hospital CAMHS inpatient services are situated far from the family home.

5 The young person may agree to accept help but then struggle with this. For example, with anorexia, the young person may agree to voluntary hospital admission but then cannot agree to weight gain, and so detention under the Mental Health Act (MHA) is necessary.

6 In CAMHS patients who are on a section of the MHA, there is often more than one diagnosis – for example, anorexia and adjustment disorder, or psychosis and autism spectrum disorder. This dual diagnosis means the child's illness is too challenging to be managed at home by parents and carers.

7 Hallucinations may be the result of post-traumatic stress disorder or an attachment disorder, rather than psychosis.

8 Bullying has a severe effect on the mental health of children, especially those who are vulnerable.

9 Poor maternal and paternal mental health is associated with poor outcomes in children, but not all children whose parents have mental health problems are at risk. Sociocultural contexts and psychological processes interact and serve as either protective factors or risk factors for the mental health of parents and children. Often there are protective factors provided by another family member, typically a grandparent. Loss of this person, whether through bereavement, dementia

or separation, can have a significant impact on the child. Other protective factors can include schooling and clubs or activities.

10 Self-harm can escalate with any changes, such as approaching discharge from hospital where anxiety is increased. Discharge care plans need to consider how to manage short-term and long-term risks carefully.

11 Features of borderline/emotionally unstable personality disorder can present from a young age and are generally referred to as adjustment disorders by CAMHS clinicians. Often a clear diagnosis of personality disorder is not made until the age of 18, although ICD-11 allows a diagnosis of Personality Disorder to be made at any age – there is no lower limit. Some behaviours are normal features of adolescence – rebellion, anxiety, preoccupation with sex or self-image, experimentation with drugs, wild ideas, tantrums and outbursts, for example. Others may be related to relationship and family difficulties. Reasons for a personality disorder diagnosis *not* being made include the hope that the child may mature and their problem behaviour lessen. There can be a stigma attached to a diagnosis of personality disorder, which in adult psychiatry often has a poor response to treatment, poor prognosis and thus negative connotations.

12 If childhood disorders are not treated, they often continue into adulthood in a different form. Ongoing conduct disorder is associated with the onset of sociopathic personality disorder. Depression and anxiety may remain and be expressed in the range of adult disorders.

In the following chapters, four categories of mental disorders in children – **Behavioural disorders in children**, **Emotional disorders in children**, **Developmental disorders in children** and **Psychotic disorders in children** – are identified and discussed in more detail. Mental disorders in children can be complex, and diagnostically may involve more than one disorder.

For each disorder the following will be considered:

- Prevalence
- Symptoms and behaviour
- Causes

- Treatment and prognosis
- Likely outcomes in adulthood
- Information for the Family Court

Where case studies are included to illustrate particular issues, they have been anonymised.

Further information

NHS – Mental health of children and young people in England

https://dera.ioe.ac.uk/32622/1/MHCYP%202017%20Summary.pdf

Mental Health Foundation – Children and young people

https://www.mentalhealth.org.uk/a-to-z/c/children-and-young-people

NHS – Children and young people's mental health services (CYPMHS)

https://www.nhs.uk/using-the-nhs/nhs-services/mental-health-services/child-and-adolescent-mental-health-services-camhs/

Young Minds – Mental disorders

https://youngminds.org.uk

Chapter 4

Child and Adolescent Mental Health Services (CAMHS)

(See also **Chapter 19** Reports and Assessments and the Family Court.)

4.01 Child and Adolescent Mental Health Services (CAMHS) are NHS services that assess and treat children and young people with emotional, behavioural and mental health difficulties. It is also known in some settings as the Children and Young People Mental Health Service (CYPMHS).

These services were established in 1995. Before this, child psychiatry services were provided in Child Guidance Clinics and Child Behaviour Clinics.

CAMHS is structured in four tiers according to the seriousness of the child or young person's condition. A child or young person is defined as those aged under 18. Although CAMHS have provided a service for children and young people up to the age of 18, there is a growing recognition of the challenges faced by young adults in transitioning into adult services. The NHS Long Term Plan (published in 2019) recognises the need to support young adults appropriately. There is a commitment to implement new approaches to mental health services for young adults, with a comprehensive offer for 0–25-year-olds reaching across mental health services for children, young people and adults.

The support from CAMHS covers problems including:

- depression
- eating problems
- low self-esteem
- relationship problems
- anxiety and phobias
- obsessions and compulsions
- sleep difficulties
- self-harming

- suicidal behaviour
- violent and angry behaviour
- the effects of abuse and traumatic events
- gender dysphoria
- substance misuse
- early-onset psychosis.

CAMHS also covers serious mental health disorders such as psychosis, bipolar affective disorder, schizophrenia and anorexia nervosa. In some areas, the service encompasses developmental disorders such as autism and attention deficit hyperactivity disorder, but services will vary from one area to another.

Each CAMHS team focuses on the needs of children and young people. They assess, diagnose and treat those experiencing emotional, behavioural and mental health difficulties and offer support to families. Usually, a child or young person is referred to CAMHS by their GP or their school for an assessment. Referrals may also be made by other agencies and professionals, such as social workers. More recently, CAMHS teams are accepting self-referrals from young people and their parents or carers.

Within the tiered model of CAMHS, young people are allocated according to perceived need or complexity. Many services are beginning to move away from this 'tiered' approach towards more integrated care models.

THE CAMHS FOUR-TIERED MODEL

4.02

Tier 1 – These are universal services involved with early intervention and prevention. They offer general advice and treatment for those children and young people with less severe mental health problems. The service is mostly provided by:

- GPs
- health visitors
- children's centres
- school nurses
- teachers
- social workers
- youth justice workers and voluntary agencies.

These services are not primarily delivered as part of a mental health service but are involved with the assessment and or support of children and young people experiencing emotional and mental health problems. They contribute towards mental health promotion, identify problems early in the child's development and, if necessary, refer them to more specialist services. Most of their work that they do with young people and their families is done through outpatient appointments, while the young person continues to live at home.

Tier 2 – These services are for children and young people with less severe problems, or who are within specific groups and at increased risk of developing mental health problems. Services are delivered by a range of statutory and voluntary agencies, offering consultation, assessment, short-term interventions and joint work. The services are provided by specialist primary mental health practitioners who at Tier 2 level, tend to be CAMHS specialists, working in teams in the community and primary care settings (although many will also work as part of Tier 3 services).

The services can include, for example:

- mental health professionals employed to deliver primary mental health work; and
- psychologists and counsellors working in GP practices, paediatric clinics, schools and youth services.

Tier 2 practitioners offer consultation to families and other practitioners. They identify severe or complex needs requiring more specialist intervention, assessment (which may lead to treatment at a different tier), and training to practitioners at Tier 1 level.

Tier 3 – These services are for children and young people with moderate to severe mental health difficulties that require the input of a specialist CAMHS team. They are delivered by a multi-disciplinary team of CAMHS professionals, usually working in a community mental health team or in a child and adolescent psychiatric outpatient service.

Team members include:

- child and adolescent psychiatrists
- social workers
- clinical child psychologists
- community psychiatric nurses
- child psychotherapists
- family therapists
- occupational therapists
- speech and language therapists
- art, music, and drama therapists.

Tier 4 – These are highly specialised treatment services for those with severe mental health problems that require intensive interventions. The tier includes both day and in-patient hospital treatment, and some specialist outpatient services.

These are generally services for the small number of children and young people who are at the greatest risk of declining mental health or serious self-harm; who may require a period of intensive input for assessment and treatment. The service may include treatment for eating disorders, gender dysphoria, learning disability and autism spectrum disorder.

Team members come from the same professional groups as listed for Tier 3. A consultant child and adolescent psychiatrist or clinical psychologist are likely to have clinical responsibility for overseeing the assessment, treatment and care of each patient.

CAMHS TREATMENTS AND THERAPIES

4.03 The CAMHS approach to treatment is based on a combination of medical and psychological interventions. This is different from adult mental health, where the primary model of intervention is medical. Generally, the interventions and treatments available differ according to the level of the tier delivering the service. In Tiers 3 and 4, the intervention will usually involve family therapy, work with parents and work with the child, which can be a combination of psychological and pharmacological interventions and approaches. Interventions such as counselling and psychotherapy are tailored to the young person's needs and their stage of development.

Assessment – Treatment interventions for the child or young person will always be considered in the context of their 'system'; that is their family, peers and community influences. A full developmental history is taken of the child and their family. This puts into context the individual in relation to their developmental experiences and environmental factors, to help understand their behaviour and other presentations.

Interventions – An essential part of every intervention is the development of a therapeutic relationship between the young person and the professional supporting them, providing a person-centred approach, alongside the treatment or intervention. Young people often find it difficult to understand or recognise their feelings, or are reluctant to talk, so informal interventions such as art and drama therapy, narrative therapy or animal-assisted therapy may be used in all tiers of CAMHS. In the case of younger children, play therapy can help the child feel safe enough to explore their feelings through play.

Behavioural therapy, such as cognitive behavioural therapy (CBT), is widely used in CAMHS. This treatment focuses on the problem as identified by the child or young person, not as others may see it and is an effective way of helping them to understand and manage unhelpful behaviours. Rapid eye movement desensitisation and reprocessing (EMDR) is a form of psychotherapy using rhythmic eye movements to dampen the power of traumatic memories and is particularly effective in treating post-traumatic stress disorder (PTSD). Family therapy is a psychological counselling approach used in CAMHS to help families improve communication and resolve conflicts.

Medication – In CAMHS, medication is used together with psychological interventions. Medical practitioners such as GPs and child and adolescent psychiatrists will make a medical diagnosis and are able to prescribe medication. In some circumstances, suitably qualified nurses may also prescribe medication. They choose medicines with the aim of influencing the child or young person's psychological and mental state, bringing about changes in mood and behaviour. The medication most prescribed is to treat ADHD, depression and anxiety. Antipsychotic medication may be used for the management of aggressive behaviour and conduct disorder.

Information for the Family Court

4.04 A number of the children and young people involved in Family Court proceedings will have come into contact with CAMHS services; possibly more so in public law work, where the local authority brings proceedings. CAMHS professionals, usually child and adolescent psychiatrists and psychologists, may be asked by the court to provide an expert witness report. Their input can make a significant contribution in complex cases where issues are finely balanced.

Further information

NHS – Children and young people's mental health services (CYPMHS)

https://www.nhs.uk/mental-health/nhs-voluntary-charity-services/children-young-people-mental-health-services-cypmhs/

Young Minds – Your guide to CAMHS

https://youngminds.org.uk/find-help/your-guide-to-support/guide-to-camhs/

RC Psych – Who's who in CAMHS: for young people, parents, teachers and carers

https://www.nhs.uk/mental-health/nhs-voluntary-charity-services/nhs-services/children-young-people-mental-health-services-cypmhs/

An Introduction to Child and Adolescent Mental Health

Pavord and Williams Sage Publications Burton, ISBN: 978 1 44624 945 1

Part II

Mental disorders and illness in children and young people

Chapter 5

Behaviour disorders in children

TYPES OF DISRUPTIVE BEHAVIOURS IN CHILDREN

- **Misbehaviour** – The child is boisterous and cheeky (teachers will be able to make a comparison with the child's peers).
- **Oppositional defiant disorder** (ODD) – Is characterised by temper outbursts, arguing with adults, disobedience, deliberately annoying others, passing on blame, being easily annoyed, resentful, spiteful and vindictive.
- **Conduct disorder** (CD) – This has more severe behaviour disturbances than ODD. The child has repetitive, persistent and seriously antisocial, aggressive or deviant behaviour. This can be carried out alone, or with friends (though usually antisocial friends) who may engage in antisocial behaviours such as shoplifting or stealing cars together.
- **Attention deficit hyperactivity disorder** (ADHD) – The child is restless and inattentive.
- **Disinhibited attachment disorder** – This can develop in children who have not had the opportunity to form selected secure emotional attachments due to insensitive or inconsistent parenting. The child is distractible, restless and socially disinhibited.
- **Generalised anxiety disorder** – The child may be inattentive and restless, but not socially disinhibited.
- **Autism spectrum disorder** (ASD) – The child may have difficulty recognising and understanding their feelings and those of others, developing and maintaining friendships and mixing in social groups.
- **Epilepsy** – This a condition of the brain which leads to seizures. There are different kinds of seizures, including jerking of the

body (convulsions) and repetitive movements. *Petit mal* epilepsy is where the child does not visibly fit but becomes trance-like.

- **Bipolar affective disorder** (BPAD) – The young person's mood has periods of elation, and/or irritability, in addition to restlessness, followed by periods of deep depression/apathy.

Multiple diagnoses *are common when children present with challenging behaviour. For example, a diagnosis of ADHD also increases the risk of conduct disorder, depression and personality disorders. ADHD is common in children who also have autism spectrum disorder or learning disabilities.*

CONDUCT DISORDERS (CD)

(See also Chapter 13, Behavioural disorders in adults.)

5.01 Conduct disorders are the most common behavioural disorders and manifest themselves in defiance, aggression and antisocial behaviour.

There are three types of conduct disorder: oppositional defiant disorder (ODD); conduct disorder (CD): and disinhibited attachment disorder (DAD). The first two are linked by aggressive and destructive behaviour and will be described together below.

Prevalence

5.02 Conduct disorders affect 6 per cent of children aged five to 16 years.

Symptoms and behaviour

5.03 The diagnosis of conduct disorder is made when the child or young person shows repetitive, persistent and serious antisocial aggressive or defiant behaviour.

Antisocial behaviour typical of a conduct disorder includes:

- fighting (with frequent initiation of fights)
- deliberate destruction of others' property

- lying to obtain items
- stealing by shoplifting
- stealing from a victim (mugging)
- use of a weapon
- frequent truancy from school
- bullying others
- breaking into others' property
- running away from home or living accommodation
- staying out after dark despite parents' rules
- being cruel to other people and animals (including causing physical harm)
- deliberate fire-setting
- forcing another person into sexual activity against their wishes.

Oppositional defiant behaviour in younger children includes:

- temper tantrums that are unusually frequent and severe for the child's development level
- arguments with adults and deliberately refusing requests or defying rules
- often deliberately annoying others
- being touchy and easily annoyed by others
- blaming others for the child's own mistakes
- being angry, resentful, spiteful and vindictive.

Oppositional defiant behaviour in older children may progress to:

- early use of drugs and alcohol
- aggression towards others
- contact with the criminal justice system due to behaviours.

Causes

5.04 In Chapter 1, in the section on attachment, the psychologist John Bowlby noted a lack of attachment had severe effects on children. His study 44 Thieves focused on children in a home for delinquent boys, and he found many of the predisposing and perpetuating factors for conduct disorders among those boys:

Predisposing factors – These include: social adversity; parents' own experience of poor parenting; ADHD in parents; parental unemployment; poor support; family discord, so partners don't support each other; domestic abuse; maternal depression; inconsistent discipline; ADHD in the child; language or reading difficulty in the child; a child separated from their mother for six months or more during the first five years of life.

Parents describe some children as 'difficult' from birth. The parents may say their child is not feeding, not sleeping and not complying with their wishes. This can permanently impair attachment.

Perpetuating factors – These include the continuity of the disruptive behaviour, so the child develops a bad reputation within the community and at school; parental discouragement and helplessness; parental isolation by other parents; the child's rejection by peers so they join a delinquent peer group (this then leads to worsening behaviour when the group is under the influence of drugs and/or alcohol); truancy and school failure.

Treatment and prognosis

5.05 Treatments are described as 'solution-focussed', with parent management training and therapy for the child to improve emotional regulation and self-esteem. Problem-solving training for the child, and school interventions, may also help. The main problem of treatment is families dropping out because of the factors described above; the same factors that predispose the child to conduct disorder.

Any additional disorder – typically ADHD – should be treated as appropriate. Until this treatment is initiated, concurrent treatment for conduct disorder may have poor results.

Conduct disorders are the most common reason for a child to go into care, as they are difficult for parents to manage. Often a child or young person's behaviour becomes a vicious circle – the child is difficult to manage so is subject to care proceedings, and consequently becomes even more difficult to manage.

Likely outcomes in adulthood

5.06 A diagnosis of conduct disorder may follow a prior diagnosis of oppositional defiant disorder (ODD). Conduct disorder and ODD in childhood have been found to predict the subsequent development of antisocial personality disorder in about one-third of children. Outcomes for these children are generally poor. This proportion may be an underestimate as it only includes *diagnosed* personality disorders. Also, this figure probably excludes adults who are in the criminal justice system.

Children with conduct disorders are more likely to leave school without qualifications, have a criminal record in adulthood (seven times greater risk than other children), become drug dependent, suffer early death due to impulsive and reckless behaviour, and 20 times more likely to go to prison.

Most personality disorders begin in the teen years, but almost all people diagnosed with personality disorders are over 18. This is partly because there is a stigma associated with the diagnosis, but also because often, there is a poor response to psychological treatment because of the symptoms of the disorder. Some experts speculate that emotionally unstable personality disorder (EUPD) symptoms naturally 'burn out', or that people grow out of the symptoms of impulsivity as they mature.

Information for the Family Court

5.07 Both the young person and their parents may have poor experiences of authority figures. Parents may blame themselves, the child and each other, projecting this anger and blame on to others.

Attention deficit hyperactivity disorder is common in people with conduct disorders and is associated with disorganisation. Good timekeeping and following rules may be difficult for them.

Case study – Conduct disorder – Trudi's story (see Appendix: Case studies, p 316.)

DISINHIBITED SOCIAL ENGAGEMENT DISORDER (DSED)

5.08 Children with an oppositional defiant disorder or conduct disorders may be unable to form close attachments with others. They do not appear to want or need comfort or support from caregivers. Children with disinhibited social engagement disorder are quite the opposite. They may be over-zealous in their efforts to form an attachment to others. The disorder is a relatively new inclusion in both DSM (Code: 313.89) and ICD (F94.2).

Prevalence

5.09 There are high-risk groups such as children in residential care, among whom the prevalence is reportedly as high as 20 per cent.

Symptoms and behaviour

5.10 The child shows the following behaviour lasting for more than one year and with an onset before the age of five:

- no fear of adult strangers; no shyness when meeting new people for the first time;
- behaviour that is overly friendly or talkative to strangers;
- hugging or cuddling of unknown adults;
- no hesitation around strangers, even when departing with an unfamiliar person; and
- failure to look to parents or primary caregivers for permission to approach strangers.

Not every child who is eager to make contact with strangers has DSED. Typically developing toddlers hit milestones based on independence and physical separation from parents. These children may explore away from their caregivers and gravitate towards others. Some children have naturally outgoing personalities and may approach other adults in an overly enthusiastic way. Children with DSED have impulsive behaviour in all settings, not only in the context of meeting strangers.

Causes

5.11 The child has usually experienced a pattern of extremes of insufficient care, such as social neglect or deprivation in the form of persistent lack of having basic emotional needs for comfort, stimulation, and affection met by caregiving adults. It is likely there have been repeated changes of primary caregivers that limit opportunities to form stable attachments (for example, frequent changes in foster care) and/or rearing in unusual settings that severely restrict opportunities to develop selective attachments, such as in institutions with high child-to-caregiver ratios.

Treatment and prognosis

5.12 Treatment for DSED for children living with or returned to their biological families, or in foster care usually includes the child's entire family unit. Talking therapies may occur individually and in groups. Psychotherapeutic treatments meant to put the child at ease may include play therapy and art therapy.

Likely outcomes in adulthood

5.13 Symptoms of DSED may continue into the teenage years. Children and young people are at an increased risk of harm from others because of their willingness to connect with strangers. They have trouble forming loving connections with other children and adults.

Information for the Family Court

5.14 Children with conduct disorders are likely also to have attention deficit hyperactivity disorder. In turn, statistically, their parents may also show some features of these conditions.

During proceedings, such parents may find it difficult to maintain focus and listen, so giving time, recapping and checking understanding can be helpful.

Further information

Symptoms of disinhibited social engagement disorder

https://psychcentral.com/disorders/symptoms-of-disinhibited-social-engagement-disorder/

Public Health England – The mental health of children and young people in England

https://assets.publishing.service.gov.uk/government/uploads/system/uploads/attachment_data/file/575632/Mental_health_of_children_in_England.pdf

Royal College of Psychiatrists – Behavioural problems and conduct disorder: for parents, carers and anyone working with young people

https://www.rcpsych.ac.uk/mental-health/parents-and-young-people/information-for-parents-and-carers/behavioural-problems-and-conduct-disorder-for-parents-carers-and-anyone-who-works-with-young-people

Young Minds – Responding to anger

https://youngminds.org.uk/find-help/for-parents/parents-guide-to-support-a-z/parents-guide-to-support-anger/

TOURETTE'S SYNDROME (TS)

5.15 Simple tics are quite common in childhood. They are not usually serious and often improve over time. Tourette's syndrome is a neurological disorder and tics can be complex in nature. These are muscular (known as 'motor') tics and vocal tics, which start in childhood, usually around the age of seven.

Prevalence

5.16 Around 1 per cent of the population has Tourette's syndrome. It is more common in boys than girls, by a factor of four to one.

Symptoms

5.17 Motor tics begin in the face with eye-blinking but can involve the whole body, so the child skips or hops. Vocal tics can be just sniffing, throat clearing or coughing, but complex tics may consist of making animal noises such as barking, or words. When you think of someone with Tourette's syndrome, you might picture them shouting out obscenities, but less than 20 per cent of people who attend specialist clinics do this. Another aspect of vocal tics is when the person with Tourette's copies what others say or do.

People with Tourette's syndrome are prone to impulsive acts, such as inappropriate or disinhibited social behaviour. Self-harm is common, occurring in 30 per cent of children with Tourette's. Three quarters have sleep disorders.

Children with Tourette's report an 'urge' to tic, like the sensation just before a sneeze. Ticcing is reduced when the child is occupied and increases when the child is excited or tired.

Causes

5.18 Tourette's syndrome is seen in children with other disorders, which indicates a strong genetic component. Around 60 per cent of children with Tourette's have ADHD, and they show more disruptive behaviour than children with ADHD alone. Approximately 30 per cent have obsessive-compulsive disorder (OCD), and 10 per cent have autism spectrum disorder (ASD).

Tourette's syndrome is more common in children who were premature babies and babies of had a low birth weight.

Treatments and prognosis

5.19 Psycho education and reassurance is the first line of treatment; this alone may help. Medications used to treat psychosis can be beneficial; these include haloperidol and risperidone. Behaviour therapies can help too; these therapies can treat other disorders, such as ADHD, without the symptoms of Tourette's being made worse.

Tic severity increases until the age of 10 to 12, then tends to reduce. However, nearly two-thirds of children with complex tics are diagnosed with a personality disorder as an adult. There is a risk of depression, which worsens with age.

Likely outcomes in adulthood

5.20 Although there is no cure for TS, the condition in many individuals improves in the late teens and early 20s. As a result, some may become symptom-free or no longer need medication for tic suppression. Although the disorder is generally lifelong and chronic, it is not a degenerative condition. Individuals with TS have a normal life expectancy. TS does not impair intelligence. Although tic symptoms tend to decrease with age, it is possible that neuro-behavioural disorders such as ADHD, OCD, depression, generalised anxiety, panic attacks, and mood swings can persist and cause impairment in adult life.

Information for the Family Court

5.21 Tourette's syndrome and associated disorders result in an overactive and impulsive child. The strain of this can lead to parental depression, breakups and problems in relationships with wider family and friends. The genetic component means a parent may also be affected.

In circumstances where a parent or carer has such a disorder, reasonable adjustments should be made in court, depending on the requirements of the individual – being mindful of signs of stress, fatigue and lack of concentration.

Further information

NHS – Tourette's syndrome

https://www.nhs.uk/conditions/tourettes-syndrome/

Tourettes Action

https://www.tourettes-action.org.uk

ADHD Foundation – Tourette's

https://www.adhdfoundation.org.uk

Tourette Syndrome – The Facts

Robertson and Cavanna, Paperback ISBN-13: 978-0199298198

TRUANCY

5.22 Truancy does not always indicate a conduct disorder. Truancy, as a group activity, is usually the result of giving in to peer pressure to skip school. However, a child might truant alone for different reasons. These include being bullied, mental health issues, boredom, lack of ambition, poor grades (especially being held back a year), being behind on schoolwork, low self-esteem, drug and alcohol use, having no friends or social involvement at school, and pregnancy.

In the UK, different cultural groups place different emphasis on school attendance. For instance, Chinese parents tend to value academic achievement very highly, whereas children from the Traveller community often have poor school attendance.

The difference between truancy and school refusal

5.23 Many children will experience brief periods of difficulty in attending school. These may be triggered by issues with learning or difficulties with peer relationships. For some children, the main source of worry is about leaving their home or separating from the family. The child or young person may refuse to go to school or find ways to avoid it, for example, complaining of physical illness or symptoms. Truancy occurs when a young person misses school without their carer's knowledge. Sometimes children refuse entirely to attend school. This may be triggered by extreme anxiety and is often referred to as 'school phobia'.

Education welfare officers work closely with schools, the young person and their family to identify and resolve attendance problems. For children who are unable to attend mainstream school, alternative education provision can be arranged. This can include settings such as pupil referral units (PRUs), one-to-one home tuition and residential schooling.

Further information

Family Lives – Truancy

https://www.familylives.org.uk/advice/teenagers/school-learning/truancy/

Chapter 6

Emotional disorders in children

6.01 Emotional disorders are the second-most widespread group of disorders with anxiety the most common presenting symptom.

ANXIETY DISORDERS

(See also **Chapter 11** Emotional disorders in adults.)

Prevalence

6.02 Anxiety is the most common mental illness in childhood and adolescence – between 5 and 18 per cent of young people are affected.

The term 'anxiety disorder' covers a group of conditions consisting of separation disorder, generalised anxiety, panic disorder, social phobia and specific phobias.

It can be helpful to consider the different types of anxiety disorders and the typical age at which each disorder presents. Symptoms are similar in all disorders; it is the triggers that are different.

Type of anxiety disorder	Prevalence (% of children in the population who are affected)	Typical age of onset	Common symptoms in children	Behavioural change resulting from anxiety
Separation anxiety disorder	2–4 %	Peaks at 7 years	Worries, distress, abdominal pain, nausea, vomiting.	Refusal to sleep alone. School refusal.

Type of anxiety disorder	Prevalence (% of children in the population who are affected)	Typical age of onset	Common symptoms in children	Behavioural change resulting from anxiety
Generalised anxiety disorder	3%	Adolescence	Sweating, sleep disturbance.	Avoidance of situations.
Panic disorder	5%	Late teens	Fear of losing control. Breathlessness, blushing, vomiting, or fainting.	Avoidance of situations.
Specific phobias	2–4%	Over 5 years	Fear symptoms centred on object or situation. Child may have anticipatory fear.	Avoidance of situations.
Social phobia	1–7%	11–15 years	Fear of embarrassment.	Avoidance of situations, leading to isolation, withdrawal and depression.

The child's coping strategy (behaviours) can worsen the situation, especially when it's a short-term solution.

The following behaviours may be seen in younger children:

- avoidance – the child uses somatic (body) symptoms to withdraw from the situation, such as complaining of a stomach ache to avoid school;
- seeking comfort – the child wants to go to the doctor or visit A&E for their somatic symptoms;
- aggression; and
- compulsions and rituals – repeated counting, praying or washing, for example.

In older children, coping strategies can include:

- self-harm (usually cutting);
- overeating;
- starving;
- gaming;
- gambling;
- taking drugs, especially cannabis for its sedative qualities;
- use of solvents (though this is decreasing as recreational drugs are more available);
- use of alcohol; and
- use of medication prescribed for other people, such as diazepam (Valium) or analgesics.

Behaviours such as bedwetting (nocturnal enuresis), can also indicate anxiety, although it's important to note that bedwetting is common and occurs in one in seven of seven-year-olds.

It's more significant if a child who has been previously dry at night starts to wet the bed when no medical cause can be identified. Clinicians are alert to this being a possible indicator of psychological stress and child abuse, and so would investigate further.

Symptoms and behaviour

6.03 Anxiety is a feature common to many mental disorders and is often the most disabling symptom of other disorders. Constant anxiety is a real experience of children and adolescents who suffer from mental disorders.

Each developmental stage of childhood has 'normal' fears for the child's age, including some that may progress into adulthood.

Age	Fear
9 months to 3 years	Sudden movements, loud noises, separation from care-giver
3 to 6 years	Specific animals, the dark, monsters/ghosts
6 to 12 years	Performance anxiety, death of a family member
12 to 18 years	Social anxiety, fear of failure
Adulthood	Illness, death

Causes of generalised anxiety

6.04 Clinicians will want to rule out conditions and or substances that can present like anxiety disorders in children. For example, a child with asthma may become anxious when short of breath due to inflammation of the airways and then fears a recurrence of this unpleasant sensation. The child may become fearful when alone, so they develop separation anxiety and panic disorder. Other medical conditions that can cause anxiety in children include heart problems that can give an irregular heartbeat, or an overactive thyroid gland, or epilepsy, as the child can have a sensation of acute anxiety just before a fit.

Street drug use, especially of stimulants, can also cause anxiety symptoms. Often overlooked is the effect of caffeine, present in many soft drinks, including heavily advertised energy drinks popular with youngsters.

There is also a genetic link. If the parent has a panic disorder, this can result in anxiety disorders in their children – typically separation anxiety. All childhood anxiety disorders are more common when both parents are affected.

Anxiety in children is also linked to a lack of parental emotional availability, which is more common in families coping with the stress of poverty, those living in overcrowded conditions and when relationship problems or domestic violence occur.

An attachment disorder, as described in **Chapter 1**, can cause an anxious and avoidant child.

Treatment and prognosis

6.05 Treatments are mainly psychological, and include:

- building resilience in the child and family;
- play therapy for young children, in which the child acts out and learns to cope with the feared situation;
- drama therapy for older children;
- family therapy; and
- cognitive behaviour therapy (see below).

Cognitive therapy – Requires the child or young person to be able to reason and engage, and the family to assist by looking at their own beliefs. The therapy is to help the child control their emotions and behaviour.

The aim is for the child to learn to manage their thoughts. Thoughts are described as 'core beliefs', which we all have and which are shaped by early events in our life. Later events lead to 'assumptions', and these can cause automatic negative thoughts, with bodily responses such as sweating, nausea and feelings of panic.

The child is encouraged to challenge unhelpful thoughts and weigh up the evidence against expected negative events. The family is involved in trying to trace the onset of the anxiety and to encourage and work with the child.

Psychological treatment – This can help up to 80 per cent of children with anxiety disorders. However, this depends on the type of anxiety, the engagement of the child and their family, and the coping strategies used by the child at the time of referral.

Medication – This can be helpful, for example, short-term use of benzodiazepines or antidepressants (most commonly selective serotonin reuptake inhibitors [SSRIs] such as fluoxetine [Prozac]).

Likely outcomes in adulthood

6.06 The risk of depression in adults who have been anxious as children is two to three times higher compared to adults who have not experienced on going anxiety as children. Factors such as avoidance, poor school attendance and educational underachievement are relevant as they can exacerbate anxiety during adolescence and into adulthood.

Children with generalised anxiety disorder have a higher rate of conduct disorder in adolescence, possibly related to the use of harmful coping strategies. These can continue into adulthood, often leading to substance misuse, self-harming and eating disorders.

Advice for the Family Court

6.07 There is a high likelihood that an anxious child has an anxious parent.

Assist parties and witnesses who are anxious and fearful about participating by providing them with any written information in good time beforehand, starting on time and allowing breaks for the person to manage their anxiety. Repeat information and allow time for it to be absorbed.

It may be helpful to check the child's understanding, by asking 'can you repeat to me what I've just said?' (not 'do you understand?'). Make sure they have understood the next steps or stage in the proceedings, and provide writing materials for them to make notes.

Case study – Anxiety disorder – Michael's story (see Appendix: Case studies, p 319.)

Further information

NHS Inform – Anxiety disorders in children

https://www.nhsinform.scot/illnesses-and-conditions/mental-health/anxiety-disorders-in-children

Anxiety UK – Children

https://www.anxietyuk.org.uk/?s=children

Young Minds – Anxiety

https://youngminds.org.uk/find-help/conditions/anxiety/

Action for Children – Children's anxiety

https://www.actionforchildren.org.uk/support-for-parents/children-s-mental-health/children-s-anxiety/

Clinical Topics in Child and Adolescent Psychiatry

Sarah Huline-Dickens ISBN1909726176

CHILDHOOD DEPRESSION

(See also **Chapter 11** Emotional disorders in adults and **Chapter 16** Mental disorders in older adults.)

6.08 Depression is the second-most common emotional disorder in children and young people. Children with depression may have symptoms of anxiety and vice versa.

Children and young people who have ADHD or autism have an increased risk of depression (the presence of two or more disorders in the same child is known as **co-morbidity**). Severe depressive disorder with psychotic symptoms can occur in young children but is more common in adolescence.

Prevalence

6.09 Depression is more prevalent in older children, with up to 4 per cent of young people between 15 and 19 years affected. It is more common in girls than in boys.

Symptoms and behaviour

6.10 Children are not as articulate as adults in expressing their emotions. It is unlikely that they will say 'I'm depressed', as an adult might, so depression can be underdiagnosed. Children are more likely to show signs of distress through their actions.

The warning signs and symptoms of depression in children fall into four categories:

Emotional signs – *Typical moods or emotions experienced by children suffering from depression include:*

- **Sadness** – The child may feel despondent and hopeless. They may cry easily. Some children will hide their tears by becoming withdrawn.
- **Loss of pleasure or interest** – A child who has always enjoyed playing sports, for example, may suddenly decide not to join in. They may complain of feeling 'bored' or reject an offer to participate in an activity which they've always enjoyed in the past.
- **Anxiety** – The child may become anxious, tense and panicky. The source of their anxiety may give a clue to what's causing their depression.
- **Inner turmoil** – The child may feel worried and irritable. They may brood or lash out in anger because of the distress they are feeling, but are unable to express.

Cognitive signs – A depressive mood can bring on negative, self-defeating thoughts. These are harmful as the child then becomes resistant to words of encouragement or advice. Once the depression lifts, the child will be much more receptive to help. The signs to look for are:

- **Difficulty organising thoughts** – People with depression often have problems concentrating or remembering. In children, this can lead to an inability to complete tasks or difficulties in school.

- **Negative view** – Depressed children can feel very pessimistic.
- **Worthlessness and guilt** – Depressed children may obsess over their perceived faults and failures, feel tremendous guilt and declare themselves worthless.
- **Helplessness and hopelessness** – Depressed children often believe there is nothing they can do to relieve their feelings of depression. In particular, a child with depression may think this is 'just the way it is' because this is their only experience.
- **Feelings of isolation** – A child who has been picked on frequently may become very sensitive to slights from their peers. This leads them to avoid groups and social situations.
- **Suicidal thoughts** – Thoughts of death are not limited to adults. Children may also wish that they were dead and express these thoughts.

Physical signs – depression causes changes in bodily functions.

- **Changes in appetite or weight** – Children who usually have a healthy appetite may suddenly lose interest in eating. Children may also respond in the opposite way, overeating, to the point of obesity and using food to self-medicate their feelings.
- **Sleep disturbances** – Children with depression may have difficulty falling asleep and staying asleep. They may wake too early or oversleep, and they may have trouble staying awake during the day at school.
- **Sluggishness** – Children with depression often talk, react and walk more slowly. They may be less active and playful than usual.
- **Agitation** – Depressed children may show signs of agitation by fidgeting or not being able to sit still.

Behavioural signs – these signs are usually the most obvious.

- **Avoidance and withdrawal** – Children with depression may avoid everyday or enjoyable activities and responsibilities. They may withdraw from friends and family, so their bedroom becomes their sanctuary. They may resent anyone coming into their sanctuary.
- **Clingy and demanding behaviour** – Some depressed children become more dependent on family and appear insecure.

- **Excessive distraction activities** – A depressed child may lack control over certain activities, for instance they may spend long hours playing video games or overeat.
- **Restlessness** – Fidgeting, acting up in class, or reckless behaviour can be signs of depression in children.
- **Self-harm** – Depressed children may cause themselves physical pain or take excessive risks. Young children do not have wider concepts of self-harm as their older peers do. Therefore, it is more significant if a seven-year-old child takes an 'overdose' of three paracetamols because they believed it would cause them to die, than if a 16-year-old takes the same amount as a 'cry for help'.

The warning signs and symptoms of depression tend to differ according to the ages of the child or young person, as shown in the table below:

Age	**Symptoms of depression in children**	**Behavioural change resulting from depression**
Under 5 years	Sadness Loss of appetite or comfort eating Anxiety Panicking Insomnia Lack of energy Agitation and or irritability	Cries easily Refuses food, even favourite foods Weight loss or gain Unpredictable outbursts Clingy or demanding behaviour Difficulty settling to sleep Little play with other children Destructive behaviour – of their own and others' possessions
5–8 years	Sadness Withdrawal and isolation Slowing up Lack of interest Irritable Poor concentration Agitation	Crying Avoidance of situations or friends Walk and talk sluggishly Repeated comments of being bored Lashes out at family and fights at school Perceived as not trying at school School refusal Fidgety at school, disruptive

6.10 *Emotional disorders in children*

Age	**Symptoms of depression in children**	**Behavioural change resulting from depression**
8–11 years	Depression Thoughts of self-harm Thoughts of suicide Loss of pleasure or interest Isolation Loss of appetite Increase in appetite, so comfort eating Insomnia Worry and turmoil Feelings of worthlessness and guilt Feelings of hopelessness	Tears or, alternatively, blank with no emotions Self-harm, such as cutting Suicide plans and attempts – **take seriously. Children of this age may not consider suicide as 'final'** Doesn't join in activities previously enjoyed, spends time alone Weight loss or gain Looks distressed and anxious and says is a failure Pessimistic about the future
11–15 years	Depression Thoughts of self-harm Thoughts of suicide Loss of pleasure or interest Isolation Loss of appetite or increase in appetite so comfort eating Insomnia Poor concentration Worry and turmoil Feelings of worthlessness and guilt Irritability	Talks of feeling depressed and worthlessness Self-harm is common and often hidden Spends time alone on solitary activities which can become obsessional – games or social media sites Lack of self-care Poor school performance and truancy Sleep reversal so sleeps during the day Suicide plans such as storing tablets and attempts – **take seriously** Lashing out at others

Age	Symptoms of depression in children	Behavioural change resulting from depression
Over 15 years	Depressed mood Insomnia Avoidance of situations or friends Lack of interest	Talks of feeling depressed and worthlessness Sleep reversal, so sleeps during the day Isolation from family and friends Poor self-care, can lead to self-neglect Self-medication with drugs Self-medication with alcohol Self-harm School refusal or truancy Obsessive gaming, Suicide plans – **take seriously**

Causes

6.11 Depression is caused by a combination of risk factors that fall into three categories: predisposing; precipitating; and perpetuating.

Predisposing factors – In childhood depression these include:

- **Genetics** – Depression in a parent increases the child's risk by 10 times.
- **Disadvantaged family factors** – Children living with a lone parent, multiple siblings, an unemployed parent, in a poor socio-economic situation, or an isolated family group due to cultural factors, are more likely to experience depression.
- **Chronic physical ill-health or disability** – Whether in the child or their family, long-term illness or disability can lead to social isolation. Chronic pain is another risk factor for depression.

There are no cultural groups that are more predisposed to depression. Any higher rate of depression is thought to be related to the socio-economic deprivation that minority ethnic groups can be more likely to suffer.

Precipitating factors – Such as bereavement, separation and severe trauma, are often linked to the onset of depression. Cumulative stress, such as the child repeatedly witnessing parents' rows or domestic abuse, is as important.

Perpetuating factors – These maintain the child's depressed mood. For instance: physical disability may lead to bullying; overeating and obesity can cause low self-esteem and bullying; and some children have very critical self-thoughts with low self-esteem.

Treatment and prognosis

6.12 Interventions at school can help improve a pupil's coping skills, but it requires the co-operation of the parents or carers to be effective.

Successful therapeutic interventions aimed at children and young people in schools are typically:

- offered in a group setting – often a class;
- offered over a series of weeks, usually sessions of 30 minutes to 1 hour, over 10 to 24 weeks;
- led by professionals – teachers or psychologists;
- skills-based with a strong emphasis on experiential practice *in situ;*
- influenced by cognitive behavioural therapy (CBT) principles;
- partly comprised of fun and enjoyable role-play experiences.

Interventions to support parents also can be provided, by such services as Sure Start, Family Centres and CAMHS. This helps parents to establish boundaries and routines, such as bedtime, when to get up and when to leave the house, with an expectation that the child will arrive at school on time.

As in the scenario about Michael (see anxiety disorder case study at p 319) treatment consists of psychological support, which can include drama or play therapy, and for older children such interventions as cognitive behaviour therapy (CBT).

The evidence for the effectiveness of antidepressant medication in children is not as strong as for adults. Current NICE guidelines recommend that it is used alongside psychological therapies and that these should be tried first. Inpatient treatment may be necessary if there is a high risk of suicide or self-harm.

Ten per cent of children with depression recover within three months, and 40 per cent by one year; however, 30 per cent do not recover within two years. This has a major effect on the child's educational achievement and future employment opportunities.

The 10 per cent of children who do not recover within two years are at high risk of their depression continuing into adulthood. We know that adults can self-medicate, for example, with drugs and alcohol, for depression in harmful ways. The risks of self-harm and suicide are significant.

Advice for the Family Court

6.13 Children with depression may blame themselves for their parents' relationship breakdown and be unable to accept it is not their fault. The experience of family breakup and disharmony may be too much for them to cope with, meaning there may be a risk of self-harm, or possibly suicide. Alternatively, a depressed child may be so lacking in motivation and interest that they appear indifferent or hostile to what is potentially a huge change to their life.

Case study – Childhood depression – Rohan's story (see Appendix: Case studies, p 320.)

Further information

NHS – Mental health of children and young people in England

https://www.england.nhs.uk/mental-health/cyp/

NHS – Depression in children and teenagers

https://www.nhs.uk/conditions/stress-anxiety-depression/children-depressed-signs/

Verywellmind – An overview of childhood depression

https://www.verywellmind.com/childhood-depression-1066805

Universal approaches to improving children and young people's mental health and wellbeing

https://assets.publishing.service.gov.uk/government/uploads/system/uploads/attachment_data/file/842176/SIG_report.pdf

EATING DISORDERS

(See also **Chapter 11** Emotional disorders in adults.)

ANOREXIA NERVOSA

6.14 Anorexia nervosa is a mental illness which manifests itself as an eating disorder. Children and young people with anorexia try to keep their weight as low as possible by not eating enough food or exercising obsessively – sometimes both. They often have a distorted view of their body, believing they are fat even if they are underweight.

Prevalence

6.15 Although anorexia can affect people of any age or gender, it is most common in young women. It typically starts in the teenage years, though pre-teens are becoming more susceptible to images of the 'perfect body' as promoted in magazines and on social media that can lead to eating disorders.

Symptoms and behaviour

6.16 The eating disorder becomes all-consuming, and the child can spend all their time thinking about how to avoid food and lose weight, leaving no room for social activities or schooling. But this displacement behaviour means they do not have to think of painful issues such as family discord, their sadness or isolation, or bereavement. There is much debate about whether websites promoting anorexia ('pro-ana' sites) can be the cause of eating disorders. The general view is that they are not, but they are a way for vulnerable young people to compare their weight loss in unhealthy competition.

Causes

6.17 Factors that can predispose a young person to develop anorexia include the existence of an eating disorder in a parent (usually the mother) or their siblings. An emphasis on perfectionism within the family, coupled with a vulnerable child (perhaps slightly overweight) can be fertile ground for the development of anorexia. The disorder is being seen in younger children, which corresponds to the younger age of the onset of puberty and confirms a hormonal component.

Often a traumatic event, such as bereavement or separation, precipitates the weight loss. Bullying, especially if for being overweight, is a major factor. Changing schools, for example, from primary to secondary, and having to cope with a new system, is particularly difficult for some children, especially if they have an additional disorder such as autism.

In children who are sexually abused, the weight loss and lack of menstruation in girls resulting from anorexia are described by psychotherapists as a retreat to the safety of childhood and escape from the trauma of abuse.

Treatment and prognosis

6.18 Weight gain to a safe level, even if not to a completely healthy weight, is vital. In life-threatening cases of weight-loss feeding may have to be by nasogastric tube, even under restraint. In children and young people who refuse nutrition, such an intervention would require being sectioned under the Mental Health Act 1983.

Patients are given a target weight, either according to their body mass index (BMI) or their physical/hormonal development (for example an ultrasound scan of a teenage girl's ovaries to show they are functioning). The young person and their family may be offered psychological treatments. The person must be at a reasonable weight to able to engage with the therapy. At too low a weight, their concentration is affected by their malnutrition.

Eating disorders have the worst prognosis of all mental disorders. Young people can recover, but the prognosis is worse the younger the child is at the onset of the condition.

There is a shortage of NHS beds for young people with eating disorders, so patients can be sent to a hospital a long way from home, which causes an additional set of difficulties. Among anorexia patients who are hospitalised, 20 per cent die due to either low weight, rapid weight loss or suicide. At very low weight, the young person's heart rate is slowed. The development of irregular heart rhythms, due mainly to low blood potassium levels, puts them at risk of cardiac arrest. Approximately 10 per cent of patients treated for anorexia develop bulimia as a weight-loss strategy, vomiting or using laxatives to avoid food absorption. Another strategy is compulsive exercise.

There are long-term health consequences of being severely underweight. Brittle bones due to vitamin and mineral deficiencies and low hormone levels mean an increased risk of fractures. In young women, menstruation will be affected, and their future fertility is at risk. Many people with anorexia develop another disorder, such as depression or emotionally unstable personality disorder with self-harm.

Likely outcomes in adulthood

6.19 Approximately 20 to 25 per cent of children with anorexia continue a severe form of the disorder into adult life. Around 40 per cent develop bulimia (overeating followed by vomiting), with weight within the normal range.

Children with anorexia may miss schooling and social contact as they are too focused on weight loss; this can mean they don't develop socially and risk becoming 'frozen' socially at the age when the anorexia developed, limiting their social contacts and future relationships.

Advice for the Family Court

6.20 Children and young people with anorexia usually do their utmost to disguise their weight loss and how little food they are eating; for instance by wearing baggy clothing. They may be hunched and sensitive to cold. Covert exercising is common such as flexing and moving their legs. If offered drinks or food, they may show fear and become distressed.

Children and young people who are severely underweight spend much time thinking about avoiding food or disposing of food they feel forced to eat. Their focus on food may lead them to appear indifferent and unmoved by major changes in their life or family.

Case study – Anorexia nervosa – Lucy's story (see Appendix: Case studies, p 322.)

Further information

BMJ – Eating disorders in children and young people

https://www.bmj.com/content/359/bmj.j5245

Young Minds – Eating problems

https://youngminds.org.uk

NHS – Overview of anorexia nervosa

https://www.nhs.uk/conditions/anorexia/

BULIMIA

Prevalence

6.21 Bulimia is less common than anorexia. The average age of onset of bulimia is around 18, but it can start as early as five years of age.

Symptoms

6.22 Bulimia is the consumption of large quantities of food (called bingeing), and then trying to compensate for that overeating by vomiting, taking laxatives or diuretics, or fasting (called purging).

It's normal for people who aren't suffering from an eating disorder to choose to eat a bit more or 'overindulge' sometimes. This is different from a binge. During a binge, the child or young person does not feel in control of how much or how quickly they're eating. Food eaten during a binge may include things the person would usually avoid, especially carbohydrate foods. Episodes of bingeing often lead to distress, guilt and shame.

The binge/purge cycles associated with bulimia can dominate daily life and lead to difficulties in young people's relationships and social situations. Bulimia can cause serious physical complications as well. Frequent vomiting erodes tooth enamel, and sufferers use methods to make themselves sick that cause them harm. Laxative misuse reduces the potassium level in the blood and affects the regularity of the heart rate.

Causes

6.23 Young people can move between diagnoses if their symptoms change – there is often overlap between different eating disorders. Bulimia may develop from another eating disorder, typically anorexia or binge eating.

Hormonal changes during puberty are linked to an increased risk of developing eating disorders like anorexia and bulimia. It seems that hormones such as oestrogen have a role to play in how the genes that have been linked to eating disorders are expressed.

Some children may become bulimic as a way of managing difficult emotions. Bingeing on food is a way they cope with overwhelming emotions, perhaps stress or anxiety about school performance or difficulties with relationships. The purging (most commonly in the form of self-induced vomiting) is then used to rid the body of calories ingested.

There is an association with ADHD, particularly in girls, which is thought to be related to being in less control of their impulses.

Treatment

6.24 Medications such as antidepressants, are rarely prescribed for children and young people under the age of 18. They will usually be offered family therapy and other therapies such as cognitive behavioural therapy (CBT), adapted to help with symptoms of bulimia.

Likely outcomes for this disorder in adulthood

6.25 Approximately 50 per cent of young people will recover from bulimia within ten years of their diagnosis, but an estimated 30 per cent will experience a relapse of the disorder with long-term effects on their health including an increased risk of diabetes and brittle bones, mood changes and reduced fertility.

Further information

Bulimia Nervosa

https://www.beateatingdisorders.org.uk/types/bulimia

Bulimia information

https://www.nhs.uk/conditions/bulimia/

COMPULSIVE OVEREATING DISORDER

6.26 Children and teenagers may go through cycles of gaining some extra weight before a growth spurt; this type of weight gain usually evens out as the child continues to grow. However, for some children and teenagers, overeating may be a sign of an eating problem. These could include emotional eating or an eating disorder, such as binge eating or bulimia.

Prevalence

6.27 According to a UK study, 12 per cent of young people binge eat during mid-adolescence.

Symptoms and behaviour

6.28 Overweight children may be suffering from 'emotional' or 'disordered' eating patterns. Some may have a degree of depression and an actual binge eating disorder. If that's the case, the child may be using food and maladaptive eating behaviours to take care of emotional needs. For example, food may be what the child is using to self-soothe, to regulate their mood, to repress feelings in an effort to feel better. Overeating can cause a child to feel guilty or embarrassed.

Causes

6.29 In children, there is a strong link between overeating and symptoms of attention-deficit hyperactivity disorder (ADHD). Children with ADHD have an increased likelihood of becoming obese adolescents, with both boys and girls being at risk. The association between ADHD and obesity is poorly understood. However, individuals with ADHD may use binge eating to cope with the frustration associated with poor attention and organisational difficulties.

As with anorexia, a child is more likely to develop an eating disorder if a parent, sibling, or another relative also has an eating disorder; they are seven to 12 times more likely to develop one than a child with no family history of eating disorders. Children diagnosed with chronic illness are also at higher risk, particularly those diagnosed with insulin-dependent diabetes mellitus (type 1 diabetes). Children who struggle with depression, anxiety, and other mental illness may also be at increased risk.

Rare causes of overeating and obesity include Prader-Willi syndrome. This is a rare genetic condition that causes a wide range of physical symptoms, learning difficulties and behavioural problems. It's usually noticed shortly after birth. The excessive appetite typical of the condition can lead to children seeking inedible food such as frozen or decayed food. This behaviour would be very unusual in a child without the syndrome.

Treatment and prognosis

6.30 Treatment of any predisposing or underlying disorder such as anxiety or depression may help, plus cognitive therapy to develop healthier coping strategies. However, the habit of overeating to cope with challenges is difficult to break, and children who overeat have a high risk of becoming overweight adults.

Likely outcomes for the disorder in adulthood

6.31 In adulthood, binge eating can be accompanied by the use of alcohol and or drugs as immediate tension and stress relievers. Obesity as a result of binge eating presents many health problems (cardiovascular, diabetes, respiratory and joint problems and diabetes) and a reduction in life span.

Advice for the Family Court

6.32 Children and young people with a binge eating disorder are using food to cope with painful feelings. There may be associated avoidance of weight gain by vomiting or use of laxatives, leading to secrecy. Most children suffer guilt and self-disgust if their loss of control is accompanied by these behaviours. This then influences mood and self-esteem.

The child or young person may be bullied in person or on social media and may be ridiculed if their appearance is different from their peers. They may also be excluded from social activities or sports. Alternatively, if the child's family and social circle are also overweight or obese, there may be a family denial of the problem.

Further information

Prevalence of binge eating in adolescents

https://www.ncbi.nlm.nih.gov/pmc/articles/PMC4655585/

OBESITY

6.33 Obesity is defined by a body mass index (BMI). People with a BMI of 25 or above are overweight and those with a BMI of over 30 are clinically obese.

Prevalence

6.34 Ten per cent of reception age children (age four to five) are obese, with a further 13 per cent overweight. At age 10 to 11 (year 6), 20 per cent are obese, and an additional 14 per cent overweight.

Causes

6.35 Children are becoming obese at an earlier age and staying obese for longer. According to the King's Fund, this is a population health and an inequalities problem. It is recognised that children living in deprived areas are more likely to be obese. At age four to five, 6 per cent of those in the least deprived areas are obese, compared with 12 per cent of those in the most deprived areas.

Treatment

6.36 Restriction of calorie intake accompanied by increased exercise is the recognised way to lose weight. In a child is overweight and not obese, the strategy of maintaining the same weight while the child grows can help. The Government's childhood obesity strategy published in August 2016 was criticised for not addressing the challenges of reducing consumption of fast food, soft drinks and confectionary. It ignored the advice of Public Health England and introduced no new rules around restricting price promotions, marketing and advertising, labelling, information, or giving local authorities stronger regulatory powers.

Likely outcomes of childhood obesity

6.37 Childhood obesity is associated with various health conditions, including asthma, early-onset type 2 diabetes, and cardiovascular risk factors. Children who are obese are also more likely to suffer from mental health and behavioural problems. In addition, being an obese child can have long-term health consequences, as childhood obesity is a strong predictor of adult obesity.

Further information

Prevalence of childhood obesity

https://www.nuffieldtrust.org.uk/resource/obesity

Childhood Obesity A Plan for Action August 2016

https://www.gov.uk/government/publications/childhood-obesity-a-plan-for-action

Prevalence of Childhood Obesity in England 2019

https://commonslibrary.parliament.uk/research-briefings/sn03336/

GAMBLING, GAMING AND SOCIAL MEDIA ADDICTIONS

(See also **Chapter 11** Emotional disorders in adults.)

GAMBLING ADDICTION

6.38 Gambling is more common among boys than girls and increasingly recognised as a reason for truancy. Gambling includes card games, lottery tickets, scratch cards and online gambling. Children gamble as a risk-taking behaviour, or as a learned behaviour from parents, or a self-soothing activity to distract from adverse experiences in childhood. There can also be a compulsive element similar to that of substance misuse and repeated self-harm.

Prevalence

6.39 This is difficult to estimate, but the indications of gambling's increasing prevalence among children are concerning. Some studies have suggested that as many as 12 per cent of young people gamble regularly. Alarming data reported by the UK Gambling Commission's report on children and gambling trends, 2019.

Google Scholar See all References in 2018, revealed that the number of child gamblers in the UK quadrupled in just two years. According to this report, 55,000 11- to 16-year-olds have been classified as problem gamblers, with an additional 70,000 11- to 16-year-olds considered at risk of developing a gambling problem. This rate of gambling among young people is believed to be higher than the rates of drinking alcohol, smoking cigarettes or taking illegal drugs.

Treatment and prognosis

6.40 The first NHS gambling clinic for children opened in 2019 as part of a new network of services for addicts, being rolled out as part of the NHS Long Term Plan. Treatment is psychological, using cognitive therapy.

Prognosis is unclear. School attendance may be affected, reducing future employment prospects. Also, if a young person continues to gamble heavily and commits a crime to fund their habit, this could lead to a criminal conviction.

Further information

Gambling in childhood

Gambling Commission: www.gamblingcommission.gov.uk

Young People and Gambling Survey 2019

https://www.gamblingcommission.gov.uk/PDF/Young-People-Gambling-Report-2019.pdf

The Risk of Gambling Disorders in Children and Adolescents

P Ferrera et al The Journal of Paediatrics. July 2019. www.jpeds.com/article/S0022-3476(19)30425-1/fulltext

GamStop – Free online self-exclusion

https://www.gamstop.co.uk

GAMING ADDICTION

6.41 Gaming addiction has been defined by the World Health Organisation as 'a pattern of persistent or recurrent gaming behaviour so severe that it takes precedence over other life interests'. There have been growing concerns about the amount of time children and teenagers spend playing online computer games and the impact it can have on their mental health.

Prevalence

6.42 The exact prevalence is unknown as it is a behaviour that probably gives more concern to parents than to children. In 2018, a survey in the UK found half of parents feared their children were becoming addicted to computer games.

Symptoms and behaviour

6.43 The child talks about their game incessantly, plays for hours on end and gets defensive, or even angry and aggressive when made to stop. They ignore their daily needs, and they often have physical symptoms from spending too much time gaming, such as dry or red eyes, soreness in the fingers, back or neck, or complaints of headaches. Children may appear preoccupied, depressed or lonely, as some games can be quite isolating.

Causes

6.44 Child psychiatrists suggest that online gaming is more popular among boys. Boys with autism spectrum disorder may be especially likely to become addicted to gaming as they develop obsessional behaviours more readily, and gaming avoids face-to-face social contact.

Treatment and prognosis

6.45 In 2019, the NHS launched the first specialist gaming clinic, the Centre for Internet and Gaming Disorders, alongside the National Problem Gambling Clinic. Treatment starts with action by parents, who are helped to enforce rules and work with the child with the aim of establishing or re-establishing healthy alternative activities.

Case study – Gaming addiction – Eddie's story (see Appendix: Case studies, p 325.)

Further information

Royal College of Psychiatrists – When the fun stops: ICD-11's new gaming disorder

https://www.rcpsych.ac.uk/news-and-features/blogs/detail/cultural-blog/2019/10/23/gaming-disorder-and-tips-for-parents-an-interview-with-professor-mark-griffiths?searchTerms=social%20media%20addiction

SOCIAL MEDIA ADDICTION

6.46 This is the equivalent of gaming and gambling addiction and is more common in adolescent girls. Potentially, social media addiction can be more harmful than gaming and gambling because of the psychological impact of negative comments. Cyber bullying and 'trolling' are widespread across social media platforms.

Many forms of social media encourage users to judge one another on their appearance and to compare their looks, clothes and lifestyle against others, with images often airbrushed and filtered to present a physical ideal that's unattainable in reality. Heavy users see a constant stream of photos and videos, carefully selected and retouched to be as beautiful or exciting as possible, perhaps including friends' activities and events to which they haven't been invited. Children, especially girls, develop Fear of Missing Out (FOMO). All of this can take its toll on their mental health.

Social media has a more sinister side too. Disguised or anonymous bullying ('trolling') can be deeply distressing. Grooming is also a risk, with paedophiles drawn to sites popular with children and young teenagers. Sites that promote anorexia – known as 'pro-ana' sites – may exacerbate, eating disorders in children and, again, these compound the effects of peer pressure and competition. A further danger comes from self-harm and suicide sites, which are still accessible despite some social media companies announcing measures to eradicate them.

Parents are advised to develop family guidelines around the use of social media and devices and to be aware of their own screen-time and habits before trying to restrict their child's behaviour.

Further information

Prevalence of problematic smartphone usage and associated mental health outcomes amongst children and young people

https://bmcpsychiatry.biomedcentral.com/articles/10.1186/s12888-019-2350-x

Technology use and the mental health of children and young people

Royal College of Psychiatrists, 2020 https://rcpsych.ac.uk/docs/default-source/improving-care/better-mh-policy/college-reports/college-report-cr225.pdf

OBSESSIVE-COMPULSIVE DISORDER (OCD)

6.47 Obsessive-compulsive disorder is a variant of anxiety. It is quite usual for children at some point in their development to have concerns about sameness and symmetry. They may insist on particular routines around bedtime or have superstitions and rituals such as avoiding cracks in the pavement. These rituals and counting are part of a child's normal development and help the child feel secure. In OCD, a child's rituals and routines become so frequent and strong that they interfere with day-to-day life.

Prevalence

6.48 Taking into account that compulsions and rituals are common in autism spectrum disorder, the overall prevalence is around 5 per cent of children.

Symptoms and behaviour

6.49 In OCD, failure to carry out the ritual, or interruption during it, causes severe distress to the child, out of proportion to the actual impact.

Causes

6.50 There are some interesting theories about the cause, as early-onset OCD can be helped by the type of antidepressants that increase the brain transmitter serotonin. It's thought that in some children, low levels of serotonin predispose them to the disorder.

Treatments and prognosis

6.51 OCD can be treated with antidepressants, either those that increase serotonin or those that increase amines. Psychological treatments designed to reduce anxiety, such as cognitive behavioural therapy and family therapy, are also used.

Early-onset OCD is a chronic condition which continues into adulthood in 50 per cent of children.

Three additional obsessional disorders in children have recently been included in the International Classification of Diseases (ICD) and Diagnostic and Statistical Manual of Mental Disorders (DSM). These are gambling, gaming and social media addictions.

Further information

Signs & Symptoms of Paediatric OCD

https://kids.iocdf.org/professionals/md/pediatric-ocd/

PTSD in Children and Adolescents

https://www.psycom.net/ptsd-in-children-and-adolescents

PERVASIVE AROUSAL WITHDRAWAL SYNDROME (PAWS)

(Also known as pervasive refusal syndrome.)

6.52 Children with this disorder withdraw entirely from all activities, not just those described in depression. In pervasive withdrawal, the child stops walking, talking, eating, drinking and taking part in any activity; it's not just the social withdrawal associated with autism. PAWS may be considered an extreme state of depression.

PAWS is rare, but life-threatening when the full syndrome is present. It occurs more often in girls. The treatment is in adolescent psychiatric inpatient units, as for extreme depression. The prognosis is poor. A long hospital admission, perhaps over a year, may be required, and the child is unlikely to recover completely.

POST-TRAUMATIC STRESS DISORDER (PTSD)

(See also **Chapter 15** Traumatic disorders in adults.)

6.53 Post-traumatic stress disorder was originally described in soldiers returning from the World War 1 and known as 'shell shock'. These men were acutely sensitive to noise and would have catastrophic reactions to certain sounds, reliving the life-threatening situations they had been exposed to and also revisiting them in their nightmares. The fear response could often be so severe that they froze.

Children may develop PTSD if they are exposed to violence, abuse or bullying, or if they are involved in, or witness, a traumatic event such as a car crash, house fire or have experience of warfare.

Prevalence

6.54 The actual prevalence of PTSD is unclear. The rate among young people may be as high as 8 per cent by the age of 18. Rates of PTSD are higher among refugee and asylum seeker children who may have been exposed to more traumas.

Symptoms and behaviour

6.55 Children with PTSD can have similar symptoms to adults, such as flash-backs, trouble sleeping and nightmares. Like adults, children with PTSD may also lose interest in activities they used to enjoy and may have physical symptoms such as headaches. Other symptoms include difficult behaviours, avoiding things related to the traumatic event and re-enacting the traumatic event again and again through play.

Causes

6.56 It is accepted that PTSD can be the result of repeated stressful events that cause the child to be afraid, such as witnessing domestic abuse or triggered by a single traumatic event. Emotional, physical and sexual abuse are all linked to PTSD. There are many child asylum seekers in the UK who have fled from conflict zones who may experience PTSD in reaction to the traumas they have been exposed to.

The stress hormone cortisol is implicated. Cortisol usually rises when a person is stressed, but people with PTSD generally have a low level, associated with emotional numbing. Children subjected to long-term violence and neglect also have low cortisol levels, and it is thought their brains become desensitised to cortisol.

Treatment and prognosis

6.57 NICE guidelines recommend individual, trauma-focused cognitive behavioural therapy intervention for young children. This is typically provided over six to twelve sessions, more if clinically indicated – for example, if the child has experienced multiple traumas.

Eye movement desensitisation and reprocessing (EMDR) can also be used to alleviate the distress caused by traumatic memories. Exactly how this works is not fully understood, but it uses the child's own rapid, rhythmic eye movements. The therapist will move their hand or an object in the child's field of vision and ask the child to follow it with their eyes. These eye movements lessen the impact of emotionally charged memories of past traumatic events, so at the same time, the EMDR therapist will ask the child to recall a disturbing event, and the emotions and bodily sensations that go with it. Then, over 90 minutes, the therapist will guide the child's thoughts to more pleasant ones. Several sessions are recommended.

NICE guidelines recommend that medications should not be prescribed for the prevention or treatment of PTSD in children aged under 18.

Likely outcomes in adulthood

6.58 Psychiatrists who work with adults, especially those with personality disorders, frequently find that there are past experiences of childhood abuse that were unrecognised and not treated. Adults often say they were ashamed to tell of their experiences, and sometimes felt too unsafe to reveal them to others. As adults, they have a fragile sense of self which is easily threatened. Untreated PTSD originating in childhood is a major impediment to developing into a mature, well-adjusted member of society.

As with depression and anxiety, adult survivors of trauma can respond to their distressing memories and nightmares with violence. A traumatised child can become an aggressive, impulsive adult. This impulsivity is worsened if they self-medicate with alcohol or drugs.

Advice for the Family Court

6.59 Children with PTSD are at risk of being traumatised by having to give their opinion to someone they regard as an authority figure, such as being interviewed by a Children and Family Court Advisory and Support Service (Cafcass) officer. They may assume they are at risk from all adults. Alternatively, a traumatised child may dissociate from the process, so they appear indifferent or almost hypnotised when discussing traumatic events and their feelings about these.

Case study – Post-traumatic stress disorder – Samira's story (see Appendix: Case studies, p 326.)

Further information

Treatment for post-traumatic stress disorder (PTSD) in children

NICE guideline [NG116]: www.nice.org.uk/guidance/ng116

Young Minds – What is PTSD?

https://youngminds.org.uk/find-help/conditions/ptsd/

PHOBIAS

(See also **Chapter 11** Emotional disorders in adults.)

6.60 Phobias are different from 'ordinary' fear. The definition of a phobia is an excessive fear that continues for over six months. Fears are a normal part of a child's development, and from the ages of three to six, there are common fears of animals, the dark, monsters and ghosts. Children's toys, books, films and games often 'demystify' commonly feared objects, creatures and situations and make them child-friendly. Examples are Pixar's *Monsters Inc*, Julia Donaldson's *The Gruffalo* or even teddy bears.

Prevalence

6.61 Phobias are the second commonest anxiety disorder, affecting 2 to 4 per cent of children.

Symptoms and behaviour

6.62 A phobia is a fear of a particular object or situation. The child presents with severe anxiety in a feared situation or the presence of a feared object. Fear can also start when the child thinks about the feared object or situation. Their anxiety symptoms might include sweating, shaking, or a feeling of choking or sickness. Other fears such as of blood, heights or flying, usually develop later in childhood.

Causes

6.63 The cause may be a specific past experience, such as being bitten by a dog, having a nightmare, or a traumatic, painful experience like having a blood sample taken. Parents with anxiety and phobias may 'transmit' them to the child by their own behaviour.

If the parent has a panic disorder, this can often result in anxiety disorders in their children, such as separation anxiety.

Treatments and prognosis

6.64 These are usually psychological. The treatment is education to help families understand the condition and provide reassurance, as well as more structured, trauma-focused cognitive behavioural therapy (CBT). In addition, graded exposure to the feared situation can help. Schools can also support the child to deal with the feared situation. Antidepressant medication may help reduce anxiety in combination with therapy.

The same phobia may continue into adulthood, so social phobia in childhood can be a precursor of social phobia in adulthood, for example.

Further information

> **Stanford Children's Health: Phobias in children**
>
> www.stanfordchildrens.org/en/topic/default?id=phobias-in-children-and-adolescents-90-P01639

SLEEP DISORDERS

6.65 Children of any age can present with sleep problems. Disordered sleep can affect the child's health and impact family dynamics and parental or sibling sleep. Lack of sleep affects concentration and memory. Children with a sleep disorder can be unusually active during the day, in contrast to adults with a sleep disorder, who are often tired. Overtired children are often irritable, and this can progress into aggression. The term 'sleep disorder' refers to the underlying cause of the sleep problem.

Prevalence

6.66 Childhood problems with getting to sleep and waking in the night are relatively common. Episodes are generally short-lived, but they can sometimes be indicative of more serious issues. Sleep is significantly disrupted in about 25 per cent of children and young people. In children with neurological disorders, the prevalence is 80 per cent.

Types of sleep disorder

6.67 **Insomnia** – In babies and children up to the age of five, the sleep-wake rhythm has not been established as the biological clock in the brain has not matured. At this age, sleep problems usually occur because of a failure to set a routine. There may be other contributory factors, such as a poor diet or possibility food additives. Insomnia is rectified by the parents or carers establishing a routine and keeping to it and changing the diet.

As the child grows older, other issues may arise which cause sleeping problems. Changes in family circumstances, attachment issues between the child and parent, and school events such as exams can all lead to insomnia. The child waking during the night may then disrupt the parents' sleep.

There are also medical and neurological causes of insomnia in childhood. It's a side effect of some medications, for ADHD treatment for instance, and 80 per cent of children with neurological disorders, such as autism and epilepsy, have long-term sleep disturbance.

Delayed sleep phase syndrome (DSPS) – Adolescents often have problems getting to bed and getting up in the morning, which is normal. But about 15 per cent of teenagers and younger adults have the condition, delayed sleep phase syndrome (DSPS) in which the person's body clock is delayed. Generally, treatment involves more than one method to change the young person's lifestyle by normalising their sleep schedule, such as adjusting the body clock and avoiding caffeine, alcohol, tobacco and excessive use of social media and online games.

Parasomnia – Parasomnia affects more children than adults. It's most common in children who have neurological or psychiatric conditions, such as epilepsy or ADHD. This sleep disorder causes abnormal behaviour while sleeping, such as night terrors, sleepwalking or talking in one's sleep. The child is unaware of their behaviour, and therefore they have no recollection of their actions when they wake. Parasomnia can be dangerous because sufferers are unaware of their surroundings. Most children grow out of it by adolescence.

Narcolepsy – Narcolepsy is a rare neurological (nervous system) disorder that affects the brain's ability to control sleep and wakefulness. Children with narcolepsy experience excessive sleepiness, which impacts all aspects of their life, including social activities and school performance. Sudden sleep episodes, known as 'sleep attacks', occur during any type of activity and at any time of the day. Treatment includes lifestyle changes and medication.

Sleep apnoea – Sleep apnoea, also known as obstructive sleep apnoea (OSA), is a rare condition that affects the airways and breathing. In children, the most common cause is enlarged tonsils and/or adenoids, which can partially block the airways. This leads to a fall in the body's level of oxygen, which causes a suspension of breathing that interrupts sleep. OSA is reported in between 1 and 3 per cent of children. However, it is diagnosed much more commonly in children with specific conditions, affecting up to 25 per cent of those who are obese, have sickle cell disease or Down's syndrome. Treatment includes surgery, medication, gum shields and nutritional advice on weight loss.

Treatment and prognosis

6.68 Treatment starts with an assessment, which includes: keeping a sleep diary; assessment of the history of sleep disturbances and precipitants; physical examination and investigations to rule out medical causes; and an assessment of parenting practices. Treatment includes sleep hygiene to promote good sleep habits and behavioural programmes to establish a routine. Exercise is often helpful, as is reducing intake of stimulant drinks. Melatonin, the sleep hormone, is available as tablets or a liquid on prescription.

The prognosis varies depending on the type of sleep disorder and the underlying cause. Some remit without treatment (sleepwalking, night terrors), but others, such as narcolepsy, are life-long. Treatment of anxiety and depression helps sleep disturbances linked that are linked to those conditions. Sleep disorders due to a lack of parental boundaries can persist into adulthood as a normal sleep-wake cycle is never established.

Likely outcomes in adulthood

6.69 As adults, people with sleep disorders may self-medicate with alcohol and or drugs and are more vulnerable to depression.

Further information

Sleep Problems in Children

https://patient.info/doctor/sleep-problems-in-children

Paediatric neurodisability and sleep disorders: clinical pathways and management strategies

https://bmjpaedsopen.bmj.com/content/3/1/bmjpo-2018-000290.full

Sleep Problems in Children

https://patient.info/doctor/sleep-problems-in-children

SOCIAL ANXIETY DISORDER AND SOCIAL PHOBIA

(See also **Chapter 11** Emotional disorders in adults.)

Prevalence

6.70 Social anxiety disorder and social phobia mostly affect adolescents, although they can begin in early childhood. The onset can be before the age of six, and so schooling is severely affected. Undiagnosed and untreated, these conditions can lead to isolation and depression. Recent estimates indicate that 6 per cent of children and around 12 per cent of adolescents meet the criteria for diagnosis of social anxiety disorder or social phobia.

Symptoms and behaviour

6.71 Social anxiety disorder is characterised by significant discomfort and avoidance of social and or performance situations. Children with this disorder struggle with excessive self-consciousness that goes beyond common shyness. They worry about being judged negatively so they stop doing the things they need (and want) to do for fear of embarrassing themselves. By avoiding the social situation, the child's anxiety about the next encounter is increased, so avoidance can build rapidly. Not only does the child fail to develop social skills with their peers, but they can become completely socially isolated.

When their anxiety is triggered, a child may experience a panic reaction (shaking, sweating, shortness of breath) or, among young children, tantrums and crying. There can also be a fear of vomiting or of losing control of their bladder or bowels.

Clinicians faced with a child who has apparent social anxiety will take a developmental history to check whether social avoidance is a result of autism spectrum disorder (ASD). In ASD, social avoidance is more about an inability to communicate or lack of interest in communicating, rather than anxiety about, and avoidance of, particular social situations.

Treatments and prognosis

6.72 Treatments are as for phobias, with graded exposure to the feared situation. If untreated, social anxiety continues into adulthood as social phobia, which is a disabling condition. Some adults adapt their lifestyle to manage their phobia more effectively. They may choose to work alone, or work at night and so sleep during the day, to avoid social contact. Some socialise only with their family, avoid relationships or form relationships only online. Others use alcohol and drugs to cope with anxiety symptoms, leading to dependence and possibly other mental health problems.

Further information

Young Minds – Tips for coping with social anxiety https://youngminds.org.uk/blog/tips-for-coping-with-social-anxiety

SOMATIC SYMPTOMS DISORDER (SSD)

(See also **Chapter 11** Emotional disorders in adults.)

6.73 Somatic symptoms disorder is the term given when a person complains of a physical symptom rather than expressing feelings of anxiety or depression.

Prevalence

6.74 Recurrent and troublesome symptoms occur in 2 to10 per cent of children and adolescents in the general population. This increases from the age of three through to adolescence. About 10 per cent of children attending paediatric services have medically unexplained symptoms.

Symptoms and behaviour

6.75 In children, symptoms are widespread, such as a stomach-ache if they are anxious about a party or an event at school. The attitude of parents and carers is important. They should generally provide reassurance and sympathy when the child is distressed or worried, rather than for instance, only when they are ill. Parental over-concern or denial of a psychological cause for the symptoms are both unhelpful.

Chronic fatigue and persistent chronic pain with no identifiable cause are categorised as somatising illness. There is a link to factitious disorders, in which someone deliberately creates or worsens physical symptoms to obtain medical attention. For instance, a child with dermatitis, which is itself a potentially serious condition that requires skin creams, baths, and occasionally steroid applications, may pick at the skin causing infection.

A less common presentation of somatisation is when the child has sudden and severe symptoms, such as appearing blind, paralysed or with seizures. These children can be subject to many invasive hospital tests and interventions to try and establish whether there is a physical cause such as a brain tumour.

Causes

6.76 Predisposing factors include families where parents suffer somatic symptoms or where there is limited communication about emotional matters, parental over-involvement or a parental history of physical or mental illness.

Important factors in the children are emotional lability (rapid and exaggerated mood changes), vulnerability and low self-esteem, but a high drive to achieve. In these children, precipitating factors include anxiety and depression, life stresses, problems with their peer group, cognitive limitations on their academic performance, and teasing or bullying.

Treatment and prognosis

6.77 This involves paediatricians, GPs and a liaison psychiatrist working with the child and family. Damage limitation is important to avoid unnecessary physical tests which reinforce the behaviour. Most children with somatising disorders do recover. However, 15 per cent of those seen in specialist services continue to have a more chronic illness. If somatisation provides a short-term solution to the child's problems (for instance, they miss the stressful event at school), then the behaviour is reinforced and is likely to continue in the longer term. This is especially likely if there are ongoing difficulties in family relationships or parental ill-health.

Likely outcomes in adulthood

6.78 Over one-third of children with somatic symptoms disorder go on to develop a mood or anxiety disorder. As adults, they have poor social outcomes, and also much pre-occupation with their health, perceiving themselves to be vulnerable to physical illnesses.

Further information

Child Mind Institute – Somatic symptom disorder basics
https://childmind.org/guide/somatic-symptom-disorder/

Chapter 7

Neurodevelopmental disorders in children

NEURODEVELOPMENTAL DISORDERS

The term 'Neurodevelopmental disorders' has a long history, yet it had not been included in previous editions of the ICD or the DSM. The term applies to a group of disorders of early onset that affect both cognitive and social communicative development, affect males more than females, and have a chronic course with impairment generally lasting into adulthood.

(The term 'neurodevelopmental' distinguishes these disorders from other more common disorders of childhood, such as anxiety and mood disorders, which are generally thought to arise from some type of psychosocial adversity and have a more episodic course.) In the ICD-11, the category 'neurodevelopmental disorders' includes the following:

- disorders of intellectual development
- developmental speech or language disorders
- autism spectrum disorders (ASD)
- developmental learning disorders
- developmental motor coordination disorder
- attention deficit hyperactivity disorder (ADHD)
- stereotyped movement disorder
- other neurodevelopmental disorders.

ATTENTION DEFICIT HYPERACTIVITY DISORDER (ADHD)

(See also **Chapter 14** Neurodevelopmental disorders in adults.)

Prevalence

7.01 ADHD affects one in 20 to one in 30 children (definitions and severities vary). Four times as many boys are affected as girls.

Symptoms and behaviour

7.02 In ADHD, the child presents with symptoms in two areas: they lack attention and are hyperactive and/or impulsive. In the US diagnostic manual DSM-5, the symptoms must occur in more than one situation (for example at school and home), be present before the age of six years and impair the child's normal functioning. The symptoms will cause the child problems in many areas, particularly in school.

Attention deficit – means the child is careless with detail, fails to sustain attention, appears not to listen, fails to finish tasks, has poor self-organisation, loses things, seems forgetful, is easily distracted and avoids tasks that require a sustained mental effort.

Hyperactivity – means the child fidgets, leaves their seat when they should be seated, is noisy in play, shouts out answers before the question is completed, fails to wait in turn or queue, interrupts others' conversations or games, and runs or climbs excessively. This behaviour provides a safety concern for parents as hyperactive young children may run out of the home and on to a busy road.

Diagnosis is dependent on the child's developmental history taken from the parents, school and the use of rating scales such as Connors 3. Before a diagnosis of ADHD is made, other reasons for the child being overactive should be excluded.

Causes

7.03 The exact cause of ADHD is not fully understood, although a combination of factors is thought to be responsible.

Genetics – The parents and siblings of a child with ADHD are more likely to have ADHD themselves. However, the way ADHD is inherited is likely to be complex and is not thought to be related to a single genetic fault.

Brain function and structure – Research has identified possible differences in the brains of people with ADHD compared to those without the condition, and there may be an imbalance in the level of neurotransmitters in the brain for those with ADHD.

Birth issues – Children at risk from ADHD include those who were born prematurely (before the 37th week of pregnancy) or with a low birth weight, children with epilepsy, and those with brain damage, and children whose parents are drug-users – probably as the child was exposed to the neurotoxic effects of drugs before birth.

Assessment and diagnosis of ADHD

7.04 A diagnosis of ADHD should only be made by an appropriately qualified healthcare professional, with specific relevant training and expertise; this is most often a specialist psychiatrist, psychologist or mental health nurse.

It is typical to use multiple stages of assessment prior to formal diagnosis. A good-quality assessment takes time and is ideally multidisciplinary, involving information gathered from a variety of sources

Diagnosis is based on:

- Clinical examination/interview with the person:

  A full clinical and psychosocial assessment, including developmental, psychiatric and physical health history, current psychosocial circumstances, mental state assessment and identification of impairments and needs. Diagnostic reliability depends on longitudinal assessment.

- Third party information:

  Partner, parent, teachers'/school reports especially for adolescents, other health or social care professionals

- Assessment tools and rating scales:

  Diagnosis should not be made solely on the basis of rating scales or observational data, however, these are valuable adjuncts.

Treatments and prognosis

7.05 ADHD can be treated using medication or therapy or a combination of both. Medication is not a permanent cure for ADHD but may help a child with the condition concentrate better, be less impulsive, feel calmer, and learn and practise new skills.

Medications – The medications most widely used for the treatment of ADHD are stimulants. Ritalin (methylphenidate) is the most common. However, it can have side effects of loss of appetite and weight loss, which can affect growth, and the stimulant effect can cause sleep disturbance. Children taking stimulants to control ADHD symptoms should have their growth monitored through regular checks of height and weight. Some medications need to be taken by the child daily, and some taken just on school days. Occasional treatment breaks are recommended to assess whether the medication is still required.

Psychological treatments – These include: groups for parents and carers to help with parenting; establishing routines; care with diet and sleep; rewarding and encouraging appropriate behaviour; encouraging exercise and activity to 'use up' excess energy. These treatments can be beneficial and reduce the need for medication.

Young people with ADHD, who have benefited from medication, but whose symptoms are still causing difficulties at home and school, can be helped by psychological treatment. This might address: social skills with peers; problem-solving; self-control; active listening skills; dealing with and expressing feelings; adjustment disorders (the term used for behaviour disorders with self-harm or violence) or anorexia nervosa. Symptom management improves a child's quality of life.

Likely outcomes in adulthood

7.06 In 15 per cent of children with ADHD, the disorder continues fully into adult life. In 50 per cent of children, the disorder continues but is less troublesome. As an adult, they are inattentive, impulsive and personally disorganised.

The problems for young people and adults with ADHD affect many areas of their lives. Difficulty concentrating means poor educational achievement. Impulsive and reckless behaviour may lead to teenage pregnancy and criminality. All of this contributes to poorer employment opportunities and lower earnings. Interpersonal difficulties with peers, employers and partners often lead to short-lived jobs and relationships.

Information for the Family Court

7.07 Children with conduct disorders are likely also to have **Attention deficit hyperactivity disorder**. In turn, statistically, their parents may also show some features of these conditions.

Reasonable adjustments for such parents appearing in court might include: using short sentences when asking questions and giving information; allowing pauses for the person to process what has been said and respond; and providing short breaks to allow the parent to refocus.

Further information

Differential diagnosis for ADHD

Clinical Topics in Child and Adolescent Psychiatry (chapter 15)

Treatment for ADHD

NICE guideline [NG87]: www.nice.org.uk/guidance/ng87

Attention deficit hyperactivity disorder (ADHD)

https://www.nhs.uk/conditions/attention-deficit-hyperactivity-disorder-adhd/

ADHD Foundation

https://www.adhdfoundation.org.uk

https://youngminds.org.uk/find-help/for-parents/parents-guide-to-support-a-z/parents-guide-to-support-anger/

Young Minds

https://youngminds.org.uk/find-help/for-parents/parents-guide-to-support-a-z/parents-guide-to-support-anger/

AUTISM SPECTRUM DISORDER (ASD)

(See also **Chapter 14** Developmental disorders in adults.)

7.08 Autism spectrum disorder (ASD) is a complex, lifelong developmental disorder that typically appears during early childhood; the onset is normally before three years of age. It usually affects a person's social skills, communication, relationships and self-regulation. ASD is a spectrum condition that affects people differently and to varying degrees. It is defined by a certain set of behaviours and comprises autism, Asperger's syndrome and pervasive developmental disorders. While there is currently no known single cause of autism, early diagnosis helps a person receive the support and services they need, which can lead to a good quality of life filled with opportunity. Although the core features of autism will be present in early childhood, they may not fully manifest themselves until later years, when social demands exceed the person's capacity to cope with them. The early-years challenges may be masked by learned coping strategies.

In ICD-11 the age of onset for ASD is now in the early developmental period rather than being specified as having an onset by three years of age, though presentations throughout the lifespan are recognised.

Prevalence

7.09 Autism spectrum disorder is one of the most common neurodevelopmental disorders. Boys are three to four times more likely to have the disorder than girls, although it is now thought that there has been an under-diagnosis of the condition in girls. Estimates of prevalence vary from 0.8 per cent to 1.5 per cent of the population, but in England the currently accepted figure is one in 100 people. There has been an increase in diagnosis which can, in part, be explained by greater public and professional awareness of the disorder and the broadening of the diagnostic criteria to encompass not just autism but conditions such as Asperger's syndrome.

Symptoms and behaviour

7.10 Autism spectrum disorder has three main features:

Difficulty in reciprocal social interaction – people with ASD have difficulty recognising and understanding their own feelings and those of others, developing and maintaining friendships and mixing in social groups.

Difficulty in communication – this can manifest in lack of eye contact, unusual speech patterns, a tendency to take things literally, reduced facial expression, a robotic voice, imitating different accents, difficulty reading body language and problems with two-way interaction.

Rigidity and focal/repetitive interests – people with ASD tend to find change difficult, wish to remain with the familiar and have intense interests, often from a young age. They may display hypersensitivity (over-responsiveness) or hyposensitivity (under-responsiveness) to stimuli. Typical patterns of behaviour include delayed response, intense or complicated body movements, and repeated hand-flapping, finger-flicking or rocking (a behaviour known as 'stimming').

Some features of ASD can be distressing for the child. Hypersensitivity to noise, colour and smells makes them anxious and upset, and sensory overload can result in 'shutdown', where the child freezes. This can be dangerous if the shutdown happens in a risky place, such as while crossing a road.

The stereotypical and ritualistic behaviours are usually the most functionally impairing symptoms of ASD. Self-harm and aggression are difficult to manage and are often the reason for a young person with ASD being in residential care.

Typical ages of diagnosis of ASD

7.11 Age 2 years, by health and childcare professionals – the condition may be identified by a health visitor doing routine developmental checks, or by a childminder or nursery keyworker, but less often by parents, unless they have a child with ASD already. Symptoms at this age include speech delay or no speech, no eye contact, obsessive behaviours and unexplained tantrums.

Age 5 to 7 years, by primary school teachers – school staff may notice the child's repetitive and compulsive behaviour, lack of eye contact, abnormal speech patterns and lack of social interaction. Stimming – repetitive actions such as handshaking or flapping, which reduce stress – becomes more apparent.

Age 11 to 12 years, by teachers in secondary school – children with ASD can find it difficult to adjust to secondary school (having different teachers, moving from class to class, being in larger buildings, encountering more pupils, having to take personal responsibility for their own timetable and homework, and so on). Typical signs are isolation from peers, obsessive solitary interests, lagging behind in discussions as the young person needs extra processing time, and remarks and responses off the point, causing teasing or bullying from peers.

Girls with ASD generally have a better ability than boys to pick up social cues and copy others. So their language difficulties are often less obvious, meaning they may be diagnosed later in childhood. Girls with ASD are vulnerable for several reasons:

- They may be excluded from social groups, and so are more likely to be targeted by bullies and abusers.
- They lack the social judgement skills needed to make suitable new friends.
- Anxiety and depression are common, more so than in girls without ASD.

Most children with ASD are looked after by parents, but severe ASD may require residential care and even hospital treatment at times.

Comorbidity

7.12 The complication with ASD is that children often have more than just autism. Around 70 per cent have at least one other diagnosis, and 40 per cent have more than one other condition. This is known as comorbidity.

A common comorbid diagnosis is anxiety. Severe anxiety can present as a thought disorder where the child 'freezes'. Mood disorders among young people with ASD increase in adolescence with self-awareness of their differences. A high proportion (studies suggest between 37 and 85 per cent) of children with ASD also meet the criteria for attention deficit hyperactivity disorder and around half have a learning disability. Psychosis is more prevalent in people with ASD than in the general population.

The term 'savant' is used when a person with autism shows a special ability, most often for mathematical calculations, art, music or cartography. In reality, this 'talent' may be just a narrow focus to the exclusion of other interests.

Causes

7.13 The exact cause of autism is still being investigated. Research suggests that a combination of factors – genetic and environmental – may account for differences in development. Autism can run in families and is among the most heritable of developmental disorders. Siblings of those with autism have a higher risk of ASD than the general population.

> ASD is not linked to vaccinations – it's a coincidence that presentation and diagnosis of more severe ASD occurs at about the same age as the measles, mumps and rubella (MMR) vaccination. The first dose of the

MMR vaccine is given around a child's first birthday and the second at three years and four months. A study in Denmark followed 650,000 children after vaccination until they were eight years old and found no link between the MMR vaccine and autism spectrum disorders.

Treatment

7.14 There is no cure for autism. However, there is a range of strategies and approaches – methods of enabling learning and development – which may be helpful. Interventions for ASD include behavioural programmes which help the child develop skills in a step-by-step way, enhancing their language, play and social development. Such programmes are intensive, have to be done for many hours a week, and use behavioural therapists working with the family. Some use one-to-one intervention at home, so the improvement may not extend to other settings.

Communication-based programmes are vital, not focused on speech but on functional communication skills, signing and picture systems (Makaton) and the Picture Exchange Communication System (PECS). These prompt children to make requests and learn to communicate spontaneously. Some communication systems focus on parent-child interaction. The Early Bird programme, developed by the National Autistic Society, is designed specifically to help parents in the period between the diagnosis of autism and the child's transition to nursery or school. There are also many programmes that aim to help children with autism improve their social understanding, such as social skills groups, social scripts and even peer training (working with the child's peers).

Social Stories™ use cartoon-type drawings and simple text to help even very young children with autism understand what might happen at a particular event or activity, or how to act appropriately in a specific situation.

Due to the very high rate of other mental health difficulties among children with ASD, research has also focused on adapting the psychological treatments used for depression, psychosis and obsessive-compulsive disorder (OCD) for young people with autism. There is no evidence that exclusion diets benefit people with ASD.

Prognosis

7.15 The impact of a diagnosis of ASD will vary according to the severity of the condition. The structure imposed by education is vital for children growing up with ASD. A child who is manageable at the age of seven or 11, with guidance or physical redirection or distraction preventing them from becoming aggressive, can be impossible to manage when an adult. Unfortunately, there are few specific services for adults with ASD.

ASD worsens in new situations, so a hospital admission can lead to a deterioration in behaviour, such as aggression and self-harm.

People with ASD are vulnerable to exploitation by others. Their wish to 'fit in' may lead to them becoming unwitting members of drug cultures (the term 'cuckoo' is used to describe a single, vulnerable person being coerced into having their home used for criminal activities). Women with ASD may seek social contact in risky ways and are, therefore, vulnerable to sexual exploitation.

The effect of ASD and additional related medical conditions (comorbid diagnoses) on families is considerable. **Epilepsy is common in people with ASD and is an additional physical and medical risk**.

The strain of caring for a severely affected child can lead to parental depression, breakups, and strained relationships with wider family and friends. The amount of parental time required for behavioural programmes may exclude the less interested or motivated parent, putting the parents' relationship under pressure.

Advice for the Family Court

7.16 An autistic child may have one or both parents with ASD. Before the hearing, it may be helpful to consider how to manage the hearing and make any necessary adjustments, such as short breaks and explaining the procedure in advance. Start on time, as some people with ASD are rigid about timekeeping and don't tolerate delay.

Check how the parent or carer wishes to be addressed and use this name at the start of questions to them to get their attention. Don't expect the person to pick up on hints or non-verbal communication. It is advisable to use short sentences, ask single, clear questions and allow time for the person to process them before moving on to the next question or topic. Check their understanding by saying: 'Can you repeat what I've just asked?' rather than 'Do you understand?'

Case Study – Autism spectrum disorder – Yushfa's story (see Appendix: Case studies, p 327.)

Further information

Autism and the MMR vaccine

https://adc.bmj.com/content/103/7/631.full?ijkey=HsMwyZDRtsKu83z&keytype=ref

Interventions for autism

Research Autism: www.researchautism.net

Autism spectrum disorder

Edited by Christopher McDougle. Oxford Medicine online 2016: https://oxfordmedicine.com/view/10.1093/med/9780199349722.001.0001/med-9780199349722

To give people a sense of what it's like to be a child with ASD, the National Autistic Society has made a short video. Go to www.youtube.com/user/NationalAutisticSoc and watch 'Can you make it to the end?'

'LONG COVID' IN CHILDREN AND ADOLESCENTS

(See also **Chapter 15** Traumatic disorders in adults.)

7.17 'Long Covid' is a term used to describe the effects of Covid-19 that continue for weeks or months beyond the initial illness. The health watchdog the National Institute for Health and Care Excellence (NICE) defines long Covid as symptoms lasting for more than 12 weeks.

Prevalence

7.18 While children are less likely to suffer severe acute coronavirus symptoms, data from the Office for National Statistics suggests that 7 per cent of children aged between two and 11 and 8 per cent of those aged 12 to 16 report continued symptoms.

Symptoms

7.19 Common symptoms of long Covid include fatigue, shortness of breath, chest pain or tightness, problems with memory and concentration, insomnia, dizziness, joint pain, depression and anxiety, tinnitus and diarrhoea.

Causes

7.20 The actual way in which coronavirus caused enduring symptoms in some children is not known, but there are several theories:

- Persisting viral infection – the children and young people likely to be most at risk of Long Covid are teenagers, who have always had increased risk of persistent fatigue and mental health problems after viral infections, such as glandular fever.
- Auto-immune disease – where antibodies develop which then attack normal cells. There are more than 80 autoimmune diseases, such as rheumatoid arthritis, which affect a wide range of body parts.
- Lasting organ damage – the coronavirus infection itself causes damage to organs, especially the lungs and nervous system. As well as a cough, the acute symptoms of Covid are a loss of smell and taste, which indicate that the nerve cells are affected by the virus.
- Post-traumatic stress disorder (PTSD) from intensive care unit (ICU) experience – or 'post-ICU syndrome' can occur in 30 to 80 per cent of survivors of ICU. Symptoms include anxiety, depression and others consistent with PTSD.

Treatment

7.21 There is no specific treatment for Long Covid at the time of writing. Self-management guidance is available. For more severe cases, physical rehabilitation may be necessary,

Prognosis

7.22 It is relatively early for a clear prognosis for Long Covid. For some patients, symptoms do continue but it is unclear why this is. Great Ormond Street Institute of Child Health is carrying out a study over the next three years focusing on young people who have had coronavirus and asking about any continuing symptoms.

Wider aspects of Covid-19 for young people

7.23 Increase in mental disorders during the pandemic – Child and Adolescent Mental Health Services (CAMHS) services report increased demand, and children and young people report increased anxiety related to the pandemic. There is an increase in self-harming behaviour, eating disorders, drug use and other addictive behaviours. Loss of structure (education, home, activities) has contributed, as has young people's uncertainty about their future.

Children with physical or mental health disorders – Restricted access to usual activities and support has had an impact on children with pre-existing conditions.

Children living in poverty – The effects of Covid-19 on employment have impacted on family finances, reducing income for many and making the basic costs of living more difficult to meet. This adversely affects children's lives, particularly in terms of nutrition, health and education.

Young carers – Young carers are often caring for a parent who suffers from poor mental and or physical health, or drug or alcohol dependency. These young people may remain under the radar and out of sight of authorities who are there to support them. The effects of Covid-19 on the physical and mental health of adults who have had the virus may also draw more young people into caring roles.

Children and young people at risk of abuse – Reduced income and restrictions on movement cause hardship and can lead to stress and conflict within families, with possible domestic violence. Calls to domestic abuse helplines surged by 50 per cent during the 2020 Covid-19 lockdown.

Less oversight of vulnerable young people may afford greater opportunities for targeting and grooming by individuals outside their families for sexual or criminal purposes. Young people who have spent more time on social media during quarantine are at increased risk of exposure to grooming.

Many 'looked after' children and young people in local authority care who have been placed out of their area have been left lonely, isolated and cut off from their friends and family back home. This is exacerbated by restrictions on meeting family and friends and travel.

Refugee and migrant children and young people – Many refugee and migrant children, and their families, are dependent on specialist advice and advocacy services to be able to access their rights and entitlements in the UK. The Covid-19 crisis has put pressure on such services, meaning risks associated with poverty, discrimination and isolation are likely to increase for refugee and migrant children.

Further information

Challenges of the Coronavirus 2019 pandemic for child and adolescent mental health

https://capmh.biomedcentral.com/articles/10.1186/s13034-020-00329-3

Royal College of Paediatrics and Child Health – the CLoCK study

https://www.hra.nhs.uk/planning-and-improving-research/application-summaries/research-summaries/children-young-people-with-long-covid-clock-study-covid-19-uph/

Royal College of Psychiatrists – Help for people experiencing anxiety during the pandemic

https://www.rcpsych.ac.uk/about-us/responding-to-covid-19/covid-19-and-mental-health/covid-19-and-mental-health

INTELLECTUAL DEVELOPMENT DISORDERS

(See also **Chapter 14** Developmental disorders in adults.)

7.24 In ICD-11, the term 'mental' is replaced by the term 'intellectual' and 'retardation' by the phrase 'disorder of development'. The new ICD-11 term is similar to 'Intellectual Developmental Disorder' (IDD) used by DSM-5. DSM-5 defines intellectual disabilities as neurodevelopmental disorders that begin in childhood and are characterised by intellectual difficulties as well as difficulties in conceptual, social, and practical areas of living.

'Disorders of intellectual development' is an umbrella term for several different conditions that affect a child's intellectual ability. It is not a disease but describes conditions that affect the normal development of the brain. Children with a learning disability find understanding information and the world around them more difficult than other children. They have a reduced ability to understand new or complex information. As well as impaired intelligence, they also have a reduced ability to cope independently (impaired social functioning).

Sometimes, disorders of intellectual development are a symptom of other conditions, for example, in Down's syndrome. A child with a disorder of intellectual disabilities may also have a mental disorder (comorbidity) and, despite all best efforts from dedicated parents and family, they may require residential care.

Government policy discourages long-term hospital care for people with a disorder of intellectual development, with or without a mental disorder. Many parents and carers do not regard a child with a disorder of intellectual disability as different or unusual; they are just themselves, and it is society that causes the stigma around their condition.

Definition of disorder of intellectual development

7.25 Major changes in the ICD-11 include the renaming of mental retardation to disorders of intellectual development. The main classifications of severity in both ICD-11 and DSM-5 include the terms 'mild,' 'moderate,' 'severe,' and 'profound'.

IQ measurement is only partially helpful, as the degree of intellectual impairment does not completely predict the child's social, educational and personal capabilities and needs.

Prevalence

7.26 The prevalence of diagnosed learning disability is 2 per cent of the population. Of these, over three quarters have moderate learning difficulties (MLD), 15 per cent have severe learning difficulties (SLD), and 1 in 20 (5 per cent) have profound multiple learning difficulties (PMLD). It is suspected that many more live with some level of learning disability and are unaware of it and are undiagnosed. There are slightly more boys with a learning disability than girls. The proportion of children with a learning disability is increasing with the survival of more premature babies and better paediatric care.

Symptoms and behaviour

7.27 A child with a learning disability is likely to find learning skills difficult and have some developmental delays. Some children may have problems with particular areas, for example, communication, reading, writing or understanding instructions. This means they can have difficulty in understanding new or complex information, learning new skills and coping independently.

Children with a mild disorder of intellectual development may have difficulties which are not apparent until they are of school age. They often exhibit difficulties in the acquisition and comprehension of complex language concepts and academic skills. At the other end of the spectrum of disorders of intellectual development, children with a profound disorder of intellectual development are likely to have very limited communication abilities and capacity for acquisition of academic skills. They may also have co-occurring motor and sensory impairments and typically require daily support in a supervised environment for adequate care

The link between disorders of intellectual development and mental disorder

7.28 Among children and young people with a disorder of intellectual development, 36 per cent also have a mental disorder, compared with 8 per cent of those who do not have such a disorder. Children with a disorder of intellectual development are also 33 times more likely to be on the autistic spectrum and are far more likely than other children to have emotional disorders.

Challenging behaviours, such as aggression, destruction and self-injury, are shown by 10 to 15 per cent of children with a disorder of intellectual development. If a young person's behaviour as they grow into adulthood becomes violent, they can only be detained under the Mental Health Act 1983 if the behaviour is associated with 'abnormally aggressive or seriously irresponsible conduct'.

The rate of schizophrenia in people with disorders of intellectual development is approximately three times greater than for the general population.

Children and young people with a disorder of intellectual development are more likely than others to live in poverty, have few friends, and have additional long-term health problems and disabilities such as epilepsy and sensory impairments. All of these factors are associated with mental health problems.

Causes

7.29 Disorders of intellectual development Learning disability is linked to problems before and after birth that reduce or prevents oxygen supply to the foetus or baby. Infections such as meningitis are also a significant cause. Children with foetal alcohol syndrome, caused by the mother's excessive alcohol intake during pregnancy, usually have learning disability alongside a range of challenging behaviours including hyperactivity, cognitive impairment, speech delay and difficulties.

Some other conditions are associated with having a disorder of intellectual development such as autism and severe epilepsy. Genetics can also play a part; the commonest genetic cause of disorders of intellectual development is Down's syndrome (see below). Sometimes there is no known cause.

Treatment and prognosis

7.30 Disorders of intellectual development are lifelong conditions. There is no cure and no medications that can improve IQ, reduce symptoms, or reverse the changes in the brain that have caused the disability. Treatments are focused on providing the right kind of support so the child is given opportunities to develop, learn new skills and, as they grow older, become as independent as possible. Some of the specialist types of educational and therapy treatments are art, music and dance therapy, occupational therapy and physiotherapy. Medication may be taken to help reduce symptoms of other conditions that may be present.

Psychological treatment for disorders of intellectual development is possible and is adapted for the child's intellectual level. Children with profound disorders typically need 24-hour support. Most children with a mild disorder live at home, requiring varying levels and types of support in response to their changing circumstances. Communication aids are becoming increasingly sophisticated. Help for parents and carers is important; they may need practical and emotional support and respite breaks.

Children with a disorder of intellectual development are likely to have complex needs. When they reach school age they will usually be assessed for an Education Health and Care plan (in Wales – a Statement of Special Educational Needs). This may lead to them attending a special school, but many are educated in mainstream schools. In England, 88 per cent of children with a moderate disorder of intellectual development, 22 per cent with a severe disorder and 17 per cent with profound multiple disorders of intellectual development are disorder of intellectual development educated in mainstream schools.

Likely outcomes in adulthood

7.31 Society's change in attitude and pressure from parents and carers is improving the outcome for children and young people with a disorder of intellectual development. There are improved opportunities nowadays for employment and independent living. The life expectancy of people with mild disorders of intellectual development learning disabilities is approaching that of the general population, but mortality rates among people with moderate-to-severe disorders are three times higher than in the general population.

Further information

Learning disability and mental disorder

https://www.nhs.uk/conditions/learning-disabilities/

Best Beginnings – Parents with learning disabilities

https://www.bestbeginnings.org.uk

DOWN'S SYNDROME

7.32 Down's syndrome is a genetic disorder. Most people have two copies of all chromosomes, but those with Down's syndrome have three copies of chromosome 21. Although all babies and children with Down's syndrome have some degree of learning disability, this is very variable.

Prevalence

7.33 Overall, one baby in every 1,000 is born with Down's syndrome, but the rate is higher among those born to older mothers. Studies suggest that the chance of a 40-year-old mother having a baby with the condition is 16 times greater than for a 25-year-old mother. Standard antenatal screening identifies babies with a higher risk of Down's syndrome in pregnancy, and a further test can confirm the condition. The birth rate of babies with Down's syndrome has fallen slightly in the UK over the past decade.

Symptoms and behaviour

7.34 Most children with Down's syndrome have mild to moderate cognitive impairment, only in some is it severe. Children with Down's syndrome have distinct facial features, commonly including a flattened face, upward slanting eyelids and short height – although not all have the same features

Down's syndrome can also cause significant health problems;

- Almost half of babies with Down's syndrome also have congenital heart disease.
- More than half of children with Down's syndrome have visual problems, including cataracts that may be present at birth. The risk of cataracts increases with age.
- Up to three-quarters of children with Down's syndrome have some hearing loss, either due to structural problems with the ear, or because children with Down's syndrome are more likely to get ear infections.
- Hypothyroidism and blood disorders such as leukaemia are more common in children with Down's syndrome.
- Hypotonia (poor muscle tone) and low strength contribute to delays in rolling over, sitting up, crawling and walking, common in children with Down's syndrome.
- Children with Down's syndrome are more likely to have epilepsy, a condition characterised by seizures. The risk of developing epilepsy increases with age, but seizures usually occur either in the first two years or after the third decade of life. Almost half of over-50s with Down's syndrome also have epilepsy.

In children with Down's syndrome, there is usually a delay in language development and memory is also affected. This varies from person to person.

Causes

7.35 It is the extra chromosomal material in Down's syndrome that is responsible for the developmental problems and characteristic physical features of the syndrome. There are no known behavioural or environmental factors that cause Down's syndrome, and it is mostly not an inherited condition.

Treatment and prognosis

7.36 Down's syndrome cannot be cured, but specific therapies can help improve skills. Speech therapy can greatly improve communication and language skills Physical therapy helps strengthen muscles and improve motor skills. Occupational therapy also aids motor skills and makes daily tasks easier. Behavioural therapy helps the emotional challenges that often accompany Down's syndrome. Most benefit is from the early introduction of such treatments.

Likely outcomes in adulthood

7.37 People with Down's syndrome are at high risk of developing dementia, with onset typically 30 to 40 years before that of the general population. However people with Down's syndrome are affected differently by dementia. Many can live full lives and are capable of continuing activities.

Further information

Down's Syndrome Association

https://www.downs-syndrome.org.uk

What conditions or disorders are commonly associated with Down syndrome?

National Institute of Child Health and Human Development: www.nichd.nih.gov/health/topics/down/conditioninfo/associated

DYSLEXIA

(See also **Chapter 14** Developmental disorders in adults.)

7.38 Dyslexia is a neurological condition that can have a significant impact during education, in the workplace and in everyday life. Each person's experience of the condition will be different. It can range from mild to severe, and it can co-occur with other learning differences. It is a life-long condition, and it can run in families.

Prevalence

7.39 Dyslexia is present in about 10 per cent of the UK population. It is more common in boys, partly because of its association with attention deficit hyperactivity disorder.

Symptoms and behaviour

7.40 Dyslexia primarily affects reading and writing skills and it also affects information processing. Dyslexic people may have difficulty absorbing and remembering information they see and hear, which can affect learning and the acquisition of literacy skills. The condition can also affect other areas such as organisational skills and timekeeping.

Dyslexia may go undetected in the early years at school, and other problems may disguise the underlying cause. A child may show signs of depression or low self-esteem and have behaviour problems at home and school. The child may become unmotivated and develop a dislike for school; in some children, this can result in truancy and lack of educational attainment.

It is important to remember that there are positives to thinking differently. Many people with dyslexia show strengths in other areas such as design, problem-solving, creative skills, interactive skills and oral skills.

Causes

7.41 There can be a family history of dyslexia, but there may be other factors that affect the development of the brain. The condition appears to be linked to certain genes that affect how the brain processes reading and language. Known risk factors include premature birth or low birth weight, or exposure during pregnancy to nicotine, drugs, alcohol or infection that may alter brain development in the foetus or newborn.

Treatment and prognosis

7.42 Whilst dyslexia is a lifelong condition, there are a range of specialist educational interventions that can help children with their learning. Generally, the earlier these interventions are started, the more effective they will be. The child's school can draw up a specific learning action plan, with the support of their special educational needs coordinator (SENCO). Most mainstream schools can offer the necessary support to a child with dyslexia, although a small number of children with more complex learning needs will benefit from attending a specialist school. Many children with the condition will be helped by the use of technology, such as working with a computer, as this better suits their way of learning and working.

Likely outcomes in adulthood

7.43 Techniques used to help children with dyslexia are also relevant and effective for adults. Making use of technology, such as word processors, can help with writing and organising daily activities. Employers should make reasonable adjustments in the workplace (Equality Act 2010) to accommodate an employee with the condition. Undiagnosed dyslexic conditions in adults can lead to them developing strategies to avoid situations they find challenging. Or they may mask their symptoms, which can lead to underperformance and not developing their full potential.

Advice for the Family Court

7.44 Dyslexia often occurs within families, so if a child has the condition, one or both parents may have it as well. Parents and carers with dyslexia may be reluctant to admit they have difficulty reading and processing information, so allow more time for written and oral information to be digested and processed. Consider allowing the use of technological aids that will assist the person's understanding and retention of information. Unlike a learning disability, dyslexia does not affect a person's level of intelligence, and any adjustments need to be made sensitively, so they are not seen as patronising or embarrassing.

Further information

British Dyslexia Association

https://www.bdadyslexia.org.uk

The Dyslexia Association

https://www.dyslexia.uk.net

Mayo Clinic

https://www.mayoclinic.org/diseases-conditions/dyslexia/symptoms-causes/syc-20353552

EPILEPSY

(See also **Chapter 14** Developmental disorders in adults.)

7.45 Epilepsy is a condition (this is the preferred term, rather than an illness) that leads to seizures. It is one of the most common disorders of the central nervous system.

Prevalence

7.46 In the UK, epilepsy affects around one in every 200 children and young people under 18. Epilepsy can start at any age, including childhood.

Symptoms

7.47 The type of epileptic seizure a child has depends on which area of their brain is affected. There are two main types of seizure: focal seizures (sometimes called partial seizures) and generalised seizures. Focal seizures affect only one side of the brain, and the child may not lose consciousness. Generalised seizures affect large areas on both sides of the brain and often result in loss of consciousness.

Signs of seizures vary widely, but can include:

- jerking of the body (convulsions)
- repetitive movements
- a tingling feeling in the limbs
- staring blankly, apparently day dreaming, a strange taste in the mouth or a strange smell in the nostrils
- a rising feeling in the stomach.

A diagnosis is made from the child's history and from an electroencephalogram (EEG) which measures brain activity. Epilepsy shows as spikes on the EEG.

The effect of epilepsy on behaviour

7.48 In some types of seizure, a child may be aware of what is happening. In other types, a child will be unconscious, and afterwards will be confused and tired with no memory of the seizure happening. Some children may have seizures when they are sleeping – 'nocturnal seizures' – which affect their sleep patterns and leave them tired and confused the next day.

Different children will have very different experiences of how epilepsy affects them, and the impact it has on their school life. Some children with epilepsy have no significant problems with their learning or behaviour.

However, children with epilepsy are at greater risk of learning and behaviour difficulties than children without epilepsy. They may find it more difficult to learn than other children as they have problems with attention, concentration and memory, and the speed with which they process information is slower than other children. The more seizures a child has, the more pieces of information they will miss. For example, if a child has hundreds of short absences in a day, they will miss many little bits of information and this will create gaps in their learning.

Causes

7.49 Epilepsy can be caused by brain damage, such as a head injury, lack of oxygen at birth, or meningitis. There seems to be a genetic component with some types of epilepsy – children who have an epileptic parent or sibling have a slightly higher chance of developing the condition themselves. Children with certain other mental health conditions are also more likely to develop epilepsy, such as those with attention deficit hyperactivity disorder or autism spectrum disorder. However, often the cause is not clear.

Photosensitive epilepsy is when seizures are triggered by flashing lights or contrasting light and dark patterns. Photosensitive epilepsy is more common in children and young people and is less commonly diagnosed after the age of 20. Some children's seizures happen in response to triggers such as stress, excitement, missed medication or lack of sleep.

Treatment

7.50 Most children and young people with epilepsy are treated with anti-epilepsy medication. Some children may have side-effects such as hyperactivity, irritability, aggression, drowsiness, dizziness, memory problems, problems concentrating and mood swings.

Prognosis and outcomes in adolescence

7.51 Some children outgrow their epilepsy by their mid to late teens. This is called 'spontaneous remission'.

Children's epilepsy is usually managed by the parent or carer. They ensure medication is taken and try to avoid precipitants to seizures. Adolescents often wish to experience late nights, alcohol or recreational drugs. These, plus excitement and emotional stress, can make seizures more likely.

Some young people find epilepsy challenging to live with, especially if they have frequent seizures or side effects from their medication. They may decide to stop seeing their doctor or taking their medication. The decision about learning to drive and driving can cause much friction. People with epilepsy are required by law to tell the Driver and Vehicle Licensing Agency (DVLA) about their condition, even if they are not having seizures.

Outcomes for people with epilepsy depend on the cause. A traumatic cause such as brain damage can shorten lifespan by an average of eight years. People with epilepsy are three times more likely to die earlier from their condition if they live in a deprived area.

Further information

Effect of epilepsy on learning and behaviour

https://www.epilepsy.org.uk/info/education/learning-and-behaviour

Epilepsy in children

https://www.epilepsysociety.org.uk/epilepsy-childhood

Death rates of neurological conditions

https://www.gov.uk/government/publications/deaths-associated-with-neurological-conditions

Young Epilepsy

https://www.youngepilepsy.org.uk

FOETAL ALCOHOL SPECTRUM DISORDER (FASD)

7.52 Alcohol can cause more damage to an unborn baby than almost any other drug. The term foetal alcohol spectrum disorder (FASD) represents the range of effects associated with prenatal exposure to alcohol. It is a permanent, lifelong disability.

Prevalence

7.53 The UK prevalence rate for alcohol consumption in pregnancy is the fourth highest in the world. It is thought that around 7,000 babies are born with FASD in the UK each year, which may be greater than the incidence of other developmental disorders such as autism. Looked-after and adopted children, who are often born into alcohol and drug misusing families, are more likely to be affected by FASD than those in the general population. A study in Bristol published in 2018 found that up to 79 per cent of children in the study population of 13,495 were exposed to alcohol in pregnancy and that to up to 17 per cent screened positive for symptoms of FASD.

The condition is underdiagnosed (masked), so potentially many children are at risk. Awareness among professionals (including GPs, specialists, and teachers) and the general public is low. Also, many individuals with FASD do not show physical features of the condition.

Symptoms

7.54 Foetal alcohol syndrome causes brain damage and growth problems. Children with the condition have a small head and are smaller than average at birth. They grow more slowly as they get older, and can be shorter than the average adult. There can be deformities of joints, limbs and fingers. They have distinctive facial features, such as small eyes, a thin upper lip, and a smooth philtrum, though these may become less noticeable with age.

Problems with brain development affect a range of functions. Children with FASD typically have poor co-ordination and balance and problems with vision and hearing. Their learning disabilities may include poor memory, trouble with attention and with processing information, difficulty with reasoning and problem-solving and poor judgment. Issues with concentration or hyperactivity and rapidly changing moods worsen these problems.

The mental, social and behavioural issues can have a significant impact on how a child with foetal alcohol syndrome copes with school. They may have:

- trouble getting along with others;
- poor social skills;
- difficulty adapting to change or switching from one task to another;
- problems with behaviour and impulse control;
- poor concept of time;
- problems staying on task;
- difficulty planning or working toward a goal.

Causes

7.55 Alcohol has a toxic effect on the foetal brain and developing body. The foetus cannot metabolise alcohol as the liver is not fully developed and cannot filter out the toxins from the alcohol. The toxins then interfere with the foetus's development. Maternal alcohol use is the sole identified cause of FASD. Binge and heavy chronic patterns of maternal alcohol use are most likely to result in FASD. Chronic alcohol use in the mother can lead to malnutrition due to reduced intake and absorption of key nutrients, increasing the FASD risk.

Treatment and prognosis

7.56 There is no treatment for foetal alcohol syndrome, and the damage to the child's brain and organs cannot be reversed. Early diagnosis and support can help with educational and behavioural strategies to meet the child's needs. FASD is a lifelong condition; severe FASD reduces life expectancy due to cardiac and renal problems. Studies have shown a life expectancy at birth of people with FASD of 34 years.

Likely outcomes in adulthood

7.57 People with FASD have a higher rate of incarceration and arrest, with approximately half facing legal trouble at some point. The prison population has a much higher proportion of people with FASD than the general population. Crimes are usually impulsive: shoplifting; stealing due to a lack of understanding of personal ownership; and fighting as a result of an overreaction.

Drug use in pregnancy and the effect on the foetus

7.58 There is no specific syndrome equivalent to FASD for children whose mothers have used drugs during pregnancy. However, prenatal illicit drug use is more prevalent among mothers of children with FASD, and it can lead to similar physical, cognitive and behavioural impairments that are relevant to FASD diagnosis.

Cocaine, opiates and amphetamines have been found to increase the risk of intrauterine growth restriction, low birth weight, small head circumference and congenital anomalies. Prenatal cocaine exposure may impair attention, speech and language development. Opiate exposure can lead to neonatal abstinence syndrome, which is characterised by abnormal arousal and irritability.

Prenatal illicit drug use is associated with a range of factors that can contribute to problems for the child, including low socioeconomic status, parental mental health problems, emotional and physical abuse and lack of social support. Also, mothers who use drugs are more likely to have unplanned pregnancies, not attend prenatal appointments, have pregnancy complications, and poor nutrition.

Case Study – Foetal alcohol spectrum disorder – Phillip and Jerome's stories (see Appendix: Case studies, p 328.)

Further information

The UK and Ireland incidence of Foetal Alcohol Syndrome (FAS)

Lu, A and Johnston K. Advances in Dual Diagnosis, Vol. 12 No. 1/2, pp. 99-102
https://www.emerald.com/insight/content/doi/10.1108/ADD-02-2019-041/full/html

First UK estimates of children who could have conditions caused by drinking in pregnancy revealed

https://www.bristol.ac.uk/news/2018/november/first-uk-prevalence-estimate-fasd.html

Prenatal alcohol exposure: identification improves outcomes

https://www.guidelinesinpractice.co.uk/paediatrics/prenatal-alcohol-exposure-identification-improves-outcomes/454774.article

Life Expectancy of People with Fetal Alcohol Syndrome

https://www.ncbi.nlm.nih.gov/pubmed/26962962

FASD and the Law – Criminal Justice

https://www.nofas.org/criminal-justice/

GENDER DYSPHORIA (GD)

(See also **Chapter 14** Developmental disorders in adults.)

7.59 Gender atypical behaviour is common among young children and may be part of their normal development. Cross-gender behaviours may start between the ages of two and four years – the same age at which most typically developing children begin showing gendered behaviours and interests.

Gender dysphoria (GD) is extreme discomfort caused by a discrepancy between a person's gender at birth – 'assigned gender' – and the gender they feel themselves to be – 'affirmed gender'. Children with gender dysphoria can experience anguish as they can feel 'trapped' inside a body that does not match the gender that feels right to them.

The reason why some people experience GD is not fully understood. It is likely that the development of gender identity is multifactorial and influenced by both biological and social factors. GD can be more distressing in adolescence due to the pubertal development of secondary sex characteristics and increasing social divisions between genders. As a result, adolescents with GD can be at risk of self-harm, despair and can become vulnerable to relationship difficulties, social isolation and stigma.

Prevalence

7.60 The prevalence of GD in the general population of children in the UK is unclear, but estimates are that about 3 per cent of children referred to Child and Adolescent Mental Health Service teams present with GD. The number of adolescents referred to specialised gender identity clinics appears to be increasing. This number does not reflect those who may have consulted their GP or sought private support.

Symptoms and behaviour

7.61 For a diagnosis of gender dysphoria, the young person must show at least six of the following, and associated significant distress or impairment in function, lasting at least six months:

- a strong desire to be of the other gender or insistence that they are the other gender;
- a strong preference for wearing clothes typical of the opposite gender;
- a strong preference for cross-gender roles in make-believe or fantasy play;
- a strong preference for the toys, games and activities stereotypically used or engaged in by the other gender;
- a strong preference for playmates of the other gender;

- a strong rejection of toys, games and activities typical of their assigned gender;
- a strong dislike of their sexual anatomy;
- a strong desire for the physical sex characteristics that match their affirmed gender.

Causes

7.62 There is no identified cause of GD, but theories include attachment difficulties in childhood, brain hormonal sensitivity and differences in brain anatomy. Some other mental disorders have been linked with a higher incidence of GD. For instance, it's more common in children and young people who are severely depressed or have autism spectrum disorder or a severe adjustment disorder. The young person's lack of 'social identity' and separateness may cause them to feel so alienated that they search for an explanation.

Treatment and prognosis

7.63 After counselling and assessment, hormone treatment to suppress puberty or prevent further sexual development may be used, possibly for several years to give the young person time to make decisions about their gender identity. These treatments stop the development of secondary sex characteristics, such as breasts and widened hips in girls or the deepening of the voice and growth of facial hair in boys. They also prevent the added distress of the body acting in a way that does not align with the young person's affirmed gender. Some young people may then go on to take sex hormones, and some of those will have gender reassignment surgery in adulthood.

Of children diagnosed with GD, only 10 to 30 per cent continue with this diagnosis after the onset of puberty into adolescence and beyond. However, the incidence of associated mental health problems is high. These include anxiety, depression and a higher risk of self-injury and suicide. In a study of transgender teens, more than half of transgender males and almost 30 per cent of transgender females reported attempting suicide. An adolescent who is experiencing distress because of their gender identity, especially if they are bullied or ostracised, is also at heightened risk of substance abuse.

Parental attitudes are key to a young person's wellbeing.

Case study – Gender dysphoria – Jay's story (see Appendix: Case studies, p 330.)

Further information

Stigma in psychiatry seen through the lens of sexuality and gender

Michael King. BJPsych International July 2019
www.cambridge.org/core/journals/bjpsych-international/article/stigma-in-psychiatry-seen-through-the-lens-of-sexuality-and-gender/FF24E21150B556BD429F39102B7FF2CE

Assessment and support of children and adolescents with gender dysphoria

Gary Butler et al
https://adc.bmj.com/content/103/7/631

SPECIFIC LEARNING DISABILITIES (SPLD)

7.64 Specific learning disabilities (SpLD) differ from learning disability as they do not affect general intelligence, whereas a learning disability is linked to an overall cognitive impairment. SpLD is a neurodevelopment disorder that is usually identified in a child's school years, although it may not be recognised until adulthood.

Specific learning disability refers to a difference or difficulty with particular aspects of learning, such as the ability to listen, think, speak, write, spell or do mathematical calculations, and will impact to varying degrees on everyday activities. Examples of specific learning disorder are dyspraxia, dyslexia, dyscalculia, dysgraphia and attention deficit hyperactivity disorder, but are usually referred to under the term of SpLD. Individual presentations can be complex and include more than one disorder overlapping.

Further information

Royal College of Psychiatrists – Specific learning disabilities: for parents and carers

https://www.rcpsych.ac.uk/mental-health/parents-and-young-people/information-for-parents-and-carers/specific-learning-disabilities-for-parents-and-carers

Helen Arkell Dyslexia Charity – What Is An SpLD?

https://www.helenarkell.org.uk/about-dyslexia/what-is-an-spld.php

EDUCATION, HEALTH AND SOCIAL CARE PLANS (EHC PLANS)

7.65 The term 'Special Educational Needs' is used to describe learning difficulties or disabilities that make it harder for children to learn than most children of the same age. Children with Special Educational Needs (SEN) are likely to need extra or different help from that given to other children of their age.

There are four areas of Special Educational Needs:

- communication and interaction;
- cognition and learning;
- social, emotional and mental health difficulties; and
- sensory and/or physical needs.

Most children with special educational needs have them met in a mainstream school or an in early years settings, although some children with more complex needs benefit from more specialist help offered in a special school. More boys than girls present with special educational needs, with boys representing around 73 per cent.

Education, Health and Care Plan (EHC plan)

7.66 An EHC plan can be issued to a child or young person between the ages of 0 and 25 years. The plan identifies the educational, health and social needs of the individual and sets out the additional support required to meet those needs. The assessment is carried out by the

Local Authority who have the legal duty to carry out the process. An EHC plan can result in additional funding and support for a child or young person.

The most common need for an EHC plan is for children and young people with a diagnosis of Autistic Spectrum Disorder and for those in need of additional support with speech, communication and language.

Special Educational Needs and Disability Tribunal (SEND)

7.67 SEND is an independent tribunal which hears parents' and young people's appeals against Local Authority decisions about the EHC plan. The tribunal also hears appeals against discrimination by schools or local authorities due to a child's disability.

The appeals heard against Local Authority decisions regarding special educational needs include refusals to:

- assess a child or young person's educational, health and care (EHC) needs;
- reassess their EHC needs;
- issue an EHC plan;
- change what's in a child or young person's EHC plan;
- maintain the EHC plan.

The tribunal also deals with appeals against decisions to refuse young people in custody:

- an EHC assessment;
- an EHC plan after assessment;
- a placement to a suitable school, or other educational institution, after their release.

The SEND tribunal looks at the evidence put before it and decides whether the Local Authority's decision followed the law and had regard to the SEND code of practice. It will make a decision based on what is right for the child or young person at the date of the hearing.

Further information

Special Educational Needs – advice for parents and carers

https://www.familylives.org.uk

IPSEA – EHC needs assessments

https://www.ipsea.org.uk/ehc-needs-assessments

Courts and Tribunal Service – The Special Educational Needs Tribunal

https://www.gov.uk/courts-tribunals/first-tier-tribunal-special-educational-needs-and-disability

The SEND Code of Practice

https://www.gov.uk/government/publications/send-code-of-practice-0-to-25

Chapter 8

Psychotic disorders in children

PSYCHOSIS

(See also **Chapter 12** Psychotic disorders in adults.)

8.01 The term psychosis is used to describe conditions where the child has hallucinations and unusual ideas and is completely detached from reality. The term 'psychotic disorders' describes illnesses that have psychotic symptoms

Psychosis can be a symptom of a serious mental illness like bipolar affective disorder or schizophrenia. In a psychotic episode, a child might hear voices, see or feel things that aren't there, feel paranoid or believe things that don't rationally make sense. These symptoms are usually of short duration and may only present for several weeks. Although it can be frightening, psychosis is treatable. Some people have one episode of psychosis and never have another, while others might need ongoing treatment.

Prevalence

8.02 Hearing voices or seeing things is not uncommon in children. Preschool children will often talk to and interact with an imaginary friend, for example. Studies have shown that up to one-fifth of young people have had the experience of hearing voices or sounds when there is no-one around, or seeing visions. This is very different from the voices associated with psychosis.

Psychosis is rare in children, affecting less than 0.5 per cent. It is a serious disorder and usually requires hospital treatment, which may be voluntary or more likely to be on a section of the Mental Health Act 1983.

Symptoms and behaviour

8.03 Children suffering psychosis may hear voices and see people or objects that do not exist (auditory and visual hallucinations), or they may smell things or feel touched by things that are not there. They have frightening and persistent ideas that people are against them, and they cannot be convinced by trusted care-givers that these ideas are not true. These are known as paranoid delusions. Young children with psychosis say the voice is in their brain whereas adults usually report voices as coming from outside.

Other disorders with psychotic symptoms include severe depression, schizoaffective disorder and bipolar affective disorder, in which there are mood symptoms (elation and or depression) and delusions or hallucinations. These symptoms are 'mood-congruent', which means they are of a depressive quality, such as the child being told by voices that they are going to die, or feeling that parts of their body are not functioning.

Causes

8.04 The most typical causes of psychotic symptoms in adolescents are recreational drugs, including amphetamines, ecstasy, LSD and especially cannabis. The use of drugs and their withdrawal can cause symptoms. Psychotic symptoms may also occur during times of severe stress and sleep deprivation.

Children with autism can have psychotic symptoms. So can children with epilepsy, especially if the seizures originate in their brain's temporal lobe. In older children and adolescents, hallucinations can be part of an adjustment disorder, which is later diagnosed as an emotionally unstable personality disorder.

Treatment and prognosis

8.05 Psychosis is usually treated using medications called antipsychotics or neuroleptics. There are also treatments such as cognitive behaviour therapy or counselling to help overcome the experience of psychosis. As the treatments and prognosis of the different psychotic disorders vary, they are considered in the following pages under each condition.

Further information

Psychosis in children

https://www.nice.org.uk/search?q=psychos+in+children

Psychosis in children: diagnosis and treatment

https://www.ncbi.nlm.nih.gov/pmc/articles/PMC3181648/

What is psychosis?

https://youngminds.org.uk/find-help/conditions/psychosis/

BIPOLAR AFFECTIVE DISORDER

(See also **Chapter 12** Psychotic disorders in adults.)

8.06 Bipolar disorder is a mood disorder most often diagnosed in older children and teenagers, but it can occur in children of any age. As in adults, bipolar disorder in children can cause mood swings from the highs of hyperactivity or euphoria (mania) to the lows of serious depression. The criteria used to diagnose bipolar disorder in children and adolescents are the same as those used for the adult population.

Prevalence

8.07 There are estimated to be around 4 million cases of mood disorders, including bipolar disorder, in the UK. More than 3 per cent of children and adolescents have some form of bipolar disorder, which is about half of the incidence in adults. The most severe form of bipolar disorder affects an estimated 0.5 per cent of children or young people, and it occurs equally in both sexes.

Symptoms and behaviour

8.08 Emotional upheaval and unruly behaviours are a normal part of childhood and adolescent years, and in most cases are not a sign of a mental health problem that requires treatment. However, if the child's symptoms are severe, ongoing or causing significant problems, it may be more than just a phase.

Signs and symptoms of bipolar disorder in children include:

- severe mood swings that are different from their usual mood swings;
- hyperactive, impulsive, aggressive or socially inappropriate behaviour;
- risky and reckless behaviours that are out of character, such as having frequent casual sex with many different partners (sexual promiscuity), alcohol or drug abuse, or wild spending sprees;
- insomnia or significantly decreased need for sleep;
- depressed or irritable mood for most of the day, nearly every day during a depressive episode;
- grandiose and inflated view of their own capabilities;
- suicidal thoughts or behaviours in older children and adolescents.

Children with bipolar disorder experience symptoms in distinct episodes. Between these episodes, the child returns to their usual behaviour and mood.

A number of other childhood disorders can cause bipolar-like symptoms, including attention-deficit hyperactivity disorder, oppositional defiant disorder, conduct disorder, anxiety disorders and major depression. Diagnosis can be challenging because these and other mental health conditions often occur along with bipolar affective disorder.

Causes

8.09 It is not known why bipolar develops. Current research indicates that there are multiple biological and life experience factors that increase the risk of a child developing the disorder:

Genetic factors – It is thought that genetic factors increase the likelihood of being diagnosed with bipolar disorder by up to 50 per cent. However, it is important to note that only 6 per cent of children with a parent who has bipolar disorder also develop the condition.

Environmental factors – Certain factors make some children more likely to become depressed, which puts them at increased risk of developing bipolar disorder. These risk factors may include poverty; ongoing environmental stresses, such as a parent who is mentally ill or abusing substances; harsh or abusive parenting; violence or other trauma; abusing drugs or alcohol; or a family history of depression.

Brain chemistry/development factors – The exact mechanisms are not understood, but it is known that both genetic and environmental risk factors can alter brain chemistry and development.

Treatment and prognosis

8.10 There is no complete cure for bipolar disorder, but with early diagnosis and treatment the illness can generally be controlled, allowing children and adolescents to return to more normal functioning. Treatment methods can involve a multidimensional approach, including both medication and talk therapy.

Likely outcomes in adulthood

8.11 Bipolar disorder is a chronic recurring illness. A person with the condition is likely to experience an average of ten episodes in their lifetime. The condition can respond well to treatment, in conjunction with good compliance with medication.

Further information

Bipolar disorder: assessment and management

https://www.nice.org.uk/guidance/cg185

SCHIZOPHRENIA

(See also **Chapter** 12 Psychotic disorders in adults.)

Prevalence

8.12 Childhood-onset schizophrenia is rare in young children. An Office for National Statistics survey reported that the prevalence of psychotic disorders in children aged between 5 and 18 years was 0.4 per cent. Schizophrenia accounts for 24.5 per cent of all adolescent (10–18 years) psychiatric admissions with an exponential rise across the adolescent years. The rise in incidence increases most significantly from 15 years onwards.

Symptoms and behaviour

8.13 Schizophrenia is one of the most serious mental disorders in childhood. Not only does the child suffer hallucinations, which means they see visions, hear noises or voices, smell things and feel touched by things that aren't there, but their thinking can be distorted by distressing paranoid ideas. Another common symptom is 'thought disorder', where their thoughts are so muddled that their speech may be incomprehensible. They may also experience 'thought withdrawal', believing someone or something has removed thoughts from their mind. These symptoms may appear alongside paranoid ideas.

Symptoms can be divided into two broad areas known as 'positive' and 'negative symptoms'. A child or young person experiencing positive symptoms displays a change in their behaviour or thought processes. Some may report that their body has been altered in some way and/or that a member of their family is an imposter. When the voices the child hears are 'command hallucinations' – meaning they tell the child to do things – this is very risky and can result in harm to themselves or to others.

'Negative symptoms' is the term describing withdrawal and loss of interests and skills, for example, disinterest in other people, loss of motivation and lack of self-care. These can be evident for a year before delusions and hallucinations develop. A child with schizophrenia may also have eccentric ideas, odd perceptions and be disorganised. They can be completely distracted by their symptoms, unable to speak, or speaking in a way that cannot be understood.

Causes

8.14 Schizophrenia in younger children is associated with brain abnormalities. Children with psychosis have a smaller than average brain before the illness begins and increased loss of brain cells. Birth complications may be relevant. Before the onset of illness, children who develop schizophrenia often have delayed language acquisition, reading skills and bladder control.

There is a genetic component. If a parent has schizophrenia, the risk of their child developing the condition is ten times greater than in the general child population. Also, specific genes make children more vulnerable to many disorders, including psychotic disorders and a child showing symptoms of schizophrenia should be screened for these genes. One such genetic disorder, known as DiGeorge syndrome, can cause developmental delay and in later years and increase risk of developing mental illnesses such as schizophrenia, depression, anxiety and bipolar affective disorder.

Cannabis use in adolescence can trigger schizophrenia, especially in those predisposed to the condition. Cannabis use worsens the course of illness in patients who already have schizophrenia. Those who use cannabis before age 18 can develop psychosis earlier; the more frequent the use, the earlier the onset.

Treatments and prognosis

8.15 NICE guidelines recommend medication to help alleviate the most distressing symptoms of schizophrenia. Oral antipsychotic medication that is used for adults is also given to children but in smaller doses. Children are not given depot (injectable) medications.

If the child or young person becomes be very distressed with symptoms of their illness, putting themselves and others at risk, they may need to be admitted to hospital for treatment. This may involve being put on a section of the Mental Health Act 1983 if they are unable to agree to informal admission.

Psychological treatment can be helpful and is adapted for children. Specifically, targeted cognitive behaviour therapy is used to help the child manage their distress, due to psychotic symptoms. Psychological treatment can include treatment interventions such as drama, play and art therapy and social skills training. Inpatient psychiatric units place emphasis on continuing with the child's education at a level they can cope with.

The prognosis of early-onset schizophrenia is poor. The duration of untreated psychosis is directly related to the outcome. Unfortunately, this can be a long time in children as the disease progresses insidiously. One-third of children will not fully recover from their first episode.

Likely outcomes in adulthood

8.16 Adults who developed schizophrenia in childhood may be so disabled by the condition that they never complete their education or are able to work. Thirty per cent of people with schizophrenia never recover fully from their first episode and require 24-hour support.

Case study – Schizophrenia, early-onset – Tom's story (see Appendix: Case studies, p 332.)

Further information

Clinical Topics in Child and Adolescent Psychiatry (chapter 16)

Sarah Huline-Dickens RCPsych Publications ISBN1909726176

Psychosis and schizophrenia in children and young people

https://www.nice.org.uk/guidance/cg155/evidence/full-guideline-pdf-6785647416

Chapter 9

Vulnerability factors and mental disorders in young people

9.01 This chapter looks at the risk factors which may make young people more susceptible to experiencing mental disorders, such as family background, medical needs or lifestyle choices; it asks questions and discusses the issues raised. The chart at the end of the chapter summarises the possible risk factors and protective factors that can affect a young person's mental health.

DOES DRUG USE IN YOUNG PEOPLE INCREASE THEIR RISK OF MENTAL DISORDERS?

9.02 An NHS survey of schoolchildren published in November 2019 showed that 24 per cent of school pupils reported they had taken drugs:

- the likelihood of having taken drugs increases with age, from 9 per cent of 11 year-olds to 38 per cent of 15 year-olds;
- 17 per cent of pupils said that they had taken drugs in the last year;
- cannabis is the drug that pupils are most likely to have taken in the previous year, with 8 per cent saying they had used it.

Young people receiving specialist substance misuse treatment in secure settings reported that cannabis was the most common substance used (91 per cent of all young people in treatment). Just under half said they had problematic alcohol use, followed by nicotine (22 per cent), and powder cocaine (16 per cent).

Cannabis and other substance misuse and mental illness in young people

9.03

- There is a clear link between cannabis and psychosis. Young people who use cannabis in their mid-teens have a higher than average risk of developing a psychotic illness in adulthood.

- Cannabis affects the developing brain in other ways too. Because of the role of the body's endocannabinoid system in regulating mood and reward, brain changes resulting from early use of marijuana may interfere with motivation. This is significant for young people.
- Whether adolescent cannabis use contributes to developing psychosis in adulthood seems to depend on whether a person already has a genetically based vulnerability to the disorder.
- Cannabis lowers mood, and adolescents who use cannabis daily are five times more likely to develop depression and anxiety in later life.
- There is a proven link between cannabis use and reduced educational performance. Cannabis affects the hippocampus – the part of the brain associated with memory, concentration, and the ability to organise and use information. A reduction in the size of the hippocampus is sufficient to cause noticeable effects. This effect seems to last several weeks after use, which can cause problems for students.
- Cannabis reduces reaction time owing to its effects on concentration; this delayed reaction time would affect any young person's ability to drive safely, particularly on motorbikes, which offer less protection for the driver than a car.
- Drug use in England has changed over recent years, with most drugs now available in more potent forms, such as skunk, which is a potent form of cannabis. Ecstasy is more potent than five to ten years ago. These more potent products are more likely to trigger psychosis. Solvents, which don't cause psychosis, are rather out of fashion as other substances are more freely available. Spice and khat also cause psychosis, and young people are particularly vulnerable.
- Drugs are relatively inexpensive and freely available. At the time of writing, ecstasy is £5 to £10 a tablet. Cannabis to make five or six joints cost £10. Spice can be bought for 50p a bag in inner cities. The selling of drugs has changed from small numbers of dealers to children being approached outside school gates to join 'county lines' gangs moving illegal drugs around the country.
- Recently there has been a new trend of teenagers buying helium and nitrous oxide. Nitrous oxide is sold in small metal containers and used industrially in the production of ice cream. Inhaling these gases produces a short-term euphoric effect, but both nitrous oxide and helium can, in rare cases, cause death.
- Drugs often contain other substances which can include toxic chemicals that are harmful.

Further Information

Statistics on Drug Misuse, England NHS 2019

https://digital.nhs.uk/data-and-information/publications/statistical/statistics-on-drug-misuse/2019

The contribution of cannabis use to variation in the incidence of psychotic disorder across Europe (EU-GEI) The Lancet Psychiatry, May 2019

https://www.thelancet.com/article/S2215-0366(19)30048-3/fulltext

DOES ALCOHOL USE IN YOUNG PEOPLE INCREASE THEIR RISK OF MENTAL DISORDERS?

9.04 Alcohol does not have the same effect on young people as it does on adults. While alcohol misuse can present health risks and be the cause of careless behaviour in all age groups, it is even more dangerous for young people; adults tend to get more subdued and slowed down by alcohol, in adolescents, it's the opposite. Young people experience higher levels of impulsivity, and they tend to become more energetic and engage in more risky behaviour, for example, dangerous driving and unprotected sex, and they may become more aggressive; getting into fights.

Adolescence is a period complicated by chemical and hormonal changes to the body, linked to the development of the brain. Pathways between regions in the adolescent brain are still developing; this 'plasticity' means the brain easily adjusts to alcohol and drugs. Studies have shown that alcohol and drugs also affect the same brain regions that are present in behaviour disorders such as ADHD and ODD.

Alcohol use in a young person can be an indicator of other (potentially hidden) difficulties such as identity issues or adverse childhood experiences (ACEs). For some young people, it is a form of 'self-medication' which enables them to relieve stress, or block emotionally distressing thoughts. The use of alcohol can be more closely linked with self-medication for children who face additional adversity in their lives, including looked after children, those seeking asylum, those witnessing or involved in violence, and those trying to make sense of their gender and sexuality.

Alcohol misuse can escalate from experimentation to a serious disorder much faster in adolescents than it does in adults, and the progression is more likely to happen in young people with mental health disorders. A 2016 study of 10,000 adolescents found that two-thirds of those who developed alcohol or substance use disorders had experienced at least one mental health disorder.

Young people who use alcohol may do so to feel less anxious and depressed, they may also feel they integrate better by conforming to the behaviour of their peer group and it's possibly not as stigmatising in the way taking medication might be. The negative aspect is that alcohol use can mask underlying emotional problems, interferes with treatment for mental health disorders and worsens the long-term prognosis for a young person struggling with one, and often ends in abuse or dependence.

Studies have shown that trauma and other adverse life events are strongly associated with alcohol use in adolescents, and clinical screening should take place for past traumatic events. Conversely, it is important to note that not all children who experience adversity go on to misuse drugs and alcohol, and not all young people who use them have experienced trauma or become addicted.

Further information

Mental Health Disorders and Teen Substance Use

https://childmind.org/article/mental-health-disorders-and-substance-use/

Young Minds

https://youngminds.org.uk/search-results/?terms=alcohol

DO PHYSICAL ILLNESS AND DISABILITY INCREASE MENTAL DISORDERS?

9.05 In the UK, 8 per cent of children aged under 18 report a disability, according to the most recent Family Resources Survey. This is a continuous household survey which collects information on a representative sample of private households (19,000) in the UK. The definition of disability used in the self-report is that of the Equality Act 2010; a person is considered to have a disability if they have a physical or mental impairment that has 'substantial' and 'long term' negative effects on their ability to do normal daily activities.

The survey includes children with a limiting, long-standing illness (lasting 12 months or more), disability or infirmity, and those experiencing one or more significant difficulties or health problems. It also includes children who would have such difficulties or problems if they did not take medication. Children and young people with disabilities are more than twice as likely to live in households in lower socio-economic positions and exposed to poverty than those without a disability.

People from less advantaged socio-economic backgrounds tend to be disproportionately represented amongst those with disabilities. These households may be more vulnerable to lifestyle factors that can contribute to disability. In childhood, these children, like others amongst their socio-economic group, will be at risk of poor nutrition, greater rates of injury and poorer mental health. The additional costs in meeting the needs of a child with a disability can also itself be a major contributor to material poverty. Children who have a disability or chronic illness often experience social isolation due to missed schooling, limitations on their activities and stigmatising by others; this makes them more likely to experience depression and anxiety.

Schooling for many disabled children, such as those with cystic fibrosis, cerebral palsy or Down's syndrome, is disrupted by the need for hospital treatment.

CEREBRAL PALSY

9.06 Cerebral palsy (CP) is the most common physical disability in childhood. Approximately 1 in 400 babies born in the UK has cerebral palsy.

CP is caused before, during or shortly after birth as a result of injury to the brain due to any of the following reasons:

- limited or interrupted oxygen supply to the brain;
- a bleed within the baby's brain;
- a premature or difficult birth process;
- the mother catching an infection (rubella or toxoplasmosis) whilst pregnant; or
- changes in genes which affect the development of the brain.

The effect cerebral palsy has on children ranges from the very mild, to more severe cases that can make it difficult for the child to control their limbs. The type of CP depends on the brain area that is affected.

There are three types of cerebral palsy: spastic, dyskinetic and ataxic. Many people will have a mixture of all three types:

- **Spastic cerebral palsy** – accounting for about 70 per cent of cases, affects the muscles in the body, making them tight, stiff and weak, and thus making it hard to control movement.
- **Dyskinetic cerebral palsy** – accounting for about 10 per cent of cases, leads to muscle control being disrupted by spontaneous writhing movements, with the muscles used for speech sometimes also affected.
- **Ataxic cerebral palsy** – accounting for about 20 per cent of cases, causes problems with balance, shaking limbs, and speech difficulties.

Depending on the area of the brain affected, some children may experience associated difficulties which become apparent as they develop. These difficulties can include:

- crawling and walking, dressing, maintaining posture;
- feeding and speech (due to the lack of coordination of the muscles of the mouth);
- sleeping;
- writing;
- hearing or visual impairment;
- epilepsy; affecting one in three children and adolescents with cerebral palsy. It is most common among children who have limited mobility; or
- behavioural problems such as anxiety or hyperactivity – these affect one in four children with cerebral palsy.

A common misconception is that people with cerebral palsy *inevitably* have learning disabilities. This may have arisen because people with the condition can have problems controlling their facial movements and speech, and it can be difficult to understand them at first.

Cognitive or learning disabilities do occur, and it is estimated that 45 per cent of children with cerebral palsy have a learning disability. These may include a short attention span, motor planning difficulties (organisation and sequencing of movement), perceptual difficulties and language difficulties. However, as with any other children, there is a wide range of intellectual ability, and many perform very well at school.

Children and young people with cerebral palsy are at greater risk of mental health problems, such as depression and anxiety, in comparison with the general population of the same age. Their mental health problems are also likely to be under-diagnosed, as most assessments focus on the child's movement difficulty.

The transition to adulthood can be stressful for young people with CP. Young adults find themselves facing many new challenges, including making the transition to adult health care, post-secondary education or vocational training, employment, and independent living, whilst making and maintaining adult relationships. It is during this period that many young people first develop anxiety or depression.

Young adults with CP often have lower rates of employment or post-secondary education and less participation in social activities, and they tend to rely more heavily on their families for living arrangements.

Further information

Action Cerebral Palsy

https://www.actioncp.org

What is cerebral palsy?

https://www.mentalhealth.org.uk/learning-disabilities/a-to-z/c/cerebral-palsy

Scope

https://www.scope.org.uk

Children and young people with disabilities

https://www.kpho.org.uk/__data/assets/pdf_file/0006/83913/CYP-with-Disabilities-Needs-Assessment.pdf

WHY ARE SOME CHILDREN BULLIED?

9.07 Some children are vulnerable to bullying because they are different. Their appearance, health needs, educational ability, lifestyle or family situation may make them more likely to be picked-on, ignored or excluded by other children. Those who are particularly vulnerable include:

- Children who have difficulties in class, for example due to attention deficit hyperactivity disorder (ADHD) or dyspraxia.

- Children with physical disabilities, such as cerebral palsy, or genetic conditions such as Down's syndrome, who may not be able to participate in games.
- Children living in different family situations, such as with a mentally ill parent or a parent with a physical disability.
- Children with religious or cultural beliefs that are different from those of most of their peer group.
- LGBTQ+ children, and those with LGBTQ+ family members.
- Children who miss school due to illness or because they are not able to participate in some activities, perhaps because of type 1 diabetes or asthma.
- Children who have an unusual appearance, such as being very tall, or short, or having a squint or acne.
- Obese children. This is an increasing issue, and bullied children may comfort eat, which worsens the problem.
- Children whose behaviour is unusual, as with tic disorders (Tourette's syndrome, for example), especially if accompanied by noises such as sniffing and grunting, or shouting and swearing.
- Children with poor social skills – as is often the case with autism and learning disability – because they are less able to participate.
- Children with low self-esteem and those who are shy and introverted.
- Children whose self-care is deficient because of their poor socio-economic status or practical difficulties with washing.
- Children who are particularly high achievers academically or in sport, drama or music ('tall poppy syndrome').

Some children are more at risk of bullying because of a combination of factors. In racist bullying, for example, a child might be targeted because of their different physical appearance, religious beliefs, accent, clothing and lifestyle.

Consequences for the bullied child

9.08 Bullying affects children in many ways, ranging from anxiety and depression to self-harm, eating disorders and even suicide. School avoidance is common, and some bullied children may become aggressive when away from the bullying situation.

Bullying can cause physical symptoms, particularly in younger children, who are less able to describe how they feel. Symptoms such as headaches, stomach aches, lack of appetite and nausea are symptoms of distress and may help the child avoid the situation when they are bullied. Overeating for comfort with obesity makes the child even more vulnerable. Sleep disturbances, such as insomnia and nightmares, are common.

Young people who are bullied may be vulnerable to being exploited. Desperately seeing acceptance and companionship, they can be lured into becoming drug mules or being sexually exploited. Being in a gang, however risky, can protect against bullying.

The consequence for the child who becomes a bully is that they feel powerful and learn that their behaviour is effective. A bullying child is likely to become a bullying adult.

Further information

Consequences of bullying behaviour

https://www.ncbi.nlm.nih.gov/books/NBK390414/

IS THERE A LINK BETWEEN ETHNICITY AND MENTAL DISORDER?

9.09 There is no clear evidence of a direct link between specific ethnic groups and mental disorder in children. However, surveys have indicated that children from a white ethnic background (more so boys) were more likely to have a mental disorder than children identifying as black or minority ethnic. Socio-economic deprivation is an important factor. Mental disorder is four times higher among children living in poverty, whatever their ethnic background. Government data tells us that black and Asian people are more likely to live in the most deprived neighbourhoods.

Black and minority ethnic children who suffer racial discrimination are likely to experience low self-esteem and high levels of anxiety and depression. They and their families are also less likely to engage with services that could intervene early to prevent mental health problems escalating.

There are no recent statistics on child and adolescent mental health by ethnicity in the UK.

9.09 *Vulnerability factors and mental disorders in young people*

A report by the Centre for Mental Health in 2015 found that in children aged 11 years, the prevalence of severe mental health difficulties was higher in white British boys than among those of mixed ethnic backgrounds, and that girls of mixed ethnic backgrounds were at greater risk than white British girls.

Percentage of 11-year-old children with severe mental health problems (total difficulties) by ethnicity: parent ratings, UK, 2012.
Source: Centre for Mental Health: Report 2015

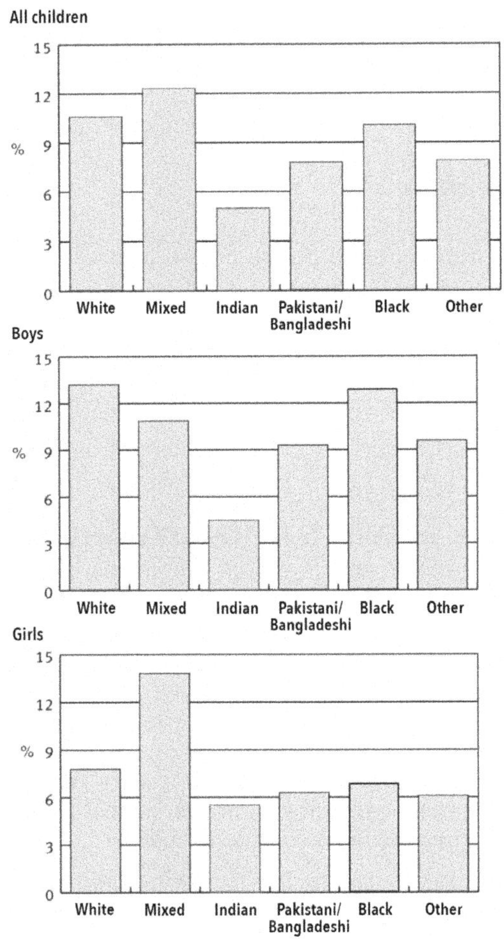

Further information

Black, Asian and Minority Ethnic (BAME) Communities Mental Health Foundation, 2019

https://www.mentalhealth.org.uk/a-to-z/b/black-asian-and-minority-ethnic-bame-communities

People living in deprived neighbourhoods Office for National Statistics. 2019

https://www.ethnicity-facts-figures.service.gov.uk/uk-population-by-ethnicity/demographics/people-living-in-deprived-neighbourhoods/latest

Mental health findings from the Millennium Cohort Study

http://cdn.basw.co.uk/upload/basw_120221-1.pdf

IS SELF-HARM *ALWAYS* LINKED TO MENTAL DISORDER?

9.10 Professor Louis Appleby at Manchester University leads the National Suicide Prevention Strategy. Statistics from their reports and surveys show that 20 per cent of young women and 8 per cent of young men admit having self-harmed. Self-harm is rising in girls aged 13 to16. Most say they do it to cope with stress.

Why is self-harm a coping mechanism? It is a way for young people to cope with overwhelming and distressing thoughts or feelings. Cutting is a typical way to self-harm, and this might give temporary relief from the emotional pain the young person is feeling. Feelings of guilt and shame can follow, which then continues the cycle of self-harm. The temporary relief, typically, from cutting, can become the young person's usual way of dealing with life's difficulties. However, the prevalence of mental disorder in young people has only shown a small rise in 20 years (from 10 per cent in 1999 to 11 per cent in 2017).

Should self-harm be taken seriously? Yes. The Manchester Self-Harm Project (MASH) followed up young people who had self-harmed and found this 'rule of 50':

- 1 in 50 young people who attend accident and emergency departments with self-harm die from suicide.

9.11 *Vulnerability factors and mental disorders in young people*

- The risk of suicide increases by 50 times the year after self-harm.

Further information

Self-harm in young people https://www.mentalhealth.org.uk/publications/truth-about-self-harm

WHY DO YOUNG PEOPLE COMMIT SUICIDE?

9.11 The clinical view of adolescent suicide is that the adolescent brain is prone to volatile moods and impulsivity. So when a young person has suicidal thoughts, they are more likely not to consider the consequences. Suicide in young people is rarely caused by one thing; it usually follows a combination of previous vulnerability factors and recent events. For example, cumulative risk factors within the family, such as the young person or a family member suffering from a mental or physical illness, or childhood abuse, bullying, alcohol or drug misuse. These factors can cause difficulties within the home, at school and subsequently, social isolation and then a 'final straw event' can precipitate a suicidal act.

Facts about suicide in young people

9.12 Professor Louis Appleby of Manchester University led a study in 2017, of 'psychological post-mortems', which examined the recording in the coroners' court when a suicide verdict was reached. Permission was sought from the coroners, who were very willing, and the families, who were often keen to talk about their child.

- Since 2010, the suicide rate in young people has risen in both boys and girls. The rate of suicide is 2.5 times higher in boys than girls (this does not include attempted suicides).
- Young people in prison are 18 times more likely to commit suicide than other young people.

Self-harm was reported in 52 per cent of under 20s and 41 per cent of 20 to 24-year-olds who died. Nine per cent of the young people aged under 20 who died had been 'looked after children', who had high rates of housing problems and suicidal ideas. Almost all had recent contact with at least one support service, but a third were not in recent contact with mental health care.

In 33 per cent of suicides, the families reported that the suicide was completely out of the blue as the young person had not reported suicidal ideas or plans. Around 60 per cent in both age groups were known to front-line agencies. Approximately 40 per cent had been in recent contact; in only 26 per cent this was mental health care.

Ethnicity and suicide in young people

9.13 In the UK black and minority ethnic (BAME) groups overall have a higher risk of associated factors for suicide attempts, but suicide is low among young Asian men and high in young Asian women compared with other ethnic groups.

Internationally, suicide rates are much higher in the USA, New Zealand and Australia than in the UK. Studies show a higher rate of risk factors such as child poverty, teenage pregnancy, or families where neither parent works in these countries. Ethnic minorities such as young Maori and Pacific Islander men are at high risk.

Social media's contribution to the risk of suicide in young people

9.14 Social media is a relatively new phenomenon and can influence suicide-related behaviour.

There is increasing evidence that the use of social media affects and changes people's lives, especially those of young people, as their use of the internet becomes more ingrained in their daily lives.

Internet sites advising on methods of suicide may discourage young people from seeking specialist help. There is evidence to suggest that social media promotes unrealistic standards of success, self-image and desirability that may affect young people's self-esteem and can encourage thoughts of self-harm and suicide.

Professor Appleby has seen a worrying trend for suicidal young people to attempt to kill themselves by hanging. There seems to be a myth among young people that hanging is painless and immediate.

Professor Appleby has worked with the media, urging them to portray the reality of hanging accurately. The aim is to emphasise that it is not immediate, causes a painful death, and if unsuccessful, can result in survivors having paralysis and brain damage.

Further information

Suicide by children and young people

University of Manchester, 2017 https://www.hqip.org.uk/wp-content/uploads/2018/02/8iQSvl.pdf

HOW ARE CHILDREN AFFECTED BY DOMESTIC VIOLENCE?

9.15 The term 'domestic violence and abuse' is used to describe an incident, or pattern of incidents, that includes coercive or controlling or threatening behaviour and violence or abuse between anyone intimately involved with each other or who are family members. These incidents may be physical, sexual, emotional or financial. Abuse can also occur from outside the home, for example, such as unwanted calls, messages and tracking from mobile phones and bullying via social media.

Victims are not confined to one gender or ethnic group. Domestic violence also includes 'honour-based' violence, female genital mutilation (FGM), and forced marriage.

The ONS, Crime Survey 2019, estimated that 2.4 million adults aged 16 to 74 years had experienced domestic abuse in the previous year (1.6 million women and 786 thousand men) an increase of 24 per cent over the year before – recent reports indicate that these figures are rising. In relationships where there is domestic violence and abuse, it is estimated children witness about three-quarters of the abusive incidents and about half the children in such families and themselves have been hit or beaten. Consequently, children not only witness the abuse, but they also experience it and are living in homes in fear of what might happen next.

Domestic abuse has a devastating impact on children and young people that can last into adulthood. One in seven children (14.2 per cent) and young people under the age of 18 will have witnessed domestic violence in their childhood.

Exposure to domestic violence and abuse harms a child's emotional, psychological and physical development. Children who are exposed to violence are more likely to have difficulty at school, abuse drugs and alcohol, act aggressively, suffer from depression and other mental health problems and are more likely to engage in criminal behaviour as adults. Some children will feel socially isolated and find it difficult to make friends easily, due to confusion over what is socially acceptable behaviour. They may develop symptoms of post-traumatic stress disorder, experiencing flashbacks and nightmares; they may also develop physical symptoms. As adults, children who have witnessed violence and abuse are more likely to become involved in violent and abusive relationships with others.

Further information

NSPCA – Domestic abuse

https://www.nspcc.org.uk/what-is-child-abuse/types-of-abuse/domestic-abuse/

Domestic violence and abuse – the impact on children and adolescents

https://www.rcpsych.ac.uk/mental-health/parents-and-young-people/information-for-parents-and-carers/domestic-violence-and-abuse-effects-on-children?searchTerms=Domestic%20abuse%20and%20children

Summary of risk factors and protective for mental disorder in children

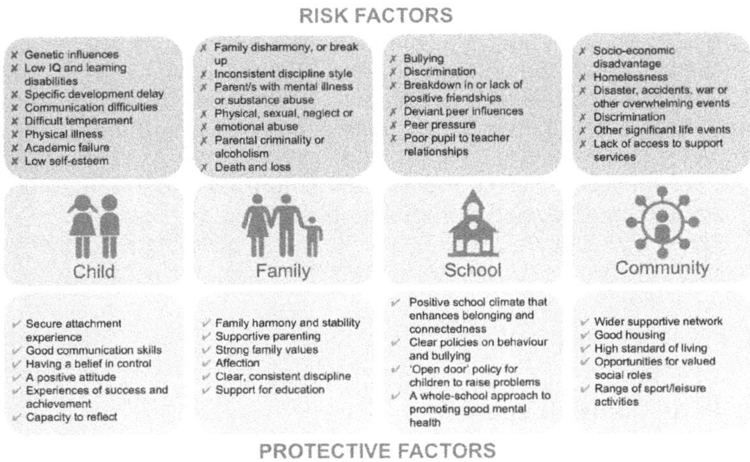

[5]

Further information

The mental health of children and young people in England (PHE Report 2016)

https://dera.ioe.ac.uk/32622/1/MHCYP%202017%20Summary.pdf

Family Resources Survey 2018/19

https://www.gov.uk/government/statistics/family-resources-survey-financial-year-201819

UK Poverty 2019/20

https://www.jrf.org.uk/report/uk-poverty-2019-20

Chapter 10

Mental disorders, relationships and parenting

10.01 This chapter discusses how some mental disorders may affect the behaviour of a parent or carer to such an extent that they are unable to carry out the parenting role safely or appropriately. This difficulty may be short-lived or permanent, depending on the adult's mental disorder.

Many parents with mental disorders are able to meet their children's needs. It is not inevitable that parents with mental disorders cannot nurture their children. However, if the disorder is untreated, it may affect the parent's motivation and ability to care for their child.

Some mental disorders may have a subtler effect on parenting, which only becomes evident as the child gets older. Examples include autism spectrum disorder and attention deficit hyperactivity disorder, where the parent's lack of social awareness or social skills can have a profound effect on the child's development. Parents with severe anxiety, especially social phobia, or severe obsessive-compulsive disorder, may also have difficulty coping with social situations, thus isolating the family and the child.

In this chapter we look at the mental disorders most likely to cause problems within the family when a parent is unwell, starting with those disorders that can have the most severe impact on relationships and parenting.

DEPRESSION AND POSTNATAL DEPRESSION

10.02 **Effect on the relationship between partners** – in severe depression the person may spend all their time in bed, not sleeping or oversleeping, lacking concentration and motivation for even self-care, so will have little emotional response to a partner. They may believe they are suffering a life-threatening illness. Suicidal thoughts are common, and they may make suicide plans.

Effect on parenting skills – depressive illness before pregnancy, or developing during pregnancy or after birth (postnatal depression), has a significant impact on the mother's ability to bond with the baby. The parent's lack of self-care will diminish their ability to care for a child. Unless there is a functioning carer, the child may be at risk of neglect.

Postpartum psychosis – this is particularly dangerous for the baby as the mother can be deluded, thinking the baby is an alien, contains a spirit, or has magical or unusual powers. The mother may mask the symptoms, and this can be lethal for the baby if the mother, without warning, acts on or tests out her beliefs about her baby. In severe depression, the parent's delusion that life is not worth living can, in rare cases, result in suicide and infanticide.

Depression and fathers – bonding between the father and baby can also be disrupted. Surveys show 10 per cent of men suffer depression after the birth of a baby, perhaps triggered by the change in their role, feeling sidelined, disruption to their routine, or sleep deprivation.

The parent can be a danger to their partner and children if they have delusions or command hallucinations (for example, voices telling them to carry out an act) and are paranoid so don't trust anyone or ask for or accept help. If the delusions involve the child or partner, this can be a lethal risk.

SCHIZOPHRENIA AND SCHIZOAFFECTIVE DISORDER

10.03 Effect on the relationship between partners – Psychotic symptoms, such as hallucinations and paranoia, are hugely disruptive. Paranoia can be directed towards the partner.

Schizoaffective disorder is also characterised by mood changes from elation to depression, which affects the parents' relationship. The mood changes can be unpredictable. Often people with these conditions do not recognise when they are becoming unwell or in need of treatment. Negative symptoms mean the person lacks motivation, which causes difficulties for the unaffected partner.

Effect on parenting skills – psychotic symptoms, such as hallucinations and paranoia, result in irritability and reduce tolerance of children's behaviour. The parent may be too disabled by their psychotic symptoms to respond to their child's needs. Paranoia may be directed towards the child. Negative symptoms cause a lack of motivation in all areas, leading to apathy and, therefore, an inability to care for the child, as well as a lack of social stimulation and contact for the child.

FABRICATED OR INDUCED ILLNESS (FII)

(Also known as Munchausen's syndrome by proxy.)

10.04 Effect on the relationship between partners – in FII, a parent or carer repeatedly seeks help for made-up illness in their child. Typically, they travel to different hospitals to avoid detection. The parent or carer's behaviour is usually driven by a severe personality disorder, which hugely affects their ability to sustain a relationship. Any challenge by their partner about the reality of the disorder is likely to end the relationship.

Effect on parenting skills – In FII, a parent or carer, usually the mother, manufactures or mimics illness in their baby or child.

This condition needs to be acted upon as it can be extremely dangerous for the child.

BIPOLAR AFFECTIVE DISORDER (BPAD)

10.05 Effect on the relationship between partners – the mood swings of bipolar disorder are disruptive in a relationship. During a manic episode, the affected person often does not agree that they are unwell.

Manic behaviour can be risky, embarrassing (eg overtalking or sexual disinhibition), and harmful in the long term (eg overspending). The unaffected partner can often see the relapse coming, which is frustrating when the person affected cannot, and also sense the depression developing after a manic spell.

Effect on parenting skills – the manic phase of bipolar disorder may result in child neglect due to lack of concentration, or the pursuit of grandiose enthusiasms. A manic phase is often precipitated by sleep deprivation, a common situation after childbirth. Women who have bipolar disorder are particularly at risk of relapse in the first ten days after giving birth, not just due to sleep deprivation but also the hormonal changes after birth.

The unpredictability of having a parent with bipolar disorder can be damaging for the child. They risk being neglected in a depressed episode, but overexcited and treated irresponsibly when the parent or carer is high – perhaps staying up all night with them, missing school, or being encouraged to behave inappropriately. There's also the potential for embarrassment or bullying when friends witness the parent's inappropriate behaviour. Additional risks relate to the parent being unaware of their own dangerous behaviour, such as driving when unwell.

DRUG-INDUCED PSYCHOSIS

10.06 Effect on the relationship between partners – this is a disorder with a sudden onset directly related to drug use. Skunk (potent cannabis), crack cocaine and khat are drugs that typically cause psychosis. The drug-taker has delusions (which they may act on) and is paranoid, disorientated, hallucinating and potentially aggressive. If this is a purely drug-induced disorder, and not schizophrenia, it should resolve within seven days. If the other partner is not a drug-user, such relapses may be difficult to tolerate in a relationship.

Effect on parenting skills – the acute symptoms of paranoia and disorientation are a danger to the child, not just through neglect, but also through being exposed to risks during the time the parent is unable to care for them. The home environment is likely to be risky due to drug-taking equipment being accessible to the child.

ACQUIRED BRAIN INJURY (ABI)

10.07 Effect on the relationship between partners – the impact on the carer is such that divorce rates are higher post-ABI than with any other illness or injury (80 per cent). Partners find coping with the cognitive, behavioural and personality changes challenging. The person is likely to be impulsive, irritable and disinhibited, but can also be apathetic and uncaring.

Effect on parenting skills – the symptoms and behaviour make it very difficult for a parent or carer with brain injury to care for a child in a sustained and consistent manner. The mixture of impulsivity, apathy and poor concentration is risky. Also, many people with head injuries experience extreme sleepiness, sleeping for 16 or more hours a day, unable to wake even if a fire alarm sounds. Another adult would need to be present to ensure safe care of children.

AUTISM SPECTRUM DISORDER (ASD)

10.08 Effect on the relationship between partners – the lack of reciprocal social interaction in ASD means the parent can be unable to recognise when another person is upset. They may not realise that they are talking about a topic that the other person has moved on from. People with ASD can have difficulty recognising when another person is distressed, and may not easily make new friends due to anxiety in social situations. An additional problem is the high rate of other disabling and distressing mental illnesses in people who have ASD. These can include depression, social anxiety, attention deficit hyperactivity disorder and obsessive-compulsive disorder.

Effect on parenting skills – the affected parent or carer may have difficulty recognising social cues in their child, and communication problems may mean they give the appearance of being aloof and uncaring. The parent or carer's lack of eye contact and difficulty recognising emotion may make them unable to respond appropriately to a child. However, basic care needs may be carried out well.

LEARNING DISABILITY

10.09 Effect on the relationship between partners – the difficulties are not so much in making relationships – many people with learning disability successfully do so. More problematic is maintaining them, with the day-to-day responsibilities of self-care, domestic living, and self-direction. Women with a learning disability may be vulnerable to sexual and emotional exploitation.

Effect on parenting skills – the affected parent›s impaired skills can have a significant effect on their ability to recognise their baby or child's needs. However, depending on the degree of learning disability, and if the parent can accept appropriate support, the outcome can be positive.

SEVERE PERSONALITY DISORDERS

10.10 Effect on the relationship between partners – being in a relationship with someone who has a personality disorder is challenging. Typical features of a personality disorder include: not trusting other people; lack of emotion; feelings of emptiness; extreme fear of rejection; reckless and impulsive behaviour; being overly dramatic and striving always to be the centre of attention (may include self-harm); perfectionism and being excessively critical of others; and an inability to see the bigger picture.

Most people with a severe personality disorder think the problem is with others rather than themselves. Self-medication with alcohol and or drugs adds to impulsive behaviour and makes supporting a partner and family difficult as they tend not to maintain employment.

Effect on parenting skills – the same factors leading to difficulty in relationships apply to the parenting of a child. People with personality disorders are likely to have been neglected or abused in childhood themselves, so they have no positive parental role models to use with their children. When a parent cannot tolerate their baby or child›s demands, there is a high risk of physical abuse. An emotionally unstable personality disorder, with changeable moods and self-harm, can severely impair the ability of even a motivated mother to manage her baby's needs. Sociopathic personality disorder, with a resulting callousness towards others' needs, can be a problem in a father who is then 'sidelined' by his partner who is caring for their baby. Domestic violence is a risk.

DRUG AND ALCOHOL ABUSE

(Alone or in combination with a mental disorder.)

10.11 Effect on the relationship between partners – periods of intoxication and withdrawal mean the affected parent is focused only on the need for their next substance fix. Typically, the parent who abuses alcohol and/or drugs will promise to abstain. Promises like this become increasingly unbelievable, and this breaks trust in the relationship. Drug and alcohol use is one of the leading causes of domestic violence, with money being diverted into funding the habit. Female partners can be pressurised into prostitution to supply money.

Effect on parenting skills – drug and alcohol use, either abuse or dependence, result in inconsistent responses to the baby or child's needs during periods of intoxication and withdrawal. Drug-seeking behaviour takes precedence over child care, such as providing regular meals and routine. Irritability and impulsivity may result in physical abuse of the child, in addition to the emotional neglect.

Young children may be at risk of needle stick injuries from drug-taking equipment in the home, or from accidentally taking drugs. Children may be deliberately encouraged by an addicted parent to experiment with substances. Studies suggest that at least one-third of looked-after children come into care with a parental history of alcohol misuse.

EATING DISORDERS

10.12 Effect on the relationship between partners – a relationship with a person who has an eating disorder can be strained by their preoccupation with weight loss, restricting food, excessive exercise and narrowing of interests to that of losing weight. It can be difficult for an unaffected partner to empathise with the fear of weight gain and the subsequent avoidance of social situations requiring the person to eat at a family social event, or in public.

Men with eating disorders tend to become preoccupied with body shape, particularly muscle bulk. Excessive time spent in the gym means neglect of their partner. Steroid abuse can be present and typically causes mood swings, irritability and aggression, which can be directed towards the partner.

Effect on parenting skills – anorexia nervosa is a potential, but rare, cause of a mother underfeeding her baby for fear it will become obese. Usually, women with anorexia who succeed with pregnancy (being underweight reduces fertility) do have a healthy baby. Issues can arise later with the child's feeding, or in adolescence when a daughter may copy her mother's food restriction or be affected by the mother's social withdrawal to focus on weight loss. For men, the time spent in the gym means neglect of their parenting responsibilities. The irritability due to steroid abuse can result in intolerance towards the needs of children.

SEVERE ANXIETY

10.13 Effect on the relationship between partners – both the bodily symptoms and the fears and dread caused by severe anxiety can be almost paralysing. In phobias and social anxiety, it can be difficult for an unaffected partner to empathise with the fear and the subsequent avoidance of situations. Much of the breadwinning, domestic work and childcare can then become the role of the non-anxious parent, causing stress.

Effect on parenting skills – it's clear that children are affected by their parent or carer's anxious behaviour, and that this can damage the attachment between them. An anxious-avoidant parent can produce the same behaviour in their child.

POST-TRAUMATIC STRESS DISORDER (PTSD)

10.14 Effect on the relationship between partners – distressing symptoms, such as flashbacks, nightmares, repetitive and disturbing images or sensations, can lead a parent with PTSD to avoid people or places that remind them of their trauma. They may even avoid talking to anyone. Many people with PTSD try to push memories of the traumatic event out of their mind, often distracting themselves with work or hobbies. This effort may hinder their ability to be affectionate and maintain a relationship.

Effect on parenting skills – hyperarousal in a parent or carer with PTSD often leads to irritability, angry outbursts, sleeping problems and difficulty concentrating. This will impact on their ability to provide consistent child care. If the PTSD is a result of domestic abuse or rape, and the child shows a facial resemblance to the abuser or is perceived by the parent to resemble the abuser, the parent may neglect or even injure the child, with serious consequences.

ATTENTION DEFICIT HYPERACTIVITY DISORDER (ADHD)

10.15 Effect on the relationship between partners – the symptoms of ADHD may not present in a parent in the same way as in a child – ie hyperactivity is more usually a symptom in children. Disorganisation is common among adults with ADHD (although disorganisation in a parent is not always due to the condition; some people who are tackling several issues at once and suffering 'normal' stress may just be trying to cope with too much). A parent who is always disorganised, always late, losing things, and often missing appointment times and deadlines, even when important, may have ADHD, and this can be frustrating for the non-affected partner.

Some adults with ADHD self-medicate with stimulant drugs such as cocaine to ease restlessness, or cannabis or alcohol to relax.

Effect on parenting skills – impulsive behaviour and difficulty concentrating may interfere with child care. In later childhood, the parent may be unable to assist with the child's social development, depending on how they have coped with their own symptoms. This is significant as the chance of ADHD in the child is greatly increased by the parent having the condition.

Parents with ADHD can be a challenge for healthcare and legal professionals due to their disorganisation and difficulty keeping appointments. They may also self-medicate using substances, which increases impulsivity.

GAMBLING AND GAMING ADDICTION

10.16 Effect on the relationship between partners – gambling and gaming addictions can be so consuming that the addict has no emotional space for their partner. These addictions can also cause financial loss, which makes domestic abuse more likely. Other addictions, to drugs and alcohol, are common.

Effect on parenting skills – the most common issue is that the addicted parent is effectively ‹absent›, occupied with their interest. Financial losses from gambling or gaming can hugely affect the family›s financial security. Domestic abuse and physical abuse of the child can occur, depending on how the parent manages their impulsivity, guilt and rage at the inevitable loss.

Further information

Prevalence of maternal mental illness among children and adolescents in the UK

www.thelancet.com/journals/lanpub/article/PIIS2468-2667(19)30059-3/fulltext

Childhood abuse and neglect

https://www.nspcc.org.uk/what-is-child-abuse/types-of-abuse/neglect/

Part III

Mental disorders and illness in adults

Chapter 11

Emotional disorders in adults

ANXIETY DISORDERS

(See also **Chapter 6** Emotional disorders in children.)

11.01 Anxiety disorders are the most common of mental disorders. Loss, such as bereavement, separation, and unemployment, and other major life changes, build up with age, which can increase anxiety during adulthood.

Prevalence

11.02 Some surveys suggest that one in five adults suffer anxiety symptoms that require treatment.

Symptoms and behaviour

11.03 There are several types of anxiety disorder, each with different symptoms:

- **Generalised anxiety disorder (GAD)** –characterised by chronic anxiety, exaggerated worry and tension, even when there is little or nothing to provoke it.
- **Obsessive-compulsive disorder (OCD)** –characterised by recurrent, unwanted thoughts (obsessions) and or repetitive behaviours (compulsions). These behaviours, such as hand-washing, counting, checking or cleaning, are often performed with the hope of preventing obsessive thoughts or making them go away. Performing these so-called 'rituals' provides only temporary relief, and not performing them, markedly increases anxiety.
- **Panic disorder** –characterised by unexpected and repeated 'panic attacks'; episodes of intense fear accompanied by physical symptoms

that may include chest pain, heart palpitations, shortness of breath, dizziness or abdominal distress.

- **Social phobia (or social anxiety disorder)** – causes overwhelming anxiety and excessive self-consciousness in everyday social situations. Social phobia can be limited to one type of situation, such as a fear of speaking in formal situations or eating or drinking in front of others. In its most severe form, the fears may be so broad that a person experiences symptoms almost every time they are around other people.

In the older population, dementia can present with generalised anxiety.

Causes

11.04 Anxiety is caused by increased adrenaline. Some people with a family history of mental disorder are more prone to anxiety. An overactive thyroid gland can also cause people to feel anxious, and too much caffeine aggravates anxiety. Drug and alcohol withdrawal symptoms cause anxiety, along with tremors.

Treatment and prognosis

11.05 Treatment for anxiety is mainly psychological. There is a wide variety of self-help, individual and group psychological treatments aimed at helping people recognise and manage their symptoms.

Anxiety can be a time-limited or recurrent condition. Some people with an anxious personality disorder may learn to live with and tolerate a higher level of anxiety. Others become avoidant, with long-term difficulties facing social situations.

Advice for the Family Court

11.06 Anxiety is a normal emotion under stress, and court appearances are stressful. Problems can occur when the parent or carer with anxiety feels under threat. This can lead to breakdowns, such as crying, inability to stay in the situation or the anxiety turning to anger. Additional behavioural issues can result when the parent or carer self-medicates to reduce their anxiety with over-use of prescribed medications or abuse of alcohol or drugs.

Anxiety can be alleviated by ensuring the parent or carer is provided, in good time beforehand, with all the information available concerning the hearing. During proceedings, clear explanations and breaks may help.

Case study – Anxiety disorder – Melanie's story (see Appendix: Case studies, p 334.)

Further information

Anxiety UK

https://www.anxietyuk.org.uk

Royal College of Psychiatrists – Anxiety, panic and phobias

https://www.rcpsych.ac.uk/mental-health/problems-disorders/anxiety-panic-and-phobias

MILD TO MODERATE DEPRESSION

(See also **Chapter 6** Emotional disorders in children.)

Prevalence

11.07 Up to 30 per cent of people presenting to their GP have depressive symptoms, and about 10 per cent of these satisfy the criteria for major depressive disorder (MDD). Depression is almost twice as common in women as in men.

Symptoms and behaviour

11.08 Depression is characterised by sadness, loss of interest or pleasure, feelings of guilt or low self-worth, disturbed sleep or appetite, tiredness, poor concentration and lack of libido. People with depression may also have multiple physical complaints with no apparent physical cause. Depression can be long-lasting or recurrent, substantially impairing a person's ability to function in daily life. At its most severe, depression can lead to suicide. In some cases, the mood is not sad, but anxious, irritable or flat.

Causes

11.09 Predisposing factors – These include genetic factors; if a close relative (mother, father, sister, brother) suffers depression, the risk for an immediate family member increases ten-fold. Brain disorders, such as those following a stroke, head injury or Parkinson's disease, are thought to affect the brain's neurotransmitters and predispose someone to depression. Drug and alcohol use also predispose a person to depression by depleting the brain's neurotransmitters. Noradrenaline, serotonin and dopamine are the brain transmitters most closely linked to depression.

Factors that alter lifestyle are relevant. Illnesses that reduce mobility, such as a stroke, chronic lung disease or arthritis, may prevent someone doing activities they previously enjoyed and reduce their social contact. Ongoing stressors, such as chronic pain and cancer, can also predispose someone to depression. Unemployment, low socio-economic status and poor housing are relevant as all reduce options and affect quality of life, as does ongoing stress with little prospect of change.

Precipitating factors – Bereavement, divorce, loss of employment and relationship breakups can be precipitants to an episode of depression. Life-threatening illness, such as cancer, and the onset or worsening of chronic illness, such as severe asthma, Crohn's disease, diabetes and stroke, are linked to depression. Often there is more than one precipitant. Some people become increasingly vulnerable to further episodes of depression, being triggered by 'lesser' stress events.

Perpetuating factors – The predisposing, precipitating and perpetuating factors can link together. For instance, a person who is unemployed, living alone in temporary accommodation, may develop a serious depressive illness. This makes them more isolated, which in turn worsens their mood. The rate of depression increases with age as there are more vulnerabilities as people grow older, such as poor health, bereavement and social isolation.

Treatment and prognosis

11.10 Most depressive states are treated by GPs in primary care. Antidepressant medication and psychological treatments such as cognitive behavioural therapy (CBT) are proven to be of benefit.

The antidepressants most commonly used are selective serotonin reuptake inhibitors (SSRIs) such as citalopram, fluoxetine (Prozac) and sertraline. Antidepressants are not addictive and do not lose efficacy over time. Patients will need to take antidepressants for six to nine months after the resolution of their symptoms and then reduce gradually. Medication is recommended for at least six months in the first episode of depression, two years in a second episode, and long term for three or more episodes.

Psychological treatments can also be effective. CBT is typically used to help patients manage early symptoms and prevent relapse. CBT helps patients challenge their negative thoughts and beliefs.

Two-thirds of patients with depression improve with medication, sometimes within days.

Around 50 per cent of patients relapse if they stop the medication as soon as their symptoms of depression subsides. The relapse risk increases with a family history of depression, a long duration of the depressive episode, treatment resistance, any chronic medical illness and difficult social factors.

Among people who have previously been mental health inpatients, the completed suicide risk (meaning the suicide attempt is fatal) is 10 per cent. The risk of suicide is highest before treatment for depression, but can also be raised at the point of some recovery when the patient has more energy to act on their suicidal thoughts and plans.

If chronic depression leads to self-neglect, this has long-term effects on a person's physical health.

SEVERE DEPRESSION

11.11 This condition is less common than mild to moderate depression. It can be triggered by an upsetting or stressful life event, such as a bereavement, but can then go beyond a normal reaction to loss and evolve into a severe depressive episode if the mood persists. Severe depression may also be accompanied by an anxiety disorder.

Symptoms and behaviour

11.12 The person's mood is very low, and they may have delusional beliefs, such as believing their body is rotting. They may suffer from lack of energy, loss of interest or pleasure in activities and slowed thinking and movement, be bed-bound and mute, and stop eating or drinking. They can also have hallucinations which are 'mood-congruent', meaning the voices are consistent with the person's mood. For instance, the voice may tell them that they deserve to die, that they should kill themselves or that they're worthless.

Treatment and prognosis

11.13 Severe depression requires hospital inpatient treatment. If there is no response to combinations of medication, then electroconvulsive therapy (ECT) can be used. ECT is given twice a week for up to four weeks. The patient must either consent to the treatment, or a treatment plan must be approved on their behalf by a doctor appointed to give a second opinion.

POSTNATAL DEPRESSION AND POSTPARTUM PSYCHOSIS

11.14 Many women feel a bit down, tearful or anxious in the first week or so after giving birth. This is often called the 'baby blues' and is so common that it's considered normal. The effect is caused by hormonal fluctuations and does not last for more than a couple of weeks following delivery. If the symptoms last longer or start later, it could be postnatal depression. Postnatal depression can start any time in the first year after giving birth. Many women do not realise they have postnatal depression because it can develop gradually. It is not just mothers that can be affected; new fathers can also experience postnatal depression. A much rarer, but more serious condition, is postpartum psychosis, also known as puerperal psychosis.

All these types of depression can make it difficult for the mother to bond with her baby. See **Chapter 1** Bonding and attachment for further information.

Prevalence

11.15 Postnatal depression – occurs in around 10 to 15 in every 100 women within one to three days of giving birth and usually resolves within a couple of weeks. Significant depression and anxiety occur in 10 per cent of new mothers.

Postpartum psychosis – is rare, estimated to occur in between one and two in every 1,000 women. There is a higher risk if the mother has a history of bipolar or schizoaffective disorder, or if she has had postpartum psychosis previously or there is a family history of the disorder.

Symptoms

11.16 Postnatal depression – usually develops within the first four weeks of childbirth. Some common symptoms of postnatal depression include a persistent feeling of sadness and low mood, difficulty in concentrating and making decisions and feelings of inadequacy. The mother feels that she is unable to look after her baby and constantly worries something is wrong with her baby, regardless of reassurances.

Postpartum psychosis – symptoms are likely to start within a few weeks of giving birth but sometimes will not emerge until months later. Postpartum psychosis can cause severe mood swings, exhaustion, a sense of hopelessness and feelings of guilt. The mother can also experience intrusive thoughts about harming herself or her baby. If she has delusional ideas about her baby – eg, believing that it is evil or possessed – this can lead to infanticide. The mother may appear very well despite these ideas, as she is ashamed of her thoughts, so does not reveal them.

Treatment and prognosis

11.17 Psychological therapies are the usual treatments recommended for women with postnatal depression. These can be 'guided self-help' in the form of an online course, sometimes with support from a therapist, cognitive behavioural therapy or individual therapy. Medication in the form of antidepressants may also be prescribed, with symptoms usually resolving within six months.

Once diagnosed postpartum psychosis needs to be treated urgently. Treatment is usually as an inpatient in specialised psychiatric mother and baby units, with supervision of the baby to reduce risk. Treatment of the actual disorder is the same as for any other psychosis: medication and therapy. Bottle-feeding of the baby may be necessary, as some antidepressants and anti-psychotic medications are not safe to take whilst breastfeeding.

Following an episode of postpartum psychosis, there is an increased chance of the condition reoccurring. The mother has a 50 per cent chance of developing psychosis after any future pregnancy and a 30 per cent chance of psychosis at another time. Postpartum psychosis is risky for the baby if the mother acts on her delusions. There is also a risk that the mother may neglect the baby's needs, and have problems bonding with the baby.

In severe cases of postnatal depression and postpartum psychosis, there is a risk to the baby, which may only be managed safely in a specialised mother and baby unit.

Case study – Postpartum psychosis – Sachini's story (see Appendix: Case studies, p 335.)

Further information

NHS – Clinical depression

https://www.nhs.uk/conditions/clinical-depression/causes/

Royal College of Psychiatrists – Postnatal depression

https://www.rcpsych.ac.uk/mental-health/problems-disorders/post-natal-depression

PaNDAS

https://pandasfoundation.org.uk

EATING DISORDERS

(See also **Chapter 6** Emotional disorders in children.)

11.18 The most common eating disorders are:

- **Anorexia nervosa** – a person aims for an extremely low weight by restricting food and excessive exercising
- **Bulimia** – the consumption of a lot of food in a short space of time followed by actions to avoid digesting it by vomiting or purging (use of laxatives).
- **Binge eating disorder (BED)** – regular loss of control resulting in eating large amounts of food.

Prevalence

11.19 It is estimated that over one million people in the UK have an eating disorder. The condition is prevalent amongst young people, influenced by factors such as social media and the 'perfect' body image portrayed in advertising, movies and magazines and increasingly on social media. The prevalence is greater in professions where there is an emphasis on being thin, such as modelling, gymnastics, athletics and ballet. Eating disorders are four times more common in women than men.

Symptoms and behaviour

11.20 In anorexia nervosa, the symptoms are weight loss, food restriction, secret eating and extreme efforts to avoid weight gain (excessive exercise, laxative abuse, self-induced vomiting). Intensive weight loss amongst women usually results in the cessation of menstruation.

Most people with anorexia try to disguise their symptoms so hide weight loss by wearing baggy clothing. Some people will avoid looking at themselves in a mirror as they are certain they are fat, even when skeletal. This is known as having a distorted body image. Others become fixated by an ideal body shape that is emaciated and spend hours looking at themselves in the mirror. The physical symptoms of malnutrition include osteoporosis (thinning of bones and fractures), infertility, muscle wasting and hair loss.

In bulimia, large amounts of food are eaten secretly and then vomited. The same malnutrition effects as in anorexia can occur, with typically more severe dental erosion due to stomach acid – repeated vomiting results in erosion of tooth enamel. The sufferer may injure themselves by using objects to induce vomiting.

Men are less likely to wish to lose weight but become fixated on being muscled. They starve and lose body fat to increase visibility of their musculature. They may also take harmful medications to build their muscles. Men with anorexia can lose their sex drive.

Causes

11.21 There is usually a mixture of psychological, environmental and genetic factors.

Predisposing factors – Having employment or a hobby where being thin is seen as an ideal, such as the performing arts or athletics, can predispose someone to anorexia. A family history of eating disorders, depression or substance misuse increases the risk ten-fold. An obsessive and perfectionist personality with low self-esteem also contributes. Difficult family relationships are often relevant.

Precipitating factors – Anorexia can be a response to stress, depression or anxiety, for example following a bereavement. Bullying, criticism or abuse can also prompt a diet which, in vulnerable people, predisposes them to develop an eating disorder. The typical age of onset is 14 to 17 years, and coincides with times of hormonal changes. In some girls, the start of menstruation can prompt dieting. Those with anorexia can feel they are in control by restricting their food intake when they perceive there is a loss of control over other aspects of their lives.

Perpetuating factors – Those with anorexia often have a co-existing depressive condition. Coupled with low self-esteem, they may think they can only feel better about themselves by losing weight. Many live limited lives governed by the amount of food they will allow themselves. Their efforts to avoid weight gain result in secrecy, so relationships can suffer or they may live in social isolation.

Treatment and prognosis

11.22 The main goal is the restoration of a healthy weight, either as an outpatient or in hospital. The weight can be determined by the patient's body mass index (BMI) or, for women, by an assessment using an ovarian ultrasound test of the weight at which they will ovulate. Weight restoration in hospital is carried out following a dietician's advice. Several meals and snacks are given throughout the day, and under observation, during and after meals to prevent vomiting or purging. Bed rest may be needed to avoid exercising.

If the person is refusing food and their condition is life-threatening, they are fed via a nasogastric tube, if necessary under restraint, and a liquid diet is given. This compulsory treatment is only given under the provision of the Mental Health Act 1983. The patient can only engage in psychological treatment when they have gained weight to a safe level, and their preoccupation with starving is lessened by being at a healthier weight.

The prognosis of long-term anorexia is poor. Some patients move from starving themselves to a bulimic presentation. Physical complications of long-term starvation are severe, affecting the bones, muscles, brain and vital organs. People who have been anorexic for years often develop osteoporosis and heart disease.

Anorexia has the highest suicide rate of all mental health disorders. Twenty per cent of patients who have been hospitalised for treatment at some point take their own lives.

Advice to the Family Court

11.23 A person with anorexia attending a hearing may feel fatigued, appear uninterested in the proceedings, and find it difficult to concentrate. They may also have anxiety or depression. Individuals can start to look better physically, but their mental health may not improve at the same rate. High levels of stress can set back a person's recovery. Consider frequent breaks and give some thought to when it would be best for them to give evidence, as an anorexic person may feel distressed following a meal break.

Further information

Beat – Eating disorders

https://www.beateatingdisorders.org.uk/

NHS – Eating disorders

https://www.nhs.uk/conditions/eating-disorders/

FABRICATED OR INDUCED ILLNESS (FII)

11.24 Fabricated or induced illness is also known as Munchausen's syndrome by proxy. It should not be confused with Munchausen's syndrome, where a person pretends to be ill or causes illness or injury to themselves.

A fabricated or induced illness, usually perpetrated by the mother, can cause significant harm to the child. It involves a well child being presented as ill or disabled, or a sick or disabled child being presented as having a more significant problem than they have in reality, and suffering harm as a result. There are usually long-lasting consequences for the child, who will probably suffer significant physical and psychological harm. Where there is a suspicion of FII, this will normally lead to a safeguarding investigation by the local authority children's service, possibly resulting in care proceedings to determine whether the abusing carer should continue to have responsibility for the child.

Prevalence

11.25 FII is rare – a study in 2000 identified 89 confirmed cases in the UK over a two-year period equating to an incidence of one child per 100,000. The medical view from paediatricians is that this is an underestimate. This is because detection can be difficult, and most cases involve children under five years old who can't talk about their symptoms or explain what's happened.

Symptoms and behaviour

11.26 Suspicion of FII is raised when the mother takes the child repeatedly to healthcare professionals insisting the child is unwell. The child may have no actual symptoms, or those they have are fabricated by the carer or, in the most dangerous situations, have been induced by the carer. The carer may induce symptoms by giving the child unnecessary medication, smothering them to simulate fits or cessation of breathing, or even tampering with hospital equipment to make it appear the child is not breathing.

Causes

11.27 The perpetrator is nearly always female; the child's biological mother in 75 per cent of cases. A surprisingly high number have links with the healthcare profession, meaning they, or a family member, work, or have worked, in healthcare. These mothers have often themselves been abused in childhood and may admit they faked symptoms themselves to avoid abuse. There is a high rate of relationship problems in families affected by FII, and the child's illness can be used by the mother as a method of keeping the father linked to the family. Mental illness in the perpetrator is common, particularly depression and emotionally unstable personality disorder.

Treatment and prognosis

11.28 There is first an examination of the medical records of both the child and carer held by the GP and/or paediatrician responsible for the child's health. Paediatricians assist by examining all hospital attendance records to determine whether these are more than would be expected. Sometimes a parent will move home or GP surgery to avoid detection.

There is clinical guidance for paediatricians and obstetricians on when to suspect FII, as behaviour can start even before the child's birth. Obstetric complications affecting a baby may have been due to the mother interfering with her pregnancy, for example, to induce a premature birth.

Once the child is safe, it may be possible to treat the parent's underlying psychological problems. This may include a combination of intensive psychotherapy and family therapy. Work with the family can be undertaken by social workers, child psychiatrists and psychologists, paediatricians with a special interest in child mental health and adult psychiatrists. Any psychiatric disorder in or illness in the parent should firstly be excluded.

In some cases of FII, there may be no possibility of reuniting the parent and child as the parent remains either in denial or continues to try and deliberately deceive about their actions (or may be in prison). The likelihood is that the abuse would continue and that any siblings would also be affected.

Other cases have a more positive outcome. The best results are in cases where underlying parental mental illness responds to treatment, and therapy addresses the parent's guilt about harming their child. These treatments are reinforced with careful assessment of support measures. Stronger links with the extended family may be beneficial.

Likely outcomes in adulthood

11.29 A report reviewing 451 cases of FII showed a death rate of 6 per cent, with another 7 per cent of children having a long-term injury. Three-quarters of the children suffered other types of abuse, such as neglect and emotional abuse. The consequences were considerable for their education.

Children who endure FII may go on to have chronic disabling mental or physical illness in adulthood. Some become abusers of others, both adults and children. In some circumstances, there may be a possibility of reuniting the family.

Advice for the Family Court

11.30 Factors indicating the possibility of reuniting the family are when the parent admits their behaviour and engages with psychological treatment. As the parent's psychological state improves and they develop empathy for the affected child, the child's attachment with the parent becomes stronger and more appropriate. A more favourable outcome is indicated if the partner remains with the family and participates in the psychological treatment. Also, it helps if the parent has support from their extended family.

Case study – Fabricated or induced illness – Ayesha's story **(see Appendix: Case studies, p 338.)**

Further information

Munchausen by Proxy and Other Factitious Abuse

Kathryn Artingstall 2017 CRC Press ISBN 1498732216

Clinical Topics in Child and Adolescent Psychiatry (Chapter 2)
Sarah Huline-Dickens

RCPsych Publications ISBN1909726176

GAMBLING, GAMING AND SOCIAL MEDIA ADDICTIONS

(See also **Chapter 6** Emotional disorders in children.)

GAMBLING ADDICTION

11.31 Gambling addiction is also known as compulsive gambling or pathological gambling. A compulsive or pathological gambler is unable to resist their impulses. This can have severe consequences, such as financial ruin and relationship difficulties. Problem gambling sometimes also leads to crime. The urge to gamble becomes so great that tension can only be relieved by gambling more and more.

Prevalence

11.32 Gambling addiction affects about 1 per cent of adults of all ages; men more often than women. It usually begins in adolescence in men and later in women.

Symptoms and behaviour

11.33 Indications of problem gambling are that the person:

- needs to gamble with increasing amounts of money to achieve the desired excitement;
- is restless or irritable when attempting to cut down or stop gambling;
- makes repeated unsuccessful efforts to control, cut back or stop gambling;
- is preoccupied with gambling, for example: having persistent thoughts of reliving past gambling experiences; planning the next venture; thinking of ways to get money with which to gamble;
- sometimes gambles because they feel distressed, for example, helpless, guilty, anxious or depressed;
- returns to gambling after losing a lot of money, to get even by 'chasing one's losses';
- lies to conceal the extent of their involvement with gambling;
- jeopardises, or has already lost, a significant relationship, job, or educational or career opportunity because of gambling;

- relies on others to provide money to relieve desperate financial situations caused by gambling;
- is unable to explain their gambling behaviour.

Progression appears to be more rapid in women. Gambling patterns may be regular or episodic, and gambling disorder can be persistent or in remission. Gambling can increase during periods of stress or depression and periods of substance use or abstinence. Individuals who begin gambling in youth often do so with family members or friends.

Causes

11.34 Theories about the causes of pathological gambling emphasise cognitive distortions rather than mood problems. Many people with this disorder are highly superstitious or believe they can control the outcome of events when they are gambling. Development of early-life gambling disorder appears to be associated with impulsivity and substance abuse. In men, there is also an association with attention deficit hyperactivity disorder.

Treatment and prognosis

11.35 Gambling disorder is treated through therapy and support groups. Psychotherapy, either individual or in group settings, and support groups such as the 12-step Gamblers Anonymous programme, are useful. This programme adheres to abstinence principles, similar to programmes for drug and alcohol abuse.

Gambling disorder is associated with depression and anxiety, and problem gamblers have a higher risk of suicide than the general population. Gambling disorder can be persistent and can increase during periods of stress or depression and periods of substance use or abstinence.

The consequences for the individual and family are considerable. Financial harms can include borrowing from family friends and loan sharks, pawning or selling possessions, and committing illegal acts to finance the gambling. Family harms include a preoccupation with gambling so that everyday family life becomes difficult. There may also be increased arguments over money and debts, emotional and physical abuse, and neglect and violence towards partner and children leading to separation and divorce.

Advice for the Family Court

11.36 People with pathological gambling behaviour often also have problems with alcohol and other substances. Drink and drugs both increase impulsive and chaotic behaviour and cause problems with relationships and parenting. The consequences of problem gambling have an impact on family dynamics and finances. Sufferers are often unaware, or in denial, of having a problem. Alternatively, the parent may be so consumed with the damage they have done to the family, they are unable to see a way forward. Parents with a gambling disorder may find parenting a source of stress, and use gambling as an escape, neglecting their responsibilities.

A parent with a gambling disorder who is party to Family Court proceedings, may fail to attend court or arrive late and be distracted by their need to gamble. It can be helpful to set clear boundaries, so the parent can demonstrate an ability to follow these. Compulsive gambling is a recurrent problem, so the court needs to consider the success (or otherwise) of the parent's previous efforts to stop the activity.

Further information

Royal College of Psychiatrists – Gambling disorder

https://www.rcpsych.ac.uk/mental-health/parents-and-young-people/young-people/problem-gambling?searchTerms=gambling

GamCare – help for problem gamblers

https://www.gamcare.org.uk/?cn-reloaded=1

GAMSTOP – online gambling restriction

https://www.gamstop.co.uk

GAMING ADDICTION

11.37 Gaming disorder has been recognised by the *International Classification of Diseases 11th Revision (ICD-11)*. It is placed within the 'Disorders due to addictive behaviours' section along with gambling disorder. The definition describes distress or interference with personal functions as a result of persistent or recurrent gaming behaviour. To be diagnosed, the interference must be severe and present for at least 12 months.

Prevalence

11.38 Little is known about the prevalence of gaming disorder. One estimate quoted by the Royal College of Psychiatrists is 1 per cent of the population.

Symptoms

11.39 Gaming disorder, involving either online gaming or video gaming, is characterised by a compulsion to game, impaired control over gaming, and gaming taking precedence over other interests and daily activities. The individual continues or escalates their gaming despite problems in their personal, family, social, educational, occupational or other important areas of functioning.

Causes

11.40 Gaming disorder is linked to drug and alcohol use. It is suggested that individuals with difficulty in emotional regulation may engage in addictive behaviours such as gaming to avoid or manage feelings of depression. So, gaming behaviour is a type of self-medication. Problematic gamers also have high rates of attention deficit hyperactivity disorder, social anxiety and low self-esteem. People with autism spectrum disorder may prefer gaming to social interaction and then become obsessive.

Treatment and prognosis

11.41 Psychological treatments, such as cognitive behavioural therapy, are suggested. As in gambling, gaming disorder can continue as a chronic condition. The isolation from spending many hours a day gaming may lead to long-lasting social withdrawal. Prognosis is worse if the gaming is accompanied by substance abuse as this increases impulsivity.

Advice for the Family Court

(See **Gambling disorder**, above.)

Further information

Royal College of Psychiatrists – When the fun stops: ICD-11's new gaming disorder

https://www.rcpsych.ac.uk/news-and-features/blogs/detail/cultural-blog/2018/08/29/when-the-fun-stops-dr.-henrietta-bowden-jones-and-professor-andrew-przybylski-on-icd-11-s-new-gaming-disorder?searchTerms=gaming

Review of the co-occurrence of Gaming disorder and other potentially addictive behaviours

https://link.springer.com/article/10.1007/s40429-019-00279-7

SOCIAL MEDIA ADDICTION

11.42 Social media addiction is also known as social media overuse and internet addiction disorder. It is a psychological or behavioural over-dependence on social media. In the UK, 90 per cent of adults use the internet. The average daily time a person spends on social media around the world is two hours and twenty-four minutes.

Treatment centres suggest that social media addiction is present if a person spends more than five hours per day on social media sites. There is some debate over whether compulsive internet usage constitutes addiction. But even within that debate, most psychiatrists and addiction experts recognise that some people engage in internet use compulsively. The two areas where this is most common are social media use and online role-playing games.

Internet addiction can take several forms. Some people might be addicted solely to social media while others split their time between social media and pornography sites. Other internet addicts may become obsessed with reading news or following sports.

Prevalence

11.43 The prevalence of problematic social media use among adults in the UK is unclear. The prevalence of problematic smartphone usage and associated mental health outcomes among children and young people in the UK (aged 16 to 19 years) is currently reported at around 23 per cent.

Symptoms and behaviour

11.44 A person who has social media addiction is someone who prefers online activity over most other things. As a result, they may show:

- feelings of isolation and loneliness;
- variable mood and stress as their mood is dependent upon whether their posts are of interest to or liked by others;
- vulnerability to online abuse by others, such as body-shaming, sexting and grooming;
- problems in relationships with loved ones as they may just communicate with them online or neglect real-life contacts in favour of online ones.

Behaviours indicating social media addiction include:

- waking during the night to use social media;
- filming and recording all aspects of their life for others to view;
- unreasonable anxiety or irritation when internet connections are slow;
- anxiety or irritation when internet use is blocked or otherwise unavailable;
- becoming increasingly socially isolated in favour of spending time online;
- poor work performance as a result of spending too much time online;
- little desire for activities away from home (depending on whether they can access social media sufficiently to manage their compulsion out of the home, they may show little desire for activities outside the home).

Social media facilitates an environment in which people are compare their real offline selves to the flawless, filtered, and edited online versions of others. Excessive social media use can not only cause unhappiness and general dissatisfaction with life, but also reduce self-esteem, and increase the risk of developing mental health issues such as anxiety and depression. Constantly comparing oneself to others can lead to feelings of self-consciousness or a need for perfectionism and order, which can then lead to a social anxiety disorder.

Causes

11.45 **Predisposing factors** – people who are stressed, isolated or depressed may use social media as a coping mechanism to relieve their symptoms. This may work in the short term, as using social media activates the same brain circuits as gambling or the use of recreational drugs, particularly cocaine.

People vulnerable to social media addiction are those with other obsessional traits. However, adults with an autism spectrum disorder, appear more susceptible to addiction to social media, using it as a sanctuary from the daily demands of face-to-face communication. They are at high risk of being exploited, bullied and abused.

Perpetuating factors – when a person posts a picture and gets positive social feedback, it stimulates the brain to release dopamine, which rewards that behaviour and perpetuates the social media habit. For some people, social media use provides continuous rewards that they are not receiving in real life, so they engage in the activity more and more. This continuous use eventually leads to problems in relationships and work responsibilities, so the person copes by increasing social networking behaviour as 'self-medication'.

Treatment and prognosis

11.46 Treatment is similar to that of compulsive gambling. The aim is to reduce or stop the time spent online.

Treatments that can help include psychological interventions, such as cognitive behavioural therapy. Group support provides mutual accountability, which is as important in internet addiction as in any other addiction. Group members rely on one another to hold each other accountable and help carry each other through difficult times. Social media addicts can also learn coping strategies to be able to live in the digital world without returning to compulsive behaviour.

The prognosis is difficult to estimate as some use of social media is inevitable in everyday life.

Advice for the Family Court

11.47 Usually, the person who is affected denies being addicted, despite evidence from their family that this is the case. Conflict about social media use may be apparent. The neglect of family and parental responsibilities may be similar to that of a parent who is gambling.

As some devices are not allowed in a court setting, it is possible that symptoms of 'withdrawal', such as anxiety and irritability may be apparent during a hearing. Attendees at court who, are unfamiliar with the protocol, may need to be reminded that the hearing is held in private and that no cameras or recordings are allowed.

Further information

Office for National Statistics – Exploring the UK's digital divide

https://www.ons.gov.uk/peoplepopulationandcommunity/householdcharacteristics/homeinternetandsocialmediausage/articles/exploringtheuksdigitaldivide/2019-03-04

Psychology Today – Addicted to Social Media?

https://www.psychologytoday.com/gb/blog/in-excess/201805/addicted-social-media

US Addiction Center – Social Media Addiction

https://www.addictioncenter.com/drugs/social-media-addiction/

National Autistic Society – Autism and the internet

https://network.autism.org.uk/knowledge/insight-opinion/autism-and-internet-risks-and-benefits

OBSESSIVE-COMPULSIVE DISORDER (OCD)

11.48 People who have obsessive-compulsive disorder have obsessions and compulsions. An *obsession* is an unwelcome thought or image that is out of the person's control and difficult to ignore. These thoughts are usually disturbing, causing distress and anxiety. To reduce the anxiety produced by the thought, the person develops *compulsions* which lessen the anxiety in the short term.

Prevalence

11.49 Studies indicate that the lifetime prevalence of OCD is 2 per cent. Men and women are equally affected. Adult OCD usually begins in the teens or early twenties. Symptoms can vary over time, but many sufferers don't seek help until they have had OCD for many years.

Symptoms

11.50 The obsessional features can be thoughts, images or doubts. Thoughts can be single words, short phrases or rhymes that are unpleasant, shocking or blasphemous. They are often the worst thoughts the person can imagine. So, a religious person may have blasphemous thoughts; a gentle and loving parent may have thoughts of harming their child. Mental images can include images of the family members dead, or the person visualises themselves doing something violent or sexual, which is completely out of character. The affected person usually realises their thinking and behaviour are not logical, but still finds it very difficult to stop.

These thoughts can be alarming for the sufferer and their family. Even if reassured that they would not act on them, the thoughts remain very distressing and intrusive. The person will try and push the thoughts away, which means they recur more frequently. Compulsions develop to reduce anxiety. These compulsions to manage the thoughts take several forms:

- **Correcting obsessional thoughts** – the person uses 'neutralising' thoughts like counting, praying or repeating a particular word.
- **Rituals** – these may involve handwashing, or arranging objects or activities in a particular way.
- **Checking** – for example, the person repeatedly checks their own body for contamination, checks that appliances are switched off, that the house is locked or that a journey route is safe.
- **Avoidance** – involves steering clear of anything that is a reminder of worrying thoughts, such as avoiding touching particular objects, going to certain places, taking risks or accepting responsibility. One example is someone avoiding their kitchen because of sharp knives.
- **Reassurance** – the person repeatedly asks others to tell them that everything is all right.

All the compulsions can take up so much time that it can become impossible to leave the house, go to work or socialise.

Causes

11.51 Predisposing – research suggests that some people are more vulnerable to developing OCD than others. Perfectionist personalities, for instance people who are meticulous and methodical, with high standards, may be more likely to develop OCD. These qualities are generally helpful but can slip into OCD if they become too extreme.

Precipitating – an incident or trauma brings on OCD in two-thirds of cases. Sudden responsibility such as childbirth or change of employment can also cause OCD.

Perpetuating – avoidance of the thought and the ritual element of the compulsion increases anxiety to increase.

Treatments and prognosis

11.52 Treatments are usually psychological. Cognitive behavioural therapy aims to identify practical skills for the person to manage their behaviours. Exposure therapy (or desensitisation) involves gradual exposure to the feared object or situation along with relaxation therapy over a number of sessions. Medication such as antidepressants can be used in the short term to reduce the anxiety associated with OCD.

As the person's behaviour and need for reassurance affect the family, family counselling, explaining the disorder and involving the family to help the person manage their behaviour, can help.

The prognosis with treatment is variable. About one-third of patients who complete a course of treatment find that their OCD symptoms wane. Another third will have some respite and find symptoms become manageable. However, symptoms can recur with stress or depression.

Advice for the Family Court

11.53 A person with OCD may have difficulty getting to the venue on time due to their need to complete certain rituals. Anxiety about the hearing is likely to produce an increase in symptoms – a visit to the venue before the hearing date may reduce anxiety on the day.

There may be a need for a person with OCD to manage intrusive thoughts by carrying out a particular action, which will cause them to appear distracted when speaking or being questioned. If the person is currently symptomatic, they will need breaks and should be given time to process questions and to make their responses. If they are unable to concentrate due to their symptoms, it may not be possible to proceed with the hearing. Written information sent beforehand can help ensure the person has sufficient time to absorb this before the hearing.

(See also Advice for the Family Court for Anxiety in adults, above.)

Further information

Royal College of Psychiatrists – Obsessive-compulsive disorder (OCD)

https://www.rcpsych.ac.uk/mental-health/problems-disorders/obsessive-compulsive-disorder?searchTerms=ocd

OCD-UK

https://www.ocduk.org

Rethink Mental Illness – Obsessive-compulsive disorder (OCD)

https://www.rethink.org/advice-and-information/about-mental-illness/learn-more-about-conditions/obsessive-compulsive-disorder-ocd/

Obsessive-Compulsive Disorder: For People Living with OCD, Carers, and Clinicians

CUP, Drummond and Edwards ISBN 9781911623755

PHOBIAS

(See also **Chapter 6** Emotional disorders in children.)

11.54 The definition of a phobia is an extreme fear of a particular animal, thing, place or situation that continues for over six months.

Prevalence

11.55 Although specific phobias often begin in childhood, their incidence peaks during midlife and old age. Onset in childhood is most commonly between ages 5 to 10. Phobias are more common in women than men in all age groups. In women, phobias increase with age. In men, they decrease with age.

Phobias persist for several years or even decades in 10 to 30 per cent of cases, and are strongly predictive of onset of other anxiety, mood and substance use disorders. The developmental course of phobias, which progress from fear to avoidance and then to diagnosis, suggests the possibility that interrupting the course of phobias could reduce their prevalence.

The most common phobias include fear and anxiety concerning heights (acrophobia), creatures, especially spiders (arachnophobia), social situations (social phobia), enclosed spaces (claustrophobia) and open spaces (agoraphobia).

Symptoms

11.56 Although specific phobias often begin in childhood, they become more common during midlife. Phobias in adults involve both fear and avoidance. For people who have specific phobias, avoidance can reduce their level of distress but can lead to a restricted lifestyle if the person's aim is to avoid their fear. Often the phobia is linked to another fear so, for example, adults with social phobia may have a fear of embarrassing themselves or blushing or vomiting in public.

Causes

11.57 **Predisposing** – Learned responses; family dynamics such a worried or anxious parent can affect how the person copes with anxiety in childhood than in adulthood. Often the same phobia can be passed from parent to child. Research suggests that some people are more genetically vulnerable to developing a phobia than others.

Precipitating – A particular incident or trauma can cause a phobia. For example, someone who experiences a lot of turbulence on a plane at a young age might later develop a phobia about flying. A panic attack in a situation can also lead to a phobia of the situation.

Perpetuating – Avoidance of the feared situation allows the anxiety and fear to increase. Long-term stress can cause feelings of anxiety and depression, reducing a person's ability to cope and can make them more fearful or anxious about being in the same situation.

Treatments and prognosis

11.58 Treatments are usually psychological. CBT aims to identify practical skills for the person to manage their behaviours. Exposure therapy, or desensitisation, involves gradual exposure to the feared object or situation along with relaxation therapy over a number of sessions.

Phobias are often accompanied by, or accompany anxiety and or depression; medication, such as antidepressants, can be used in the short term to reduce the anxiety associated with phobias.

Phobias persist for several years or even decades in 10 to 30 per cent of cases and are strongly predictive of onset of other anxiety and mood disorders. Adults often self-medicate their anxiety with alcohol and drugs, so there is a strong link between phobias, anxiety and substance misuse disorders.

Advice for the Family Court

11.59 A visit to the venue of the hearing before the actual hearing date may reduce anxiety on the day.

If the person is currently symptomatic, they will need breaks, given time to process questions and to make their responses.

If they are unable to concentrate due to symptoms, it may not be possible to proceed. Written information can help to provide the person has sufficient time to absorb this before the hearing.

(See also Advice for the Family Court for Anxiety in adults, above.)

Further information

The Lancet Psychiatry – Specific phobias

https://pubmed.ncbi.nlm.nih.gov/30060873/

Mind – Phobias

https://www.mind.org.uk/information-support/types-of-mental-health-problems/phobias/about-phobias/

NHS – Phobias

https://www.nhs.uk/conditions/phobias/

Royal College of Psychiatrists – Anxiety, panic and phobias

https://www.rcpsych.ac.uk/mental-health/problems-disorders/anxiety-panic-and-phobias?searchTerms=phobias

SOMATIC SYMPTOM DISORDER (SSD)

(See also **Chapter 6** Emotional disorders in children.)

11.60 Somatic symptom disorder and somatisation disorder are both terms used to describe disorders when the affected person has many persistent physical complaints that are associated with excessive and maladaptive thoughts, feelings and behaviours, which are all related to those symptoms.

Prevalence

11.61 The prevalence of SSD is estimated to be 5 to 7 per cent of the general population. It is far more common in females (the female-to-male ratio is 10:1). The prevalence is approximately 17 per cent of the people who consult general practitioners regularly.

Symptoms and behaviour

11.62 Recurring physical complaints usually begin before age 30. Most sufferers have multiple somatic symptoms, but some have only one severe symptom, typically pain. Any body part may be affected, Severity may fluctuate, but symptoms persist and rarely remit for any extended period. The symptoms themselves, or excessive worry about them, can be distressing or disrupt daily life, and some sufferers become depressed. Specific symptoms and their frequency vary between cultures.

People affected are usually unaware of their underlying mental problem and believe that they have physical ailments. They typically continue to pressure doctors for additional or repeated tests and treatments, even after results of a thorough evaluation have been negative.

Patients may become dependent on others, demanding help and emotional support and growing angry when they feel their needs are not met. They may also threaten or attempt suicide. Often dissatisfied with their medical care, they typically go from one physician to another or seek treatment from several physicians concurrently.

Causes

11.63 SSD arises from a heightened awareness of various bodily sensations, combined with an inclination to interpret these sensations as indicating illness. While the exact cause is not clear, people with the condition have often experienced childhood neglect, sexual abuse, chaotic lifestyle, and may also have a history of alcohol and substance abuse.

Personality disorders are associated with SSD. Psychosocial stressors, including unemployment and impaired occupational functioning, also play a part.

Treatment and prognosis

11.64 Cognitive behavioural therapy can help to reduce anxiety and limit the person's link between a bodily symptom and a need to seek immediate medical help. People with SSD also benefit from having a supportive relationship with a primary care physician, who coordinates all their health care, offers symptomatic relief, sees them regularly, and protects them from unnecessary tests and procedures. Treatment of an additional disorder such as depression may help.

The prognosis of SSD is variable. If there is a clearly identified trigger associated with a treatable depression, the prognosis is better. However, up to 90 per cent of sufferers have symptoms lasting longer than five years. The most severely affected are so preoccupied with their health so that they can be socially isolated, unemployed, depressed and chronically anxious.

Alcohol and drug abuse are common, as these are used to self-medicate. Dependence on prescribed medication, such as analgesics is also common. Medical interventions, such as surgical procedures, have their own risks.

Case study – Somatic symptom disorder – Aurelia's story (see Appendix: Case studies, p 339.)

Further information

Ryan S. D'Souza, W M. Hooten – Somatic syndrome disorders

https://www.ncbi.nlm.nih.gov/books/NBK532253/

NHS – Medically unexplained symptoms

https://www.nhs.uk/conditions/medically-unexplained-symptoms/

SUBSTANCE MISUSE – ALCOHOL AND DRUGS

11.65 Alcohol and drugs are often used to self-medicate the symptoms of mental health problems. People can abuse alcohol or drugs to relieve the symptoms of an undiagnosed mental disorder, to cope with difficult emotions, or to change their mood temporarily. Unfortunately, abusing substances often worsens the symptoms the individual hoped to ease.

Prevalence and causes

11.66 It is estimated that around 17 per cent of adults in England drink to hazardous levels, while just over 1 per cent report levels that indicate probable dependence on alcohol. In addition, 3 per cent of adults in England show signs of drug dependence. Men are more likely to be dependent on illegal drugs than women (4.3 per cent compared to 1.9 per cent).

Alcohol and drug abuse can increase the underlying risk of developing mental disorders. People who are predisposed to a mental disorder may precipitate it by abusing alcohol or illegal or prescription drugs. For example, users of cannabis, khat and marijuana have an increased risk of psychosis, while those who abuse opioid painkillers are at greater risk of depression. Crystal meth causes mania and psychosis.

Substance abuse may also sharply increase symptoms of mental illness, or even trigger new symptoms. It can prolong an episode of illness as abuse of alcohol or drugs can interact with medications, such as antidepressants, anti-anxiety medication and mood stabilisers, making them less effective at managing symptoms. People with impulsive behaviours, such as those with personality disorders and attention deficit hyperactivity disorder, can have riskier behaviour and be more aggressive under the influence of substances. Drug and alcohol withdrawal cause severe symptoms of anxiety and panic and therefore need to be carefully managed.

Drug dependence can make people vulnerable as they rely on others for supplies and must somehow fund their habit. The drugs are toxic; more deaths occur among heroin takers than users of any other drug as it slows and stops respiration. Users become tolerant to the drug's euphoric effects, requiring increasingly larger doses.

Some drugs are more toxic than they used to be. For example, ecstasy and some forms of cannabis are more toxic now compared to five to ten years ago. Drug-taking trends may be imported from other parts of the world and copied by people with little knowledge of the drug's effects, such as with crystal meth, recently imported from the US.

Although deaths from helium inhalation are rare, many young people are unaware of the risk of asphyxiation as breathing helium over some minutes prevents oxygen from reaching the brain.

Treatment and prognosis

11.67 Treatment for both alcohol and drug dependency can include a number of different strategies, such as cognitive behavioural therapy, medication and support from self-help groups. Detoxification treatment manages withdrawal symptoms when an addict stops taking opioids like heroin or stops drinking alcohol. Treatment may be given while the individual is living at home or as a hospital inpatient. If drug or alcohol problems are severe, treatment may take place in a residential rehabilitation facility. Family therapy may be offered alongside other treatments.

It is not unusual for individuals with alcohol and drug dependence to have other psychiatric disorders. A 2014 study found that half of people with drug dependence were receiving treatment for other mental health conditions, and adults with drug dependence are twice as likely as the general population to be receiving psychological therapy.

For some younger people, drug experimentation is a life stage they mature out of – weekend ecstasy users, for example. They may turn to alcohol instead as they get older. For those who continue to use, many change drugs depending on price. Accidental death is common. Users can slide down the social scale as their motivation becomes increasingly centred on drug use.

The effects of alcohol and drug dependence have an adverse effect on families as well as individuals. Marriages where one or both partners have an alcohol or drug problem are twice as likely to end in divorce as those in which alcohol and drugs are not a problem. Partners of people with harmful use of alcohol or drugs experience higher rates of domestic abuse. Alcohol and drug misuse is implicated in a high proportion of cases of child neglect and abuse, and one study identified heavy drinking as a factor in half of child protection cases.

Advice for the Family Court

11.68 If a parent is known to use drugs, then their partner is likely to use drugs also. Users often seek out other users, or one parent might coerce the other into drug taking. Impulsive and chaotic behaviour may mean the parent fails to attend court or attends late. They may be distracted if under the influence or in withdrawal.

The fairest approach is to set clear boundaries so the parent can demonstrate an ability to follow these. If they are not able to do this, it provides evidence of their inability to do so in other situations when they are expected to be responsible with the child.

Further information

HelpGuide – Substance abuse and mental health issues

https://www.helpguide.org/articles/addictions/substance-abuse-and-mental-health.htm

Healthline – Inhaling helium: Harmless fun or health hazard?

https://www.healthline.com/health/inhaling-helium#balloons

NHS – Alcohol abuse support

https://www.nhs.uk/live-well/alcohol-support/

NHS – Drug addiction: getting help

https://www.nhs.uk/live-well/healthy-body/drug-addiction-getting-help/

Chapter 12

Psychotic disorders in adults

PSYCHOSIS

(See also **Chapter 8** Psychotic disorders in children.)

12.01 Psychosis is a term for a mental disorder with two main symptoms: hallucinations and delusions.

Experiencing the symptoms of psychosis is often referred to as having a psychotic episode. Some psychotic episodes, depending on the cause, can resolve themselves within hours or days and without treatment. Typically, this would be psychotic symptoms associated with delirium (caused by infections), sleep deprivation and symptoms caused by drug use. If psychotic episodes last for weeks or months, this is likely to indicate the presence of schizophrenia, bipolar affective disorder or severe depression.

Prevalence

12.02 The estimated prevalence of psychotic disorder in England in 2018 was 0.7 per cent of people aged 16 and over.

Symptoms and behaviour

12.03 Hallucinations occur when a person hears, sees and, in some cases, feels, smells or tastes things that do not exist outside their mind. A common hallucination is hearing voices. Delusions are firm beliefs that are not shared by others. A common delusion is someone believing there's a conspiracy to harm them. The combination of hallucinations and delusional thinking can cause severe distress and a change in behaviour. Typically, people think these experiences are real at the time.

Causes

12.04 **Predisposing factors** – Large inner cities tend to have a higher incidence and prevalence of psychosis. This is explained by higher rates of deprivation and poverty and higher population density.

A family history of schizophrenia is a significant risk factor. Between 6 and 17 per cent of people who have a first-degree relative (parent, sibling or child) with schizophrenia develop psychosis at some point during their life. Adverse life events that have been shown to increase the risk of experiencing a psychotic episode include child abuse, death of a parent, family conflict, domestic violence, early experience of alcohol, and substance use and misuse.

At risk mental state – Often psychoses are preceded by a phase known as 'at risk mental state' (or 'subclinical' psychosis). It is estimated that around 5 per cent of the general population have subclinical psychotic experiences. The proportion of people with an at risk mental state who develop a psychotic episode is 18 per cent after six months, 22 per cent after one year, 29 per cent after two years and 36 per cent after three years.

Precipitating factors – Psychosis can be triggered by regular abuse of drugs, including skunk, other forms of cannabis, khat and amphetamines, and by alcohol abuse. Although single severe stress events can carry risk, there is an increased risk of developing psychosis with multiple events. Events associated with chronic adversity carry the greatest risk. Psychosis can also result from side effects of prescribed medicine, typically steroids or medication to treat Parkinson's disease, or from a physical condition, such as a brain tumour.

Treatment

12.05 Treatment for psychosis involves using a combination of:

- **antipsychotic medicine** – which can help relieve the symptoms of psychosis;
- **psychological therapies** – the 1-to-1 talking therapy, cognitive behavioural therapy has proved successful in helping people with psychosis, and family interventions (a form of therapy that may involve partners, family members and close friends) has been shown to reduce the need for hospital treatment in people with psychosis; and
- **social support** – support with social needs, such as education, employment or accommodation.

Clinical teams called Early Intervention Teams offer a comprehensive package of treatment. Typically, the team remain involved for up to three years. Some people with psychosis are recommended to take antipsychotic medication on a long-term basis and possibly for the rest of their lives. Some, on medical advice, may be able to gradually reduce their dosage of medication and eventually stop taking it altogether if there is a marked improvement in symptoms.

Prognosis

12.06 How often a psychotic episode occurs, and how long it lasts for, can depend on the underlying cause. An important factor in recovery is the duration of untreated psychosis. A shorter psychotic episode with a more acute onset has a better prognosis.

Advice for the Family Court

12.07 If the parent or carer is currently symptomatic, they will need to take breaks and be given time to process questions and make their responses. If they are unable to concentrate due to symptoms, it may not be possible to proceed. Written information provided in advance can help ensure the person has sufficient time to absorb this before the hearing.

Also, see Advice for the Family Court in this chapter on schizophrenia.

Further information

Public Health England – Psychosis Data Report

https://www.gov.uk/government/publications/psychosis-data-report

NICE – Psychosis and schizophrenia in adults: prevention and management

https://www.nice.org.uk/guidance/cg178

Mind – Psychosis

https://www.mind.org.uk/information-support/types-of-mental-health-problems/psychosis/types-of-psychosis/

BIPOLAR AFFECTIVE DISORDER

(See also **Chapter 8** Psychotic disorders in children.)

12.08 Bipolar affective disorder (not just 'bipolar') is a mental disorder characterised by extreme mood swings. It used to be called manic depression.

Prevalence

12.09 In the general population, the prevalence is 1 to 3 per cent. Younger people are more likely to have a bipolar affective disorder; a 2014 study found that 34 per cent of 16- to 24-year-olds tested positive but only 0.4 per cent of 65- to 74-year-olds screened positive.

Symptoms and behaviour

12.10 The onset of bipolar affective disorder is usually in a person's early twenties. The disorder is characterised by extreme changes in mood, from severe lows (depression) to severe highs (mania), with regular moods in between.

Typically, those in the manic stage present with:

- talking rapidly (pressure of speech);
- poor sleep;
- grandiosity (heightened self-esteem);
- elated mood – feeling 'on top of the world';
- increased appetite;
- irritability; and
- reckless or disinhibited behaviour, such as overspending, sexual disinhibition, delusions (such as being God, royalty, or having superhuman powers) and hallucinations. These hallucinations, for example hearing the voice of someone famous praising them, can reinforce the person's belief and elated mood.

People with bipolar affective disorder are more likely to have insight into their condition when their mood dips, as often when becoming high (manic) they feel extremely well. Hospital admission may be necessary. Those with BPAD are usually detained on section, if they pose a risk to themselves and/or others and have no insight.

Treatment

12.11 The mainstay of treatment for bipolar affective disorder is mood stabilisers, medication which must be taken regularly and long term. Antipsychotic medication is also prescribed to manage the over-activity, which can lead to exhaustion. Some people remain on this medication as it also has mood-stabilising properties. Antidepressants are sometimes prescribed, but may make mood swings worse by precipitating a swing into mania. Careful blood monitoring is required for patients on mood stabilisers. Some medications should be avoided by women of child-bearing age and definitely in pregnancy

Cognitive behavioural therapy (CBT) is a psychological treatment typically used to help people manage early symptoms and prevent relapse. Cognitive analytic therapy offers a more individual and thoughtful explanation for the individual's personal development and patterns of behaviour.

Prognosis

12.12 People who have bipolar affective disorder are more likely to return to normal functioning between episodes than those with schizophrenia. Important factors are whether they have insight, and so will comply with medication, and whether there is substance misuse (patients may self-medicate with alcohol or other substances, which worsens prognosis). Cannabis use increases the duration of manic episodes.

'Rapid cycling' is a term used when a patient has more than four manic episodes in a year. This has a worse prognosis. Repeated episodes can result in impairment in executive function (the higher functioning centre at the front of the brain), and so patients can appear more able than they are.

Advice for the Family Court

12.13 If a parent with bipolar affective disorder attends court and is symptomatic, they may display the following behaviours.

If they are in a manic phase, they are likely to have problems with concentration, pressure of speech (uninterruptable) and poor concentration. The elated parent may also have no understanding of others concerns, as they may have grandiose beliefs that can affect their parenting ability.

If the parent is in a depressed phase, they may lack motivation and have poor concentration. The depressed parent may be so full of self-blame and guilt that they are unable to see any positives. They may also be at risk of self-harm and suicide.

Regular breaks will help manage any mood swings (the stress of the situation may bring these on). Where possible, present information in writing. If these adjustments do not help, it may be necessary to reschedule the hearing date.

Further information

NICE – Bipolar disorder: assessment and management

https://www.nice.org.uk/guidance/cg185

Bipolar UK

https://www.bipolaruk.org

DELUSIONAL DISORDER

12.14 Delusional disorder is a rare condition estimated to affect 0.2 per cent of people experiencing it at some point in their lifetime. It is equally likely to occur in men and women. Unlike schizophrenia, there is usually a single delusional idea which can be pursued beyond realistic expectations. Stalkers, extremely litigious people, and people who pester organisations because of their belief that they are being persecuted can all come into this category.

Delusional disorder does not respond well to medication or psychological treatment. People with this condition rarely admit they are ill. In their view, it is other people who do not take their beliefs seriously. Apart from the fixation, they may function perfectly normally in other areas of their life.

People with a delusional disorder who come to court may have boxes and files of papers to prove their point.

Further information

Cleveland clinic – Delusional disorder

https://my.clevelandclinic.org/health/diseases/9599-delusional-disorder

SCHIZOAFFECTIVE DISORDER

12.15 In schizoaffective disorder, there are symptoms of both schizophrenia and mood disturbance. The person has the paranoid ideas typical of schizophrenia, but their mood will be either elated or depressed. More women than men are affected by the disorder, and it tends to develop at a later age in women than men.

The distinction between schizoaffective disorder, schizophrenia and bipolar affective disorder is important for two reasons:

- For the patient to receive the most appropriate treatment, antipsychotic medication alone may be sufficient for schizophrenia, whereas people with bipolar disorder respond better to mood-stabilising medication. For schizoaffective disorder, the person will need both types of medication.
- The prognosis of the disorders is different. Bipolar disorder has the best prognosis, then schizoaffective disorder, and schizophrenia has the worst prognosis.

It's not unusual for a diagnosis of any of these illnesses to be changed to another, as patients may have different symptoms at different stages of their illness.

Further information

Royal College of Psychiatrists – Schizoaffective disorder

https://www.rcpsych.ac.uk/mental-health/problems-disorders/schizoaffective-disorder?searchTerms=Royal%20College%20of%20Psychiatrists%20-%20Schizoaffective%20disorder

SCHIZOPHRENIA

(See also **Chapter 8** Psychotic disorders in children.)

12.16 Schizophrenia is the most devastating of mental illnesses. Not only are there distressing psychotic symptoms, but the chronic illness itself causes negative symptoms (such as apathy, lack of emotion, monotone speech or complete withdrawal), which may be even more disabling. Schizophrenia affects men and women equally, but the onset of the disorder is generally earlier in males. Men with schizophrenia are typically diagnosed in their late teens and early twenties, while women are more likely to be diagnosed in their late twenties or early thirties.

Prevalence

12.17 The prevalence of schizophrenia in the UK is approximately 15 cases per 1,000 people.

Symptoms and behaviour

12.18 Symptoms of schizophrenia fall into two main categories, called **positive symptoms** and **negative symptoms** (see below). The symptoms vary from person to person, both in pattern and severity. Not every person with schizophrenia will experience all the symptoms, and the symptoms may change over time. Typically, patients with schizophrenia do not realise they are unwell, so lack insight, and therefore do not see the need for medication or follow-up.

Positive symptoms

12.19 **Delusions –** A delusion is a firmly-held idea that, is not based on reality, despite clear and obvious evidence that it isn't true. Delusions are extremely common in schizophrenia, occurring in more than 90 per cent of those who have the disorder. Often these delusions involve illogical or bizarre ideas or fantasies. Common delusions include:

- **Delusions of persecution** – these will often involve bizarre ideas and plots.
- **Delusions of reference** – the person might believe a newspaper or a TV personality is sending a message meant specifically for them.
- **Delusions of grandeur** – the person believes they are a famous or important figure or that they have unusual powers.

- **Delusions of control** – the person believes their thoughts or actions are being controlled by outside or alien forces.

Hallucinations – These are sounds or other sensations experienced as real when actually they exist only in the person's mind. While hallucinations can involve any of the five senses, auditory hallucinations (hearing voices or other sounds) are most common in schizophrenia. Visual hallucinations are also relatively common. Schizophrenic hallucinations are usually meaningful to the person experiencing them. Often the voices are of someone they know. Most commonly, the voices are critical, vulgar or abusive and can include command voices that instruct them to carry out actions. Hallucinations tend to be worse when the person is alone.

Thought disorder and disorganised speech – Fragmented thinking is characteristic of schizophrenia. It can be observed in the way a schizophrenic person speaks; they tend to have trouble concentrating and maintaining a train of thought. They may respond to questions with an unrelated answer, start sentences with one topic and end somewhere completely different, speak incoherently or say illogical things.

Disorganised behaviour – Schizophrenia disrupts goal-directed activity, impairing a person's ability to care for themselves, work, and interact with others. Disorganised behaviour appears as a decline in overall daily functioning, unpredictable or inappropriate emotional responses, and actions that seem bizarre and have no purpose.

Negative symptoms

12.20 Negative symptoms are the absence of normal behaviours. People living with schizophrenia commonly lose interest and motivation in life and activities, including relationships and loss of libido. They may lack concentration, experience changes in sleeping patterns, and have poverty of speech and thought. Common negative symptoms of schizophrenia include:

- lack of emotional expression – an inexpressive face;
- flat voice;
- lack of eye contact;
- lack of interest or enthusiasm;
- problems with motivation;
- lack of self-care; and
- lack of interest in the world – apparent unawareness of the surrounding environment and social withdrawal.

Negative symptoms are secondary to positive symptoms and are especially difficult to treat.

Causes

12.21 Schizophrenia is more common in males with developmental disorders than in the general population. There is early onset and high incidence in males with neurodevelopmental disorders. It is also more common in parents, children and siblings of an affected individual – an incidence of 10 per cent, compared with 1 per cent in the population. There is a genetic component too. In some families an abnormality in chromosome 22 increases the incidence of psychosis to around 25 per cent in young people, rising to 40 per cent in those aged over 25.

Cannabis can produce an acute psychotic reaction in non-schizophrenic people who use it, especially at high doses, although this fades as the drug wears off. Cannabis can cause schizophrenia. Daily cannabis use increases the risk of developing schizophrenia by three times, and using skunk increases the risk by five times.

Treatment

12.22 Antipsychotic medication is prescribed either in tablet form or long-lasting injections (depot injections). Depot injections are given to people who cannot be relied on to take oral medication. Those who refuse their depot medication relapse more slowly than those who stop the oral medication, as the depot medication remains in their system for some weeks.

Clozapine is recommended for people who continue to have symptoms (treatment-resistant) even though they are prescribed, and compliant with, other antipsychotic medications. However, if the person stops taking clozapine, the medication must be restarted at a low dose and then increased gradually to a therapeutic level. This is because clozapine has life-threatening side effects, as it can reduce the person's white blood cell count, making them vulnerable to infections, and increase the risk of heart failure.

Psychological treatments can also be beneficial. At a basic level, talking therapy helps a person to understand they are suffering from an illness. More complex psychology can be beneficial for those who have some insight that they are unwell. This might include cognitive behavioural therapy to help the person challenge or manage their symptoms, and relapse prevention to help them recognise early signs of relapse.

Prognosis

12.23 People who present with positive symptoms of schizophrenia, with an acute onset and with mood symptoms, have a better prognosis than a schizophrenic condition that has a gradual onset. The prognosis is worse the earlier in life the condition develops. People with negative symptoms also have a worse prognosis. Full recovery is unusual, with only approximately 15 per cent returning to previous functioning capabilities. Cannabis and other illicit drugs can trigger relapses, and ongoing use worsens prognosis. Each relapse and delay in restarting a therapeutic dose of medication worsens the prognosis, unlike with bipolar affective disorder.

The duration of untreated psychosis (DUP) is important for long-term functioning. The longer the DUP, the worse the prognosis. Important factors are whether the patient has insight into their condition and so will comply with medication and whether there is substance misuse.

Life expectancy among people with schizophrenia is significantly reduced – by up to 15 years – as sufferers either neglect physical health conditions or do not seek help with them. Also, they may not express physical symptoms in a way that medical services can understand. Some antipsychotic medication has the side effect of increased appetite. This, combined with a schizophrenic person's reduced motivation to exercise and take good physical care of themselves, increases their risk of diabetes, cardiac problems, high cholesterol and joint problems related to obesity.

Advice for the Family Court

12.24 When someone with schizophrenia is acutely unwell, they will have problems with concentration and communication and may be distracted by hallucinations. Their delusions may prevent them being able to co-operate, so it may be necessary to reschedule the hearing date.

For someone with chronic schizophrenia, the negative symptoms can often be more disabling. An apparent lack of motivation is likely to cause problems for the partner and the care of the children. These negative symptoms are hard to treat, so the person's behaviour may not improve.

Further information

Royal College of Psychiatrists – Schizophrenia

https://www.rcpsych.ac.uk/mental-health/problems-disorders/schizophrenia?searchTerms=Schizophrenia

Living With Schizophrenia

https://livingwithschizophreniauk.org/symptoms-of-schizophrenia/

Rethink Mental Illness – Schizophrenia

https://www.rethink.org/search-results/?q=Schizophrenia

Chapter 13

Behavioural disorders in adults

PERSONALITY DISORDERS

13.01 The term 'personality disorder' describes a range of mental disorders in which an individual's personal characteristics result in long-term problems in the way they cope with life, interact with others, or respond to events emotionally.

People with personality disorders are likely to act impulsively, with little thought for the consequences of their actions, and they often find it difficult to learn from their experiences. This often results in aggressive behaviour, bringing them into contact with the criminal justice system. It is estimated that 50 to 70 per cent of prisoners and individuals on probation, have behaviours indicating they have some category of personality disorder.

Women with a personality disorder often become pregnant several times with different partners in the hope of securing an enduring relationship. Their personality disorder and self-harming behaviour can make it difficult for them to care consistently for a baby or child. If they are unable to mature sufficiently or learn from their experience, then successive children are taken into care.

Prevalence

13.02 One NHS study found that about 5 to 10 per cent of the general population have a personality disorder, and about 30 to 40 per cent of psychiatric patients are diagnosed with the condition. Most personality disorders begin in the teen years when the personality further develops and matures.

Of the types of personality disorder, some are diagnosed more frequently in men (such as those characterised by violence and suspicion towards others), and some more often in women (such as those characterised by labile emotions). This difference between men and women is because men tend to direct their emotions of emptiness and rejection into reckless and aggressive behaviour, whereas women are more likely to internalise their feelings and have a tendency to self-harm. People with certain personality disorders are more likely to come to the attention of the police and health services, especially when there are risks to others and the individual themselves.

Some people tend to live a solitary life to avoid the feeling of rejection, so their disorder may not be apparent. The individual is just regarded as odd.

Most people with personality disorder think the problem is with others rather than their own behaviour.

Symptoms and behaviour

13.03 These vary between disorders, but common indications include:

- not trusting other people;
- lack of emotion;
- feelings of emptiness;
- extreme fear of rejection;
- reckless and impulsive behaviour;
- being overly dramatic;
- striving always to be the centre of attention (may include self-harm);
- perfectionism and being excessively critical of others;
- an inability to see the bigger picture; and
- experiences similar to auditory hallucinations but generally short-lived.

The categories of personality disorder in ICD-10 such as paranoid, emotionally unstable, dissocial, and schizoid have been replaced in ICD-11 by 'personality disorder' in category 6D, with five severity levels. In addition, there are groups of symptoms and behaviour called 'qualifiers' which will distinguish categories.

Symptoms must be present for more than two years to make a diagnosis. Personality disorders can be diagnosed at any age according to ICD-11.

The five severity Levels of Personality Disturbance proposed in ICD-11 and the likely population prevalence

Level and diagnostic number in ICD-11	Main features	% of population with this level
No Personality Disturbance (PD)	No personality disturbance	45%
PD	Some personality problems in certain situations but not universally	48%
Mild PD 6D10.0	Definite well demarcated personality problems across a range of situations	5.3%
Moderate PD 6D10.1	Definite personality problems usually covering several personality domains and across all situations	1.5%
Severe PD 6D10.2	Personality problems leading to significant risk to self or others	0.2%

These severity levels mean more people have a personality difficulty than not – which seems surprising.

The groups of symptoms and behaviour which will be rated in ICD-11 (6D) in addition to the mild/moderate/severe ratings are:

- negative affectivity (6D11.0) – the tendency to experience a broad range of negative emotions with a frequency and intensity out of proportion to the situation, over-reactive to external threats or criticism, problems, and setbacks. They have low frustration tolerance and easily become visibly upset over even minor issues or reject others' suggestions or advice;
- detachment (6D31.1) – tendency to maintain interpersonal distance (social detachment) and emotional distance (emotional detachment).
- dissociality (6D31.2) – disregard for the rights and feelings of others, encompassing both self-centeredness and lack of empathy;
- disinhibition (6D31.3)– tendency to act rashly based on immediate external or internal stimuli (ie, sensations, emotions, thoughts), without consideration of potential negative consequences.
- anankastia (6D31.4) – a narrow focus on one's rigid standard of perfection and of right and wrong and on controlling one's own and others' behaviour to ensure conformity to those standards.

Diagnosis will be made using rating scales and screening instruments such as the Standardised Assessment of Personality (SAPAS) is a brief interview-based screening instrument consisting of eight dichotomously rated items taken from the opening section of an informant-based interview

It is hoped that the changes in ICD-11 may reduce stigma of personality disorder and lead to proactive treatment – currently clinicians use the diagnosis 'personality disorder' when treatment for other disorders fails.

Causes

13.04 The causes are complex, but they are thought to result from a combination of the genes a person inherits and early environmental influences. Issues with attachment in infancy are thought to lead to conduct disorder in childhood and then personality disorder in adults. A person's relationship with their parents and family has a strong influence on how they come to see the world and what they believe about other people. The environmental factors that seem to be common and widespread among people with emotionally unstable personality disorder are linked to neglect. These include: being a victim of emotional, physical or sexual abuse; being exposed to long-term fear or distress as a child; being neglected by one or both parents; and growing up with a family member with a serious mental health condition or alcohol or drug misuse problem.

The chance of a child developing a personality disorder is increased by 10 times if either parent has a personality disorder.

Treatments and prognosis

13.05 Treatment varies depending on the type and severity of the personality disorder. It may include psychotherapy and medications. Intensive psychological treatment is the only intervention proven to benefit those who come to the attention of health and social services. Dialectic behaviour therapy focuses on self-harm, suicidality and issues about relationships, which tend to be problems early in the lives of patients with a borderline personality disorder. As these symptoms remit with time, older patients may need to deal with problems relating to feelings of emptiness and fear of abandonment.

Personality disorder symptoms can reduce over time. However, the person's behaviour, changes in mood and difficulty with relationships can lead to self-medicating with alcohol and/or drugs. This can make holding down employment difficult, while the impact on relationships may leave the person isolated.

Many people with a personality disorder frequently present for help in crisis; this is a feature of their impulsivity. This behaviour can be difficult for mental health services to manage, so such people may be less likely to receive appropriate help, and there can be a high risk of suicide.

Advice for the Family Court

13.06 Some people with a personality disorder may have had issues from a young age with authority figures and can project their previous negative experiences on to those in authority. Therefore a parent with such a disorder may have preconceived ideas and expectations before coming to court. Some parents with a personality disorder will have experienced repeated relationship breakdowns.

If dealing with a parent with a personality disorder in court, make clear to them that the court is independent. Explain they will find some information difficult to hear. People with a personality disorder have learned to shrug off or attack criticism. This is their coping strategy, so try to prepare them for when they will hear criticism and emphasise supportive comments. Make rules and stick to them, as impulsive and unpredictable behaviour is the norm for someone with a personality disorder. Keep yourself and other attenders safe in the event of a disruptive emotional reaction. Offer regular breaks.

These two case studies contrast emotionally unstable personality disorder and sociopathic personality disorder, detailing how these disorders may present to services, and how services respond.

Case studies – Personality disorders – Karen and David's stories (see Appendix: Case studies, p 341.)

Further Information

Royal College of Psychiatrists – Personality disorder

https://www.rcpsych.ac.uk/mental-health/problems-disorders/personality-disorder?searchTerms=personality%20disorder

Mind – Personality disorders

https://www.mind.org.uk/information-support/types-of-mental-health-problems/personality-disorders/about-personality-disorders/

NICE – Mental health of people in prison (including Personality disorder)

https://www.nice.org.uk/guidance/ng66/documents/mental-health-of-people-in-prison-draft-scope2

NHS – Borderline personality disorder

https://www.nhs.uk/conditions/borderline-personality-disorder/causes/

ICD-11 Personality Disorder categories

The Development of the ICD-11 Classification of Personality Disorders: An Amalgam of Science, Pragmatism, and Politics. Tyrer P, Mulder R, Kim YR, Crawford MJ. Annu Rev Clin Psychol. 2019 May 7;15:481-502. doi: 10.1146/annurev-clinpsy-050718-095736. Epub 2019 Jan 2. PMID: 30601688.

Chapter 14

Neurodevelopmental disorders in adults

The term 'Neurodevelopmental disorders' has a long history, yet it had not been included in previous editions of the ICD or the DSM. The term applies to a group of disorders of early onset that affect both cognitive and social communicative development, affect males more than females, and have a chronic course with impairment generally lasting into adulthood.

(The term 'neurodevelopmental' distinguishes these disorders from other more common disorders of childhood, such as anxiety and mood disorders, which are generally thought to arise from some type of psychosocial adversity and have a more episodic course.) In the ICD-11, the category 'neurodevelopmental disorders' includes the following:

- disorders of intellectual development
- developmental speech or language disorders
- autism spectrum disorders (ASD)
- developmental learning disorders
- developmental motor coordination disorder
- attention deficit hyperactivity disorder (ADHD)
- stereotyped movement disorder
- other neurodevelopmental disorders.

ATTENTION DEFICIT HYPERACTIVITY DISORDER (ADHD)

(See also **Chapter 7** Neurodevelopmental disorders in children.)

14.01 Attention deficit hyperactivity disorder (ADHD) is a pattern of behaviours which usually appears in childhood. The condition tends to improve with age, but it can continue into adult life. The presentation in adults is less obviously hyperactive but more of disorganisation.

Prevalence

14.02 In 15 per cent of children with ADHD, the disorder continues into adult life, but it can be less troublesome. Around 1.5 million adults are estimated to have the condition but, as reported in 2018 by ADHD Action, only 120,000 are formally diagnosed.

Symptoms and behaviour

14.03 Behaviours that can be symptoms of ADHD in childhood include being over-active, easily distracted, impulsive and unable to concentrate for any length of time. Many adults may have one of these problems, but not all of them. In adulthood, to be given a diagnosis of ADHD, these problems must be severe enough to interfere with how an individual gets on with people socially and at work.

As someone with ADHD gets older, the over-activity usually lessens but the impulsivity, poor concentration and risk-taking can get worse. These can make it hard to work, learn and interact with other people. Adults with the condition are more likely to experience depression, anxiety, feelings of low self-esteem and drug misuse. They can feel overwhelmed and struggle in less structured environments.

Causes

14.04 The exact cause of ADHD is not fully understood, although a combination of factors is thought to be responsible.

- **Genetics** – The parents and siblings of a child with ADHD are more likely to have ADHD themselves. However, the way the condition is inherited is likely to be complex and is not thought to be related to a single genetic fault.
- **Brain function and structure** – Research has identified possible differences in the brains of people with ADHD compared to

those without the condition, and an imbalance in the level of neurotransmitters in the brain among those with the condition.

- **Birth issues** – Children at risk of ADHD include those who were born prematurely (before the 37th week of pregnancy) or with low birth weight, children with epilepsy, and those with brain damage. Contributory factors also include negative early life experiences, such as children whose parents are drug-users – probably because the child was exposed to the neurotoxic effects of drugs before birth.

Treatments and prognosis

14.05 ADHD can be treated using medication or psychological interventions, but a combination of both is often most effective. Medication is not a permanent cure for ADHD but may help with the condition so a person can concentrate better, be less impulsive, feel calmer, and learn and practise new skills.

The medications most widely used for the treatment of ADHD are stimulants. Ritalin (methylphenidate) is the most common. However, it can have side effects of loss of appetite and weight loss, and the stimulant effect can cause sleep disturbance. Occasional treatment breaks are recommended to assess whether the medication is still needed.

Psychological treatments can include cognitive behavioural therapy, mindfulness techniques and group therapy. Self-help support groups can also be beneficial for both the individual and their family.

Adults with ADHD are likely to experience interpersonal difficulties with peers, employers and partners often leading to short-lived jobs and relationships. Some will find work that is compatible with their symptoms, but many studies report higher rates of employment problems, including higher turnover of jobs leading to poorer employment opportunities, lower earnings and periods of unemployment.

Advice for the Family Court

14.06 A parent with ADHD may be disorganised and late, chaotic and unable to follow the rules. They might talk over others and then get frustrated when reprimanded.

If they are presenting their case, it may be helpful to give clear and frequent summing up of the current stage of the court process and what is expected. Consider scheduling a short break in court proceedings to give the parent some respite from the situation.

Someone who had ADHD as a child, and consequently had difficulties with schooling, may have poor literacy as an adult. The person may not admit or acknowledge this.

Further information

Royal College of Psychiatrists – ADHD

https://www.rcpsych.ac.uk/mental-health/problems-disorders/adhd-in-adults?searchTerms=ADHD

ADHD Action

https://www.adhdaction.org

Differential diagnosis for ADHD

Clinical Topics in Child and Adolescent Psychiatry (chapter 15), see above

Treatment for ADHD

NICE guideline [NG87]: www.nice.org.uk/guidance/ng87

AUTISM SPECTRUM DISORDER (ASD)

(See also **Chapter 7** Neurodevelopmental disorders in children.)

14.07 Autism spectrum disorder (ASD) comprises autism, Asperger's syndrome and pervasive developmental disorders. Although onset is usually is before three years of age, an increasing number of people are being diagnosed in adulthood. Some people may recognise autistic traits in themselves, but not seek a formal diagnosis.

Autism is a lifelong disability which affects how people communicate and interact with the world. No two autistic people are the same as it is a spectrum disorder. Each person with the condition has their own personality and life experiences, and it affects people in different ways.

The following are features present in an ASD diagnosis in adulthood, and the impact these may have on someone who is a parent or carer.

Prevalence

14.08 Men are around three times more likely than women to be diagnosed with ASD. The condition can run in families, and siblings have a higher risk. Estimates of prevalence in the UK vary, but the currently accepted figure is around one in 100 people.

Symptoms and behaviour

14.09 An adult with ASD has difficulty with reciprocal social interaction. This means:

- the person may often be talking about a subject that others have moved on from;
- they may be unable to recognise when another person is upset;
- they may not easily make new friends as they are either anxious or unaware in social situations;
- their difficulties in communication – for example, lack of eye contact, unusual speech patterns, tendency to take things literally, and a robotic voice – mean others may avoid them.

People with ASD find unfamiliar situations difficult, so they may avoid trying new things. They may be hyper- or hypo-sensitive to stimuli (meaning their senses are overwhelmed or they don't respond), so bright lights, loud noises and smells may be distressing. Alternatively, they may not notice odours that other people do, such as the smell of gas, food that has gone off, or body odour. Parents who are autistic may not pick up on cues when a child is upset, as they may have difficulty interpreting facial expressions and body language, and so may be unsure how best to offer comfort.

People with ASD often have other overlapping physical and mental health conditions. These conditions can include epilepsy, gastrointestinal problems and other disabling and distressing mental illnesses such as sleep disorders, depression, social anxiety, attention deficit hyperactivity disorder, obsessional compulsive disorder, schizophrenia and bipolar affective disorder. Diagnosis of ASD can be problematic if the person also has another mental health disorder, as some conditions are overlapping.

The stereotypical patterns of behaviour in children with ASD, such as stimming (hand flapping, rocking, humming), may not be so apparent in adults. Some adults may not be diagnosed until there is a change in their circumstances that removes protective factors, such as the death of a parent.

Causes

14.10 Causes of autism are still being investigated. It is likely there is a combination of genetic and environmental factors which account for changes in brain development. Studies have found a link between parental age and autism. Older parents – mothers aged 35 or older and fathers over 40 – are more likely to have an autistic child.

Treatments and prognosis

14.11 There is no known cure for autism, but there are several treatment approaches that can help improve social functioning, learning and quality of life. Treatments include behavioural support plans, communication assessments and talking therapies, such as cognitive behavioural therapy and social skills training. There is no medication that can treat the condition, but some medications can help with related symptoms, such as depression, seizures, insomnia, and trouble focussing attention. Medication is most effective when combined with behavioural therapies.

Advice for the Family Court

14.12 Adults with ASD often have difficulty understanding other people's viewpoints. A parent with autism may find mediation difficult, as their thinking can be rigid. The parent's possible lack of understanding or empathy with people who are trying to assist, such as social workers and teachers, may cause difficulties.

The affected person may have obsessions, repetitive behaviour or routines that help them cope with everyday life, so allow for these in the hearing. Some parents with ASD may have poor educational achievement, so do not assume they are literate. Social naivety can make people with ASD appear as though they have a learning disability, which may not be the case.

At the hearing, a parent with ASD may be rigid about time, take expressions literally and fail to understand metaphors. Sensory overstimulation is likely to cause irritability and even shutdown. Someone in shutdown may be unable to communicate, will look closed down or may just keep answering 'yes'. If very stressed, they may use stimming to self-regulate anxiety.

Case studies – Autism spectrum disorder late diagnosis – Heather and Manuel's stories (see Appendix: Case studies, p 344.)

Further information

NICE – Autism spectrum disorder in adults: diagnosis and management

https://www.nice.org.uk/guidance/cg142

National Autistic Society

https://www.autism.org.uk

Mencap – Autism and Asperger's syndrome

https://www.mencap.org.uk/learning-disability-explained/conditions-linked-learning-disability/autism-and-aspergers-syndrome

INTELLECTUAL DEVELOPMENT DISORDERS

(See also **Chapter 7** Neurodevelopmental disorders in children.)

14.13 Disorders of intellectual development are lifelong. Onset is from birth, and it is often diagnosed in childhood. People are affected in different ways. Common difficulties include adapting behaviour to different situations, interacting with others and controlling behaviour. It is often confused with specific learning difficulties, such as dyslexia, which do not affect intellect.

Often the person themselves, and their family, friends and carers, would dispute that they have a disability; they consider that it is other people's perception.

Prevalence

14.14 Disorders of intellectual development affects around 2 per cent of the UK population. In 2019, the Office for National Statistics reported there are 1.5 million children and adults affected in the UK. Of these, approximately 1,130,000 are adults.

Symptoms and behaviour

14.15 Major changes in the ICD-11 include the renaming of mental retardation to disorders of intellectual development.

Essential (Required) Features for diagnosis are the presence of significant limitations in intellectual functioning across various domains such as perceptual reasoning, working memory, processing speed, and verbal comprehension. There is often substantial variability in the extent to which any of these domains are affected in an individual. The severity of a Disorder of Intellectual Development is determined by considering both the individual's level of intellectual ability and level of adaptive behaviour.

Four levels of severity are described: mild, moderate, severe, and profound.

Behavioural indicators describe those skills and abilities that would be typically observed within each of these categories – as listed in the ICD-11 Diagnostic Guidelines on Neurodevelopmental Disorders.

6A00.0 Mild Disorder of Intellectual Development

14.16 Persons with a Mild Disorder of Intellectual Development often exhibit difficulties in the acquisition and comprehension of complex language concepts and academic skills. Most master basic self-care, domestic, and practical activities. Affected persons can generally achieve relatively independent living and employment as adults but may require appropriate support.

6A00.1 Moderate Disorder of Intellectual Development

14.17 Language and capacity for acquisition of academic skills of persons affected by a Moderate Disorder of Intellectual Development vary but are generally limited to basic skills. Some may master basic self-care, domestic, and practical activities. Most affected persons require considerable and consistent support in order to achieve independent living and employment as adults.

6A00.2 Severe Disorder of Intellectual Development

14.18 Persons affected by a Severe Disorder of Intellectual Development exhibit very limited language and capacity for acquisition of academic skills. They may also have motor impairments and typically require daily support in a supervised environment for adequate care, but may acquire basic self-care skills with intensive training

6A00.3 Profound Disorder of Intellectual Development

14.19 Persons affected by a Profound Disorder of Intellectual Development possess very limited communication abilities and capacity for acquisition of academic skills is restricted to basic concrete skills. They may also have co-occurring motor and sensory impairments and typically require daily support in a supervised environment for adequate care

14.20 International Classification of Diseases (ICD-10) does refer to intelligence quotient (IQ) in classifications of the level (degree) of learning disability as follows:

- mild – IQ of 50 to 70
- moderate – IQ of 35 to 50
- severe – IQ of 20 to 35
- profound – IQ <20.

However, IQ alone is not helpful as it does not give an indication of the person's overall functioning.

A person cannot be detained in a psychiatric hospital for treatment under the Mental Health Act 'just' for a learning disability. The learning disability must present with abnormally aggressive and seriously irresponsible behaviour.

Causes

14.21 There are over 700 genetic conditions that can cause a learning disability. The best known are Down's syndrome and fragile X syndrome. Problems during pregnancy and birth can result in brain injury to the newborn. Certain types of infections during pregnancy and illnesses, such as encephalitis in early infancy, can also be causes. However, for many people, particularly those with a mild learning disability, there may be no discernible cause.

Mental health disorders and disorders of intellectual development

14.22 Between 25 per cent and 40 per cent of people with disorders of intellectual development experience mental health problems. The prevalence of dementia is much higher amongst older adults with disorders of intellectual development compared to the general population (21.6 per cent compared to 5.7 per cent at age 65-plus). People with Down's syndrome are at particularly high risk of developing dementia, with an age of onset 30-40 years younger than the general population.

Prevalence rates for schizophrenia in people with disorders of intellectual development are approximately three times greater than for the general population. Rates of anxiety and depression among people with disorders of intellectual development vary widely, but they are generally reported to be at least as prevalent as in the general population and higher among people with Down's syndrome. Challenging behaviours – aggression, destruction, self-injury and others – are present in 10 to 15 per cent of people with a disorders of intellectual development.

People with a disorder of intellectual development have higher rates of other developmental disorders, such as autism spectrum disorders and attention deficit hyperactivity disorder. They are also vulnerable to abuse due to low self-esteem, stigma and dependence on others.

Increased rates of mental disorder are related to:

- the condition that causes the disorder of intellectual development also causing psychiatric disorder (for example, people with Down's syndrome are at increased risk of developing dementia);
- communication problems leading to an inability to express feelings (for example, after bereavement, which can lead to depression or anxiety);
- higher rates of social deprivation.

Despite the high reported rates of other mental disorders in adults with disorders of intellectual development, these may be under-diagnosed. This is because they develop and present in different ways compared to in people without disorders of intellectual development, and the usual signs or symptoms may not be observable or reported. The person's language and/or abstract thinking may make emotional symptoms difficult to identify. Clinicians may also overlook psychiatric symptoms, attributing them to the disorders of intellectual development.

Treatment and prognosis

14.23 There is no treatment for disorders of intellectual development, but interventions can help maximise people's strengths.

In adulthood, a person with a disorder of intellectual development will be presented with new challenges as life changes for them, such as adjusting to the demands of a new job, or parenthood. These transitions are stressful but can be managed with the right support.

Support from professionals, such as GPs, paediatricians and physicians, speech and language therapists, physiotherapists, educational and clinical psychologists and social services, can help people develop and live independently. People with more severe disabilities require supported accommodation to have assistance with everyday tasks, such as washing and dressing, and protection and support for their vulnerabilities.

Children and young people with a disorder of intellectual development may also have special educational needs.

Patients with mental disorders are treated in the same way as all other patients – with medication and psychological treatments. Adjustments are made so that the person can understand information and engage in appropriate psychological therapy for their level of understanding.

Older people with a disorder of intellectual development are more likely to develop serious health problems, such as epilepsy or pneumonia. They may find it difficult to express their needs and be heard so communicating symptoms may be difficult, and they are more likely to die because of a late diagnosis.

Prevention and detection of physical health problems are vital, as life expectancy is reduced in people with a disorders of intellectual development. On average, the life expectancy of women with a disorder of intellectual development is 18 years shorter than for women in the general population; and the life expectancy of men is 14 years shorter than for men in the general population. The average age of death of those with profound disabilities is around 40. All people with a disorder of intellectual development are eligible for an annual health check from the age of four, but this is only done in about half the population.

Advice for the Family Court

14.24 There is no specific minimum IQ that means a person with a disorder of intellectual development is unable to care for their child. Each case must be looked at individually, considering the parent's skills as well as their deficits. Much depends on the willingness of the parent to accept help.

Around 40 per cent of parents with a disorder of intellectual development do not live with their children. The children of parents with a disorder of intellectual development are more likely than any other group of children to be removed from their parents' care. Parents with a disability are often affected by poverty, social isolation, stress, mental health problems, low literacy skills and communication difficulties.

When preparing for a court attendance by a parent with a disorder of intellectual development, consider beforehand what reasonable adjustments are needed for that person. Discuss with their social worker, intermediary, carer or friend how best to communicate. If possible, allow the parent to go first and then have the final say. Use short sentences and simple language. Remember that communication through pictures and written words is favoured by some people over spoken language.

Check the person's understanding by asking them to explain to you in their own words. When talking about time, use events, for example 'after breakfast…'. Allow sufficient time and adjust the pace to suit the individual – don't move on too quickly. Beware of a person's tendency to please, note any signs of agitated behaviour and consider possible breaks.

Further information

NHS – Health and Care of People with Learning Disabilities

https://digital.nhs.uk/data-and-information/publications/statistical/health-and-care-of-people-with-learning-disabilities

NICE – Mental health problems in people with learning disabilities

https://www.nice.org.uk/guidance/population-groups/people-with-learning-disabilities

MENCAP – The voice of learning disability

https://www.mencap.org.uk

Foundation for People with Learning Disabilities

https://www.mentalhealth.org.uk/learning-disabilities

DYSLEXIA

(See also **Chapter 7** Neurodevelopmental disorders in children.)

14.25 Dyslexia is the most common of specific learning difficulties. Those with the condition can have difficulty with reading, writing, spelling and numeracy. They may also have problems with processing written information swiftly, and there may be weaknesses in their short-term and working memory.

The Equality Act 2010 identifies dyslexia as a disability. Dyslexia can have a significant impact during education, in the workplace and in everyday life. Each dyslexic person is unique, so everyone's experience of the condition is different.

Prevalence

14.26 According to the British Dyslexia Association, the proportion of the population in the UK with some form of dyslexia is around 10 per cent. Four per cent of the population is severely affected.

Signs and symptoms

14.27 Dyslexia is a spectrum disorder. It can range from mild to severe, and symptoms may include:

- difficulty reading, including reading aloud;
- confusion of visually similar words, such as cat and cot;
- slow and labour-intensive reading and writing;
- problems with spelling – often erratic;
- mispronouncing names or words, or problems retrieving words;
- difficulty in scanning or skim-reading text (adults with dyslexia may frequently lose their place or feel like the words are jumbled or moving);
- the need to re-read paragraphs to understand them;
- difficulty in listening and maintaining focus;
- difficulty in concentrating if there are distractions;
- visual problems while reading (adults with dyslexia may be highly sensitive to glare, or the colour of the paper or words, or the font or layout of the text); and
- confusing left and right, or otherwise struggling with spatial reasoning – for example, a person with dyslexia may have trouble reading a map, particularly if the map contains written words.

Many people with dyslexia feel sensations of mental overload/switching off. Dyslexic adults also often suffer from anxiety issues. They can become fearful because of the constant frustration they feel because of their condition.

Though difficulty reading is a hallmark of dyslexia, particularly in children, most adults with the condition can read and have devised strategies to work around their reading difficulties. Those that continue to find reading difficult develop ways of coping or hiding the problem, for example avoiding activities that involve reading and writing, blaming poor eyesight or loss of reading glasses, or having another family member read or write for them. Adults with dyslexia may present a range of other characteristics, such as memory problems.

It is important to remember that there are positives to thinking differently. Many people with dyslexia show strengths in areas such as reasoning and in visual and creative fields.

Causes

14.28 Genetic – It's not uncommon for two or more children in the same family to have dyslexia. It is sometimes impossible to determine if older relatives have the condition as it may not have been diagnosed when they were younger.

Brain structure and function – Research suggests that the root source of dyslexia is a phonological deficit. (Phonology means the relationship between speech sounds in a language.) This may explain why many adults with dyslexia have trouble breaking words down into smaller parts. Some brain imaging studies suggest that this phonological deficit occurs in the left hemisphere of the brain, which is associated with processing words and language. The two hemispheres of the brain may also communicate differently in people who have dyslexia.

Association with other disorders – Both adults and children with dyslexia sometimes have attention deficit hyperactivity disorder or developmental co-ordination disorder, also known as dyspraxia, which is a condition affecting physical coordination. Dyspraxia is commonly thought to be a disorder that causes clumsiness and poor coordination, but it can cause a range of other issues, including problems with processing information, organisational and social skills.

Treatment and prognosis

14.29 Treatment for dyslexia begins with a proper diagnosis. Simply knowing that the problem is due to the condition can help some adults with dyslexia feel better about their difficulties. Other interventions that might help a person with the condition include reading, vocabulary and phonology practice. Specific fonts may make it easier for people with dyslexia to read. Adults benefit from understanding their individual learning style and pattern of strengths and weaknesses. This helps them study and work in a way which is most likely to be successful. They may find it helpful to use technological aids, such as a specialised computer, smartphone apps and digital recorders.

Dyslexia starts during early childhood and is a lifelong condition. The prognosis is worse if it is not identified. The longer-term effects range from low self-esteem, frustration and anxiety to socio-economic effects of under-achievement in education and work.

Advice for the Family Court

14.30 People with dyslexia may have problems in preparing statements and evidence for court hearings, for example planning and writing letters or reports that focus on relevant information presented logically. They may struggle to meet deadlines due to poor time management, with particular difficulties estimating how long a task will take. Some have a poor working memory and experience problems retaining information and assimilating any new documentation at short notice. They may also experience difficulty with listening at the same time as taking notes.

A person with dyslexia should be allowed time for processing written information. They may have difficulty skim reading a report which has been submitted late. Allow breaks, as people with dyslexia report experiencing mental overload and are at times unable to recall what has transpired or the outcome of the hearing. Some people with the condition rely heavily on technology, such as speech recognition software, for many aspects of their daily lives and may feel disadvantaged if they are not allowed to use it. Allow flexibility if at all possible.

Further information

The Dyslexia Association

https://www.dyslexia.uk.net

The British Dyslexia Association

https://www.bdadyslexia.org.uk

Dyslexia.UK.com

http://www.dyslexia.uk.com

NHS – Dyslexia: Teenagers and adults

https://www.nhs.uk/conditions/dyslexia/symptoms/

Medical News Today – What is dyslexia in adults?

www.medicalnewstoday.com/articles/319972

EPILEPSY AND ASSOCIATED MENTAL DISORDERS

(See also **Chapter 7** Neurodevelopmental disorders in children.)

Prevalence

14.31 Epilepsy is a condition (this is the preferred term, rather than illness) that leads to seizures. It is one of the most frequent disorders of the central nervous system and is a common and serious brain condition. It is estimated that epilepsy affects around 1 in around 100 people in the UK. Those at highest risk are children and people aged over 65. Approximately half of people diagnosed with epilepsy also have co-existing physical or psychiatric conditions.

Symptoms and behaviour

14.32 The type of epileptic seizure depends on which area of the person's brain is affected. There are two main types of seizure: focal seizures – sometimes called partial seizures – which affect only one side of the brain and may not cause loss of consciousness; and generalised seizures – which affect large areas on both sides of the brain and often result in loss of consciousness.

Different types of seizures include:

- jerking of the body (convulsions);
- repetitive movements; and
- unusual sensations such as a strange taste in the mouth or a strange smell, or a rising feeling in the stomach.

If the person's consciousness is affected, they can be disorientated and unable to respond. They may misinterpret other people's behaviour so, for instance, interpret loud speech as an attack and respond aggressively. The person may also be confused for a while, sometimes called 'post-ictal' (after-seizure) confusion. It may be hard to tell when the seizure has ended. The person might be tired and want to rest, and they may not remember the seizure afterwards.

A diagnosis is made from the person's medical history and from an electroencephalogram (EEG) which measures brain activity. Epilepsy shows as spikes on the EEG. Adults are usually investigated with a magnetic resonance imaging brain scan to look for a structural change in the brain.

Causes

14.33 Epilepsy has a number of risk factors (including a strong genetic predisposition), rather than being a condition with a single expression and cause. The genetic component is significant, as one in three people with epilepsy has a family member also affected.

In adults, epilepsy can result after a structural change in the brain, such as damage caused by a brain injury, stroke or tumour. Epilepsy can also occur in infections such as meningitis, and in elderly people with neurodegenerative diseases such as Alzheimer's.

Other causes of fits can be drug and alcohol abuse and withdrawal from their use. Less common causes are genetic conditions such as tuberous sclerosis, or neurofibromatosis, which can cause growths affecting the brain. Photosensitive epilepsy – fits caused by flashing or flickering lights – is less common in adults than in children.

Treatment

14.34 Treatment can help most people with epilepsy have fewer seizures or stop them completely. Anti-epileptic drugs are the most commonly used treatment for the condition. They help control seizures in about 70 per cent of people. They do not cure epilepsy, but they can stop seizures happening.

Which anti-epilepsy medication is chosen varies depending on: the seizure type or syndrome; side effects; the person's age (sedating medicines are avoided for an older person); effects on pregnancy and unborn children in women of childbearing age; and effects on a patient's bone health, mood and other health concerns.

If seizures are not controlled by medication, there are other options. Neurosurgery may be considered to remove a small part of the brain that's causing the seizures. Another procedure is to implant a tiny electrical device inside the body (similar to a pacemaker) that can help control the fits by altering the electrical signals in the brain. A special diet (ketogenic diet) may also help control seizures.

Seizure alarms can be alerted by a fit, or the person can press the alarm if they feel a fit coming on and put themselves in a safe position. Safety helmets reduce the chance of injury during a fit.

Prognosis

14.35 Anti-epileptic medication suppresses seizures in up to two-thirds of all people with epilepsy, but does not alter the long-term prognosis. Suppression of seizures or seizure management does improve a person's quality of life (QOL).

Outcomes for people with epilepsy depend on the cause. A traumatic cause, such as brain damage, can shorten lifespan by an average of eight years. People with epilepsy are three times more likely to die from their condition if they live in a deprived area. Those who also have learning disabilities are at higher risk of dying from the condition – the risk increases as the severity of the learning disability increases.

In the UK there are around 1,200 deaths related to epilepsy each year. Some of these deaths are caused by complications during or after a seizure. Other deaths may be due to accidents, such as falls or drowning. Recent studies show that the majority of premature deaths in people with epilepsy may be caused by another condition the person has alongside their epilepsy. These include underlying neurological problems which may have caused the epilepsy, as well as cardiovascular or respiratory problems and cancer.

When the person has a long seizure or several seizures with no recovery in between, it is called status epilepticus, or 'status'. If the convulsion continues for 30 minutes or more, this can cause lasting damage to the brain, or even death. Other deaths in people with epilepsy relate to drug or alcohol abuse and suicide. Sometimes a person dies during or following a seizure for no apparent reason, which is known as a sudden unexpected death in epilepsy (SUDEP).

Associated mental disorders

14.36 There is a crossover between epilepsy and neurological and psychiatric conditions. An estimated 20 to 30 per cent of people with epilepsy have psychiatric disorders, the most common being depression, anxiety and psychosis.

Epilepsy and depression – Depression is more likely in someone with epilepsy, with a occurrence of between 10 and 20 per cent. Depression occurs more frequently in those with partial frontal and temporal lobe seizures. It is also more common in people with poor control of seizures.

There are many possible causes of depression in people with epilepsy. The most common is an injury to a part of the brain that controls mood. Hormone levels, especially low oestrogen, can also trigger depression and can affect seizure frequency. Anti-seizure medications, such as phenobarbital, can affect mood centres and may increase the risk of depression.

Treating depression and epilepsy involves identifying the best combination of anti-seizure medications and antidepressants to maintain seizure control and improve mood. Talking treatments and therapies can also be helpful. Taking regular exercise and eating well-balanced meals may contribute to well-being.

Epilepsy and anxiety – Anxiety occurs in 19 per cent of people with epilepsy and can have a significant impact on their life. Individuals often develop anxiety after epilepsy is diagnosed, or after they have their first seizure. A common cause of anxiety in epilepsy is the fear of having a seizure, but anxiety is also related to the condition in more specific ways. It can occur not only as a reaction to the diagnosis, but also as a symptom of epilepsy or as a side effect of seizure medication. The prevalence of anxiety is higher in partial epilepsies, especially those with an origin in the temporal lobe.

Treatments for anxiety linked to epilepsy can include anti-anxiety medications and talking therapies – such as counselling, psychotherapy, group therapy and cognitive treatments – which may help reduce anxiety and make life more manageable. Feeling socially isolated or rejected due to epilepsy may also influence anxiety symptoms. Social support is, therefore, important in the life of a person with epilepsy.

Epilepsy and psychosis – Psychosis is a severe mental disorder in which the person loses contact with reality. Some forms of psychosis are closely linked to the occurrence of seizures and differ from the psychotic disorders that affect other people. The prevalence of psychosis in people with epilepsy is around 8 per cent.

Psychosis in people with epilepsy is most often classified according to the time when episodes occur in relation to seizures. Symptoms may include delusions, depressive or manic psychosis, or bizarre thoughts and behaviour. Symptoms of psychosis can occur before a seizure and last for minutes to hours. They can also occur after a seizure and can be transient or last several weeks. If psychotic symptoms continue for more than several weeks, then the person may have developed a severe chronic disorder resembling schizophrenia. The onset of psychosis is variable, but usually occurs in those who have had the condition for more than 10 years.

The treatment for psychosis is usually long-term, antipsychotic medication, alongside the treatment to adequately control seizures. During a psychotic episode, maintaining the patient's safety is the primary concern. Educating patients and their families about the psychiatric manifestations is also important.

Epilepsy and bipolar affective disorder – People with epilepsy are twice as likely to have bipolar symptoms than people with other medical conditions. The temporal lobe of the brain seems to be more strongly linked to mood disorder or mood change. Studies suggest epilepsy does not affect the onset of the first bipolar episode or the frequency of affective events. However, depressive symptoms are more severe during a relapse, and ongoing mood disturbance has many hypomanic characteristics.

Some of the medications used to treat bipolar disorder, such as lamotrigine or valproate, were originally developed to treat epileptic seizures. And there's further evidence of the relationship between mood disorders and seizures: it is thought bipolar symptoms may be missed in people with epilepsy because some of the commonly used anti-epileptic agents may be treating the bipolar symptoms as well.

Epilepsy and cognitive disorders – Memory problems are an important feature of seizures arising from the temporal lobe of the brain. Short-term memory problems are seen most often. This may be because nerve cells in the brain, responsible for memory, can be sensitive to the effect of seizures. How long it takes to recover varies from one person to another, and even after fully recovering from a seizure, some people's memory might be permanently affected.

Other frequent cognitive complaints in adults with epilepsy include feeling slowed down mentally and attention problems. Medications to control seizures can also affect memory.

Some people with epilepsy may be at higher risk of developing dementia, while individuals with some forms of dementia, mainly Alzheimer's disease and vascular dementia, are at significantly higher risk of developing epilepsy.

Epilepsy and disorders of intellectual disability – Epilepsy is more common in people with an intellectual disorder than in the general population. Twenty per cent of people with epilepsy also have disorders of intellectual development. Those with more severe disorders are more likely to have epilepsy.

Epilepsy itself does not cause severe intellectual problems, but the two can occur together and have the same cause. For example, hypoxia (low oxygen), injury or infection at birth may cause mental limitations, epilepsy and cerebral palsy.

Cognitive or intellectual problems tend to be more severe in people who either: developed epilepsy at an early age; have many seizures; have an underlying brain lesion; have poor seizure control; or didn't have their seizures controlled for a long time.

Epilepsy and suicidal behaviour – People with epilepsy are at significantly higher risk of suicide. Around 13 per cent of people with epilepsy attempt/commit suicide – a rate five to ten times that of the general population. Factors relevant to this increased risk are similar to those among people with mental disorders who commit suicide: current or past anxiety and mood disorders; mental disorders within the family; and previous suicide attempts.

Epilepsy affects the lives of people with seizures and their families. It restricts activities and may force specific behaviours, such as taking medicines, not driving, maintaining regular sleep cycles, limiting alcohol use, and making other lifestyle changes that can lead to feeling a loss of independence.

People with epilepsy may experience fear, stress, frustration and embarrassment at having seizures. Areas in the brain that control emotions and behaviour may be affected by seizures, and this may lead to increased impulsivity and, therefore, a higher risk of acting on suicidal thoughts.

Advice for the Family Court

14.37 People with epilepsy may need time for breaks and to process questions, and for the court to allow time for them to reply. It's worth noting that very brief absence seizures are often mistaken for 'daydreaming' or not paying attention, and that stress and excitement can trigger a seizure. A person with absence seizures may also miss information.

Some epilepsy medications are sedative, so may interfere with a person's concentration, particularly at a lengthy hearing. The memory problems associated with epilepsy may be masked by the person's positive presentation.

Further information

Epilepsy Society

https://www.epilepsysociety.org.uk/

NHS – Treatment of Epilepsy

https://www.nhs.uk/conditions/epilepsy/treatment/

Guidance on valproate use in women and girls of childbearing years

en/guidelines-research-services/guidelines/valproate-use/

NHS – Epilepsy Toolkit: Optimising a system for people living with epilepsy

https://www.england.nhs.uk/rightcare/products/pathways/epilepsy-toolkit/

MedDocs – Epilepsy and psychiatric disorders

https://meddocsonline.org/ebooks/some-aspects-of-epilepsy/epilepsy-and-psychiatric-disorders.pdf

Epilepsy Foundation – Epilepsy and psychological disorders
https://www.epilepsy.com/article/2016/11/epilepsy-and-psychological-disorders

ResearchGate – Psychiatric disorders in epilepsy

https://www.researchgate.net/publication/238080779_Psychiatric_disorders_in_epilepsy

Brain – Cognition and dementia in older patients with epilepsy

https://academic.oup.com/brain/article/141/6/1592/4915830

GENDER DYSPHORIA (GD)

(See also **Chapter 7** Neurodevelopmental disorders in children.)

14.38 Gender dysphoria (GD) is the unease a person feels due to a mismatch between their gender identity and their biological sex assigned at birth. Many people with gender dysphoria have a strong and lasting desire to live a life that 'matches' or expresses their gender identity.

They may report identifying as a member of the opposite sex from an early age. Many trans people and organisations prefer the term gender variance.

Prevalence

14.39 Gender variance is not uncommon. A survey of 10,000 people undertaken in 2012 by the Equality and Human Rights Commission found that 1 per cent were gender variant to some extent. Historically, more pre-gender surgery or pre-certificated women have sought treatment than men. The number of people being referred and diagnosed with the condition has increased over the last decade.

Symptoms and behaviour

14.40 Gender dysphoria is not a mental illness, but some people may develop signs of discomfort or distress, including:

- low self-esteem;
- becoming withdrawn or socially isolated;
- depression or anxiety;
- taking unnecessary risks; and
- neglecting themselves.

At some time in their life, many will seek professional advice, perhaps after long periods of cross-dressing publicly or privately. This may be influenced by their personal and social circumstances, family support, and degree of motivation.

Causes

14.41 The exact cause of gender dysphoria is unclear. Gender dysphoria is not related to sexual orientation. People with gender dysphoria may identify as straight, gay, lesbian or bisexual.

Treatment and prognosis

14.42 For some people, treatment may just involve acceptance and affirmation or confirmation of their identity. For others, it may involve significant changes to their physical appearance, such as hormone treatment and surgery.

GPs are advised to refer adults who think they may have gender dysphoria to a gender dysphoria clinic. These clinics have a multidisciplinary team of healthcare professionals who offer ongoing assessments, treatments, support and advice, including:

- psychological support, such as counselling;
- speech and language therapy (voice therapy) to help the person sound more typical of their gender identity;
- cross-sex hormone therapy (if indicated, hormone treatment is initiated by a clinic. In general, people wanting masculinisation usually take testosterone, and people wanting feminisation usually take oestrogen);
- facial hair removal – this is prescribed and funded in England, but not in Wales; and
- referral for surgery.

Individuals with GD report they experience high levels of stigmatisation and discrimination in society which negatively affects their lives at home, in education and at work. The distress caused by gender dysphoria can result in clinical depression, self-harm and suicidal acts, if unresolved. The use of non-prescribed hormone treatments by those self-medicating can cause serious physical side effects.

Advice for the Family Court

14.43 Before proceeding with the hearing, the court should establish how the person wishes to be addressed – first name (and last name) and prefix. It may cause distress if there is an error in how they are named.

Be aware of the person's previous likely experiences with authority. People who have gender dysphoria will probably have endured years of stigma, discrimination, and ignorance both of their situation and of their legal rights.

The Gender Recognition Act 2004, s 12 states: 'The fact that a person's gender has become the acquired gender under this Act does not affect the status of the person as the mother or father of a child'.

Further information

Royal College of Psychiatrists – Good practice guidelines for the assessment and treatment of adults with gender dysphoria

https://www.rcpsych.ac.uk/docs/default-source/improving-care/better-mh-policy/college-reports/cr181-good-practice-guidelines-for-the-assessment-and-treatment-of-adults-with-gender-dysphoria.pdf

BMJ – Gender dysphoria: assessment and management for non-specialists

https://www.bmj.com/content/357/bmj.j2866

BMA – Managing patients with gender dysphoria

https://www.bma.org.uk/advice-and-support/gp-practices/gp-service-provision/managing-patients-with-gender-dysphoria

NGA Law – Trans parents and legal parenthood

https://www.ngalaw.co.uk/knowledge-centre/trans-parents-and-legal-parenthood

Chapter 15

Traumatic disorders in adults

ACQUIRED BRAIN INJURY (ABI)

15.01 Acquired brain injury (ABI) refers to an injury to the brain not present at birth. ABI is a leading cause of death and disability. It is a chronic condition with hidden disabilities and lifelong consequences.

Prevalence

15.02 There are around 1.4 million people living with brain injury in the UK. Among male prisoners, 47 per cent have a history of brain injury, and 70 per cent of these injuries were before the first offence.

Symptoms

15.03 Symptoms of ABI include memory deficits, a change in behaviour, speech and language problems, problems walking and changes in sensations. The symptoms depend on the area of the brain that is injured. People with ABI typically show too much of some behaviours and too little of others. Too much anger, irritability, impulsiveness, self-centeredness, anti-social behaviour and confabulation (making up events to hide memory deficits) are difficult for family and friends to cope with. Too little behaviours may include lack of motivation, loss of initiative, and lack of social awareness. Extreme exhaustion is also very common.

Causes

15.04 ABI may be caused by trauma, for example, an accident, fall, assault or sporting injury, especially in young men. This can cause damage to the immediate area and can also shake the brain inside the skull, causing injuries elsewhere. Other causes are infections such as encephalitis and meningitis, stroke (cerebrovascular accident), tumours, and injuries resulting from oxygen deprivation, as can occur in severe chest infections and chronic obstructive airway disease. Hypoxic brain damage (brain damage caused by lack of oxygen) from drug or inhalant use is also becoming more common. Early-onset neurological disorders, such as Huntingdon's disease, can also cause ABI by damaging the brain.

Treatments and prognosis

15.05 There is no cure for ABI, but the person can be helped by physiotherapy, speech and language therapy and occupational therapy to relearn tasks.

Many people with ABI self-medicate with drugs and alcohol, which makes them more impulsive. Epilepsy can be a complicating factor. Restriction of work and social activities because of disability and practical issues, such as being unable to drive, can increase the risk of depression.

ABI is lifelong. Eighty per cent of marriages break up after one partner suffers a brain injury. If the marriage continues, the unaffected partner frequently becomes a carer for the affected person.

Advice for the Family Court

15.06 Be aware of the person's problems. They may be chaotic and miss appointments, talk about the same thing repeatedly, make inappropriate personal comments, or say they will do something but never get around to it. They will lack insight into the extent of their difficulties.

To make the court experience easier for a parent with ABI, ask single questions, making one point at a time. Speak slowly and clearly and make it clear when you are moving on to a new topic. Allow the person time to process information and check they have understood by asking them to repeat what's been said: 'Can you tell me what I've just said?'.

Try to ensure the hearing room is as quiet as possible without distractions, take regular breaks and consider a short working day.

Further information

Royal College of Speech & Language Therapists

https://www.rcslt.org/speech-and-language-therapy/clinical-information/brain-injury

Headway, the Brain Injury Association

https://www.headway.org.uk

United Kingdom Acquired Brain Injury Forum

https://ukabif.org.uk

'LONG COVID' IN ADULTS

(See also **Chapter 7** Neurodevelopmental disorders in children.)

15.07 'Long Covid' is a term to describe the effects of Covid-19 that continue for weeks or months beyond the initial illness. The health watchdog the National Institute for Health and Care Excellence (NICE) defines Long Covid as symptoms lasting for more than 12 weeks.

This condition can have a huge impact on people's lives. Many are unable to return to work or have a social life. Many have described how it affects their mental health, especially as the course of the condition is often fluctuating; just as they feel they are getting better the symptoms return. Also, it has important economic consequences for them, their families and for society.

Prevalence

15.08 About a quarter of people who have had coronavirus, experience symptoms that continue for at least a month. Around one in ten of 18 to 49-years-olds, who contract coronavirus, are still unwell after 12 weeks.

Long Covid is more likely to develop in older people, women and those who have had five or more symptoms in the first week of becoming ill. Twenty-two per cent of people aged over 70 who contract Covid-19 are affected. People with asthma are also more likely to develop Long Covid; this is the only clear link so far related to existing health conditions causing increased vulnerability to the condition. Those living in the most deprived areas, those working in health or social care, and those with another limiting health condition or disability, are also more likely to report having Long Covid.

Symptoms

15.09 Long Covid symptoms are highly variable and wide-ranging. The most commonly reported symptom is fatigue, accompanied by two patterns of symptoms:

Respiratory and cardiovascular symptoms, which include (but are not limited to) the following:

- breathlessness;
- cough;
- chest tightness;
- chest pain; and
- palpitations.

Neurological and psychological symptoms, which include the following:

- cognitive impairment ('brain fog', loss of concentration or memory issues);
- headache;
- sleep disturbance;
- peripheral neuropathy symptoms (pins and needles and numbness);
- dizziness;
- depression;
- anxiety; and
- delirium (in older populations).

Other symptoms include fever, abdominal pain, nausea, diarrhoea, reduced appetite (in older populations), joint pain, muscle pain, tinnitus, sore throat, loss of taste and/or smell and skin rashes and thrombosis.

Causes

15.10 In adults, the chances of having long-term symptoms do not seem to be linked to the severity of the initial Covid illness.

The actual cause is unclear. It is suggested that the virus may cause premature ageing of the immune system, as the symptoms appear to be due to the persistence of the virus in some parts of the body that are sheltered from the immune system. These symptoms can include damage to the brain and can cause damage to organs such as the heart, lungs and pancreas. The virus can also cause, in some cases, diabetes and blood clotting, which may result in heart attacks and strokes.

Treatment

15.11 At the time of writing, there is no specific treatment. For those with neurological symptoms, a brain scan can look for evidence of inflammation or strokes that can occur as a complication of Covid-19.

For many people, the way forward is to find ways to self-manage their symptoms, such as setting realistic goals. The following strategies may help:

- graded return to activities;
- avoiding over-exertion;
- breathing exercises to help with breathlessness;
- meditation and relaxation to ease anxiety; and
- measures to achieve good sleep.

Prognosis

15.12 Long Covid can vary in different individuals. This is not unique to Covid-19 – other viral illnesses can also have varied lasting effects.

A study led by the University of Leicester, it was found that among those who needed hospital treatment for the initial illness, it was common for symptoms to last five months or more. There are separate reports of symptoms lasting 12 months or longer – this includes people who didn't need hospital treatment initially and those who did.

Of those who were working before they had Covid-19, 17.8 per cent were no longer working and a further 19.3 per cent had experienced a health-related change to their work.

WIDER ASPECTS OF COVID-19 FOR ADULTS

15.13 Loss of employment and income – Loss of employment and uncertainty about work can have serious consequences, including depression, anxiety, psychosomatic symptoms, drops in subjective wellbeing and self-esteem, and suicide. Over twice as many unemployed people (34 per cent) experience mental distress, compared to people in employment (16 per cent). Job insecurity and restructuring also have negative impacts on employee wellbeing over time.

This is relevant for people who face uncertainly about their longer-term employment. Employees in the hospitality, leisure, travel and tourism sectors, which saw sharp downturns during the pandemic, are more likely to be young, migrants, poorly paid and in rented accommodation. There is a corresponding risk to their mental health and their families. Many self-employed people in these sectors lost their livelihoods in the pandemic, and many were also ineligible for any government support. Again, the resulting anxiety and financial strain may have had a significant impact on their mental health and their home life.

Bereavement – In normal circumstances, when people suffer loss and bereavement, around 7 per cent have a complex reaction with more severe and prolonged grief symptoms. The experience of grief itself does not necessitate intervention, but complex reactions can do.

The circumstances of the pandemic may add to the difficulties of those mourning the loss of a loved one. These include restrictions placed on visits to hospitals and care homes, and constraints on spending time with seriously ill relatives. The restrictions placed on funerals during the pandemic also deprived people of an important part of the grieving process, and it is possible that more people will suffer a complex reaction, complicated by guilt, than would otherwise be the case.

Anxiety and depression – Covid-19 is a potentially lethal infection. Inevitably, some people will remain anxious about the threat to themselves and their friends and family. Those who already suffer an anxiety disorder are vulnerable to excessive anxiety during the pandemic. People seriously affected by the virus will be admitted to intensive care, and those with pre-existing anxiety or depression are at major risk of developing post-traumatic stress disorder (PTSD) following an episode of intensive care. Routinely, 20 per cent of survivors of intensive care experience PTSD during the 12 months after discharge.

Coping strategies – Obsessional behaviour, such as online gambling, gaming and social media addiction, increase when work and face-to-face social activities are not available. There is evidence of increased use of alcohol and cannabis among the UK population during the pandemic, which may give rise to associated problems.

Effects of pandemic restrictions – People with mental disorders or conditions are likely to have had their care disrupted by limitation of services and activities due to Covid-19. The closure of day centres and daily activities may have had a profound effect on people dependent on these, causing deterioration in their mental state and life skills. This has impacted family members who are carers, who have had to take on 24-hour caring responsibilities.

Burnout and moral Injury – Medical professionals and other vulnerable groups, such as frontline workers, may experience post-traumatic stress and burnout. Covid-19 has put these workers at greater risk of 'moral injury' – a term first used for those in military service. It means the profound psychological distress that occurs when one's moral or ethical code is violated. During the Covid-19 outbreak, many of these workers were in a changed and challenging work environment where it was difficult to meet their usual professional standards and expectations. Moral injury can lead to shame, guilt and other negative thoughts, which in turn may contribute to mental health problems such as depression, anxiety and post-traumatic stress disorder.

Heightened safety risks – It has already been widely acknowledged that social distancing and lockdown measures may increase exposure to domestic violence and abuse for children and other family members already at risk. Such measures have a disproportionately adverse effect on women by potentially exposing them to further danger and reducing their access to external support networks and vital services that would normally keep them safe and well.

Further information

NHS – Long-term effects of coronavirus

https://www.nhs.uk/conditions/coronavirus-covid-19/long-term-effects-of-coronavirus-long-covid/

NHS – Living with long Covid

https://www.uclh.nhs.uk/our-services/find-service/covid19-clinics/living-long-covid

NICE – Covid-19 rapid guideline: managing the long-term effects

https://www.nice.org.uk/guidance/ng188

University of Leicester – Post-hospitalisation Covid-19 study

https://www.leicesterbrc.nihr.ac.uk/themes/respiratory/research/phosp-covid/

Royal College of Psychiatrists – Covid-19: Support for patients and carers

https://www.rcpsych.ac.uk/about-us/responding-to-covid-19/covid-19-and-mental-health

POST-TRAUMATIC STRESS DISORDER (PTSD)

(See also **Chapter 6** Emotional disorders in children.)

Prevalence

15.14 One large survey of the general population in England found that 3 in 100 adults screened positive for PTSD. It is more common in certain groups of people. For example, some studies have found that the disorder develops in about 20 per cent of firefighters, 33 per cent of teenage survivors of car crashes, and up to 50 per cent of female rape victims.

Symptoms and behaviour

15.15 In most cases of PTSD the symptoms develop during the first month after the traumatic event, but in a minority of cases, there may be a delay of months or even years before symptoms appear. Trauma symptoms can vary in intensity over time. Symptoms may worsen when the person is stressed in general, or when then have reminders of the initial trauma – they may see a report on the news about a sexual assault and feel overcome by memories. Thoughts of suicide and self-harm are common

Symptoms of PTSD can include flashbacks, nightmares, repetitive and distressing images or sensations, or physical symptoms such as pain, sweating, feeling sick or trembling. There is often irritability or outbursts of anger and irrational and intense fear. Some people become very sensitive to noise. Hyperarousal (the person's abnormally heightened state of anxiety) often leads to angry outbursts, sleeping problems and difficulty concentrating.

The opposite of this hyperactive and emotional state can also occur, with loss of interest in activities and life in general, a sense of a limited future and feeling numb and empty. A person with PTSD may also avoid people or places that bring to mind the trauma, which can lead to social isolation.

People with PTSD try to push memories of the traumatic event out of their mind, often distracting themselves with work or hobbies. There is a high incidence of alcohol or drug use as these are often used for self-medication.

Causes

15.16 Not everyone exposed to a stressful event suffers PTSD. Some people have risk factors that make them more vulnerable to developing the condition when they are exposed to a traumatic event. These include previous mental health problems, being socio-economically disadvantaged, a family history of mental illness and being exposed to trauma in the past.

Treatment and prognosis

15.17 Trauma-focused psychological treatment is the recognised. This includes cognitive behavioural therapy and eye movement desensitisation and reprocessing therapy. Medications such as antidepressants can also relieve symptoms. Self-harm and suicide risk can increase in the early phase of psychological treatment as the person relives the experience.

Studies show that about two in three people with PTSD eventually get better without treatment, although the improvement may take several months. In about one third, the symptoms last longer, sometimes for many years, and can be severe in some people.

Other mental disorders, such as anxiety and depression can also occur. Unresolved PSTD increases the risk of substance dependence for self-medication.

Advice for the Family Court

15.18 When dealing with a parent who has PTSD, bear in mind that it may be associated with other mental disorders such as depression. Be alert to mood changes such as anger and irritability.

Hypervigilance and anxiety may make a person appear agitated and restless for no apparent reason.

Alternatively, they may appear apathetic due to a loss of interest in activities and life in general.

The stress of appearing in court, or the nature of the case, may cause anxiety and flashbacks. It can be useful to ask the person informally how they can be helped to manage, with perhaps, a pre-arranged signal to indicate a need for a break. Also, ask if they are sensitive to noise or light.

Case study – Post-traumatic stress disorder – Natalie's story (see Appendix: Case studies, p 348.)

Further information

NHS – Post-traumatic stress disorder (PTSD)

https://www.nhs.uk/conditions/post-traumatic-stress-disorder-ptsd/

MIND – Post-traumatic stress disorder (PTSD)

https://www.mind.org.uk/information-support/types-of-mental-health-problems/post-traumatic-stress-disorder-ptsd/about-ptsd/

Royal College of Psychiatrists – Post-traumatic stress disorder (PTSD)

https://www.rcpsych.ac.uk/mental-health/problems-disorders/post-traumatic-stress-disorder?searchTerms=Royal%20College%20of%20Psychiatrists%20-%20Post-traumatic%20stress%20disorder%20%28PTSD%29

Chapter 16

Mental disorders in older adults

16.01 In addition to the adult mental disorders discussed in previous chapters, there are mental disorders that are more likely to occur in older people. Those aged 60 and above are at risk of developing particular mental health conditions due to neurological disorders or from the result of alcohol and drug misuse. Physical illnesses common in old age, such as diabetes, hearing loss and osteoarthritis, may also have an impact on a person's mental health.

As people age, they are more likely to experience several conditions at the same time. Mental health conditions may have an impact on physical health and vice versa. The most common mental and neurological disorders in this age group are dementia and depression.

DEPRESSION

16.02 Depression is more common in older people, affecting around 22 per cent of men and 28 per cent of women aged 65-plus. Studies show that those who experience a series of depressive episodes over their lifetime have significantly decreased memory function by the time that they are 50.

The most common triggers for mental health problems in older people are life events and changes in circumstances, such as loss of a partner, siblings or friends, and financial worries. Retirement, moving home and becoming a carer are all life changes that can have an impact on mood. Also, the increased likelihood of physical illness and consequences of reduced mobility, chronic pain and side effects can all affect mood. Some physical disorders, particularly stroke or Parkinson's disease, are highly associated with depression. Some older people are disadvantaged socio-economically, which can add to social isolation.

Medication for physical conditions, such as steroids and medication for Parkinson's, can cause depression. Increasing numbers of older people are using recreational drugs and alcohol regularly, to the point of dependency. This may be a progression from use earlier in life, or uptake later in life to ease depression or self-medicate after bereavement or to relieve loneliness.

DEMENTIA

16.03 Dementia is a progressive deterioration in the functioning of the brain, affecting memory, personality, behaviour and ability to do everyday activities such as dressing, washing, household tasks and shopping. There may be associated psychiatric symptoms, such as mood disorder and psychosis.

It is essential to obtain a collateral history, speaking to relatives, friends and care-givers if possible, as well as the patient themselves, along with a mental state examination and standard cognitive screening tests.

Not everyone with dementia has a diagnosis. This can be due to difficulty diagnosing in the early stages of the illness, the slow progression of the condition, limited public awareness of the diseases that cause dementia, or other factors.

Prevalence

16.04 A person's risk of developing dementia rises from one in 14 over the age of 65, to one in six over the age of 80, with even higher rates among those in their late 80s and 90s. Dementia can, however, occur at any age and is known as early-onset dementia if it starts under the age of 65. Early-onset dementia often has a genetic component, so blood relatives may be at risk.

Causes

16.05 There are many types of dementia, including:

- **Alzheimer's disease** – (the commonest type of dementia), which occurs when the brain shrinks (atrophies) excessively for the person's age.
- **Cerebrovascular disease** – which causes vascular dementia (impaired blood flow to the brain resulting in problems with thought processes such as reasoning, planning and memory)
- **Lewy body dementia** – in which visual hallucinations, fluctuating confusion and features of Parkinson's disease are common.

- **Frontotemporal degeneration** – where behavioural disturbance is often the presenting feature.
- **Alcohol-related dementias** – these are becoming more common and may affect adults in the prime of life.

Treatment

16.06 There is no medication currently available to cure dementia. It is usually irreversible, but an early diagnosis is important to optimise the management of the condition. Anti-dementia medication, such as rivastigmine, can slow the progression of the condition.

The lives of people with dementia can be improved by the identification and treatment of any accompanying illness, the detection and management of challenging behaviours, and the provision of information and support for carers.

Some people with dementia need treatment in a hospital or nursing home as their condition progresses. For people who cannot consent to their care arrangements, there are legal protections if these arrangements deprive them of their liberty. If receiving treatment in hospital, this may involve them being detained on a section of the Mental Health Act. If resident in a nursing home, they may become subject to Deprivation of Liberty Safeguards (DoLS). Deprivation of Liberty Safeguards (DoLS) which is part of the Mental Capacity Act 2005.

(Deprivation of Liberty Safeguards (DoLS) is to be replaced by Liberty Protection Safeguards (LPS) under the Mental Capacity (Amendment) Act 2019; the scheme has been delayed, with a timescale for implementation in April 2022.)

Case study – Dementia – Grace's story (see Appendix: Case studies, p 239.)

Further information

Mental Health Foundation

https://www.mentalhealth.org.uk

Age UK

https://www.ageuk.org.uk/globalassets/age-uk/documents/factsheets/large-print-factsheets/fs62-09-deprivation-of-liberty-safeguards.pdf

Independent Age

https://www.independentage.org

Independent Age

https://www.independentage.org

Alzheimer's Society

https://www.alzheimers.org.uk

Alzheimer's Association

https://www.alz.org/uk/dementia-alzheimers-uk.asp

PART IV

The work of the Family Court and mental health

Chapter 17

The work of the Family Court

17.01 The Family Court – One of the branches of the justice system in England and Wales; procedures are very different from the criminal courts, it deals mainly with legal disputes concerning children and the breakdown of family relationships. The court is a single jurisdiction, consisting of four tiers of the judiciary – Tiers 1 to 3 usually sit in the local magistrates' and county courts, whilst the most senior, Tier 4, sits in the High Court. The work divides mainly into two areas: private work and public work.

The High Court – More complex family cases are dealt with in the Family Division of the High Court. For example, where a child, who is subject to legal proceedings and requires protection, and the issue is not covered by the Children Act 1989; this is known as 'Other Work' of the jurisdiction. The most common type of case is where a child has been made a 'ward of court', and court consent is needed for important decisions. It also deals with cases involving specific issues, such as international child abduction and forced marriage.

Case allocation – Cases are assigned to the different Tiers, based on their type and complexity. This assigning is undertaken by a 'gatekeeping team'. The team is made up of district judges and legal advisers, who determine which level of judge a particular case will be allocated to: magistrates, a district judge, a circuit judge or a high court judge. If appropriate, cases can be transferred between the Tiers. Specially trained magistrates sit as Tier 1 judges in the local Family Court, dealing with Public and Private Law cases, the most senior judges sit in the High Court. Unlike in criminal proceedings, the standard of proof is the 'balance of probabilities', not 'beyond reasonable doubt'.

The Children Act 1989 – This provides the basis for most applications dealing with children in both private and public work in the Family Court. At its heart, is the principle which states that the best interests of the child must be the court's paramount consideration when it is deciding any issue relating to a child's upbringing or property. The Act allocates duties to local authorities, the Family Court, parents, and other agencies, such as the NSPCC, to ensure children are safeguarded, and their well-being is promoted. The Act takes the view that children are usually best cared for in their own families.

However, it also makes legal provisions, for circumstances when parents and families are unable to provide adequate care and protection for a child, or if the parents are living apart and cannot agree over care arrangements for the child.

Media and hearings – Most hearings concerning matters to do with children are heard in private. Accredited media representatives can attend family proceedings in the Family Court. To make sure that children, vulnerable adults and families are protected from unwanted publicity, the court can put restrictions on what can be reported. The media is not allowed to attend any placement or adoption proceedings, or any conciliation or financial dispute resolution appointments – this is where a judge is assisting the parties to reach an agreement.

PRIVATE WORK IN THE FAMILY COURT

17.02 Private cases are those matters heard in the Family Court between two or more private individuals, usually, the child's parents, (although it can involve others, such as grandparents and relatives) who are trying to resolve a dispute concerning a child. Generally, this is where parents have separated, or are divorced, and there is a disagreement about such matters as who the child should live with, contact arrangements, and where the child should go to school; where possible families are encouraged to reach an agreement out-of-court.

The types of court order include parental responsibility, financial applications and orders under the Children Act 1989, s 8, which are used to settle where a child lives, parental contact and responsibility, and other specific disputes.

Examples of court orders include:

- **Child Arrangements Order** –covers where a child lives, how much time the child spends with each parent, and what other kinds of contact, such as phone calls and texts, are agreed.
- **Specific Issue Order** – looks at a particular issue regarding how a child is to be brought up, such as which school they attend, their religious education and specific activities they might undertake.
- **Prohibited Steps Order** – can be applied to stop the other parent from making a decision about the child's upbringing, such as preventing a child from being taken abroad.
- **Special Guardianship Order** – gives a guardian legal responsibility without removing legal responsibility from the birth parents.

Family Mediation is the process by which separated, and divorced parents can negotiate a resolution to disagreements over family concerns with the help of an independent, professionally trained mediator. Although mediation is voluntary, the Family Court expects applicants to have made every effort to have come to an agreement over disputes, whether these are related to separation, divorce, money or arrangements for the children. Before applying to the court, it is expected that the applicant has attended a Mediation Information and Assessment Meeting (MIAM) with an accredited family mediation service, to assess whether they are suitable to participate in the process. Family mediation can help reduce hostility and improve the chances of long-term co-operation between parents and couples; where an agreement cannot be reached, the court will impose an order.

PUBLIC WORK IN THE FAMILY COURT

17.03 When local authority children's services make an application for an order to safeguard the welfare of a child, the matters are usually referred to as Public Law cases; the NSPCC also have authority to bring such cases before the court. The majority (two thirds) of Public Law applications are for care orders.

Examples of court orders include:

- **Emergency Protection Order** – which are used to ensure the immediate safety of a child by taking them to a place of safety, or by preventing their removal from a place of safety.
- **Interim Care Order** – which places the child in the care of the local authority on an interim basis, before a final hearing; the local authority must accommodate and maintain the child and shares parental responsibility with the parent(s).
- **Care Order** – which place the child in the care of the local authority and gives them parental responsibility for the child.
- **Supervision Order** – which place the child under the supervision of their local authority.
- **Secure Accommodation Order** – which restricts the liberty of a child being looked after by a local authority, by placing the child in secure accommodation.

The child's voice – In Public Law, the child is automatically a party to the proceedings and is represented by a children's guardian, who is appointed by the Children and Family Court Advisory and Support Service (Cafcass). A guardian is an independent person who promotes the child's welfare and ensures that the arrangements made are in his or her best interests. The guardian appoints a solicitor to act for the child.

'OTHER WORK' IN THE FAMILY COURT

17.04 About 70 per cent of cases heard in the Family Court are private and public law cases, the remaining 30 per cent of cases are made up of a variety of different orders and work.

Examples of 'other work' in the Family Court:

- **Domestic Violence Remedy Orders** – these are orders made to prevent domestic violence and to keep a spouse out of the family home; they are a **Non-molestation Order** and or an **Occupation Order**.
- **Forced Marriage Protection Order** – which assists victims of forced marriage and prevents the marriage from taking place.
- **Matrimonial Cases** – covers divorces, annulments and separations.
- **Mental Capacity Act 2005** – provides a statutory framework to empower and protect vulnerable people who lack the capacity to make their own decisions.
- **Female Genital Mutilation Protection Order** –intended to safeguard girls who are at risk of FGM at home or abroad.
- **Adoption Order** – which removes the rights, duties and obligations of the natural parents and bestows parental responsibility for the child permanently with the adopting parent(s).
- **Financial Remedy Order** – deals with the financial arrangements following divorce and separation.

How parents can help their child during a separation and divorce

17.05 For children, parents separating will be a distressing and confusing time and can cause or contribute to anxiety and depression. At any age, children may feel shocked, uncertain or angry at the prospect of their parents separating. They may even feel guilty, blaming themselves for the problems at home. If the parents are antagonistic, the dynamics mean less possibility of stability for them.

Child psychologists recommend patience, reassurance, and a listening ear to minimise tension as children learn to cope with unfamiliar circumstances. Providing routines that the child can rely on reminds them that they can depend on their parents for stability, structure and care. A working relationship between the parents helps children avoid the stress and anguish that come with watching parents in conflict.

There are circumstances when a parent may struggle to help their child cope; if either parent is suffering anxiety or depression, they are less likely to be able to offer the emotional support to the child, or a regular routine; this is also the case when either parent suffers a more serious mental disorder or physical illness.

To help children and young people deal with divorce and separation, remind them that both parents love them. Also, be honest when talking about the situation, but keep in mind the child's age and understanding; avoid blame and avoid sharing negative feelings the adults have about each other.

Further information

Courts and Tribunal Service – The family justice system

www.judiciary.uk/about-the-judiciary/the-justice-system/jurisdictions/family-jurisdiction/

Judicial College – Family Court Bench Book

https://www.judiciary.uk/wp-content/uploads/2016/10/family-court-bench-book-jan-2018.pdf

Cafcass – Family mediation

https://www.cafcass.gov.uk/grown-ups/parents-and-carers/divorce-and-separation/family-mediation/?highlight=mediation

NSPCC – Children and Divorce

https://www.nspcc.org.uk/keeping-children-safe/support-for-parents/separation-and-divorce/

Chapter 18

Safeguarding children and local authority care

18.01 Under the Children Act 1989, every local authority has a statutory duty to safeguard and promote the welfare of children in their area who are in need. They have particular responsibility for children identified as being a **child in need,** by providing a range and level of services appropriate to the child's needs. Young people (those under 18) who've been admitted to hospital for assessment and/or treatment of a mental disorder, are automatically regarded as a child in need.

Children and young people who are taken into care or accommodated by local authority children's services are known as 'looked-after children'. Where there are difficulties with relationships at home, parents may agree for a child to be accommodated by the local authority, or a young person may make the request themselves. The local authority will apply to the Family Court to make the child a subject of a court order if they need to intervene because the child is at risk of significant harm.

SAFEGUARDING INTERVENTIONS

18.02 **Child in need** – Identifying a child in need is undertaken through a formal process, known as a Children Act 1989, s 17 assessment. This is carried out by the local authority children's service. There are criteria that set out the reasons for an assessment, which establish if a child and their family need support. If they do, a child in need plan will be produced, setting out the help that will be provided. The plan will include a time frame and will be reviewed at regular intervals. Should there be significant ongoing concerns about a child's welfare, a child protection conference will be arranged.

Child protection plan – A child protection conference is held by children's services to determine how best to safeguard the child and promote their future safety, health and development. The meeting will include the professionals involved, such as the child's social worker, health visitor, GP, and police. The child's immediate family, other relatives and, where appropriate, the child, may also attend. The meeting will decide whether the child is at risk of significant harm and, if so, whether a child protection plan is necessary. If a child is identified as being at continuing risk of significant harm, they will formally be made subject to a child protection plan (known previously as being on the at-risk register). The plan sets out what steps and provisions are needed to safeguard a child's welfare and minimise the risks of harm to the child. It also outlines ways of monitoring and evaluating progress.

Reasons for children being on a child protection plan.

Reason	Percentage of children
Abuse or neglect	63%
Family dysfunction – parenting capacity inadequate in the long term	14%
Family in acute stress/temporary crisis	8%
Absent parent	7%
Child disability	3%
Parental illness	3%
Other	2%

Care and supervision orders – Local authority children's services have a duty to prevent children suffering ill-treatment and neglect. Under the Children Act 1989, s 47 they have a duty to investigate reports of a child being at risk. If the children's service has reasonable cause to suspect that a child is at risk of significant harm or has suffered significant harm, and there is no other viable alternative, they can take out care proceedings and make an application to the Family Court for a supervision order or care order. Any such proceedings are done in consultation with the local authority's legal department, who examine the strength of the evidence.

Looked-after child – Is the term used for a child in the care of the local authority. Depending on the circumstances, a child can either be voluntarily accommodated, under the Children Act 1989, s 20; that is with an agreement between the parent(s) and the local authority. Or, alternatively, where such agreement is not appropriate, a child may be removed from their family by means of a care order made by the Family Court, if considered to be at risk if they remain in the parental home. In these circumstances, the children's service will place the child with other suitable family members, foster carers, or in a children's home. An unaccompanied asylum-seeking child, who has no-one with parental responsibility to care for them, also becomes a looked-after child and the responsibility of the local authority. There are around 80,000 children in the care of local authorities in England and Wales.

The age profile of children in care and placements – The ages of children and young people being looked after increases as they get older and enter their teenage years as the chart shows:

Age	Percentage of the total number of children in local authority care
Under 1 year	5%
Aged 1 to 4 years	13%
Aged 5 to 9 years	18%
Aged 10 to 15 years	39%
16 years and over	24%

Around 70 per cent of looked-after children are placed in foster care. Of the remainder, 12 per cent are placed in children's homes or semi-independent living accommodation, for example, hostels or flats, or secure children's accommodation if they are a significant risk to themselves or others. Around 7 per cent are placed under supervision with their parents, and 4 per cent live independently or in residential employment.

A local authority's duties to those leaving care – A child stops being 'looked after' when they are adopted, return home, or they turn 18. However, the local authority is required to support a young person leaving care at 18 until they are at least 21, and this can be extended to 25 if they are still in education or training. The young person may continue to live with their foster family, known as a 'staying put arrangement', until the age of 21. This enables a young person leaving care to remain in a secure and stable home while they make the transition into adulthood.

CHILDHOOD ABUSE AND THE CONSEQUENCES

18.03 **Factors –** There are a number of factors that contribute to child abuse and neglect. These include:

- **socio-economic factors,** such as poverty and poor housing;
- **substance misuse** – drugs and alcohol;
- **domestic abuse** – including sexual violence and exploitation; and
- **mental health problems.**

These factors have a significant impact on the ability of the parent to provide a nurturing environment for the child, and they may be compounded if the parent or carer lacks support from family or friends. There are also factors that relate specifically to the child, such as those with a mental or physical disability, who are more vulnerable to abuse and neglect.

Neglect and physical abuse – Neglect can cause profound, long-term damage to a child's emotional, social and physical development and have a significant impact on their future life. In babies, brain development passes through sensitive periods where appropriate stimulation results in the development of particular skills, such as language. Without stimulation, development of such skills may be severely delayed or even permanently compromised. Neglect at critical times in infancy and childhood may therefore lead to serious problems later, some of which may be difficult or impossible to rectify. All forms of abuse and neglect during childhood, known as 'adverse childhood experiences', are associated with poor mental health, anti-social behaviour and thoughts of self-harm and suicide. The consequences of physical abuse – referred to as 'non-accidental injury' – range from minor to severe injuries, brain damage and possibly death.

Domestic violence – The effects of domestic violence on children can be severe. Some children may become withdrawn and find it difficult to communicate. Others may act out the aggression they have witnessed, or blame themselves for the abuse. Many studies have found strong links with poorer educational outcomes and higher levels of mental health problems. One study found that around half of adults who experienced domestic abuse before the age of 16 also experienced domestic abuse later in life, compared with 13 per cent of those who did not experience abuse before the age of 16. Experience of abuse was far higher among females than males, whereas the perpetrators of abuse were more likely to be male.

Sexual abuse – Childhood sexual abuse is known to be associated with a wide range of mental health conditions. Survivors of childhood sexual abuse are at risk of self-harming behaviours and eating disorders, and there is an increased likelihood of depression or borderline personality disorder. Studies have shown that the mental disorders of anxiety, depression, post-traumatic stress disorder and schizophrenia are more common in those who have suffered abuse as children. The risk of suicide in adulthood is increased.

Effects of abuse on adulthood – The effects of childhood abuse in later life can be profound and wide-ranging. They may include attention problems, learning disorders, and issues with emotion recognition, regulation and social perception. People who were abused as children may have difficulty forming friendships due to impulsivity and violent behaviours. Studies have also shown increased involvement in criminal behaviour.

Childhood abuse is a risk factor in the development of depression, anxiety and other psychiatric disorders throughout adulthood. Adult survivors of childhood abuse are also more likely to misuse substances. Physical health problems, such as obesity, and somatising disorders, such as chronic pain, are more common. For both men and women, sexual abuse in childhood can have an impact throughout adulthood on relationships, resulting in repeated failed and abusive relationships.

CULTURAL SAFEGUARDING ISSUES

18.04 Some communities in the UK have cultural practices and beliefs that can put children and family members at risk and so there may be safeguarding concerns. These include:

Forced marriage – This is a formal marriage or informal union in which one or both parties have not expressed free and informed consent. Child brides are forced to drop out of school, have children before they are mature, and can be subjected to a life of violence and abuse.

Female genital mutilation (FGM) – This is the ritual cutting or removal of a female's external genitalia – a practice illegal in the UK. In some communities, FGM is carried out routinely on babies or young girls in the belief that it reduces female libido, so the girls will be more likely to remain virgins until marriage and stay faithful to their husband. FGM has immediate and long-term health risks of chronic pain, infections, infertility, birth complications, danger to newborn babies, and psychological consequences.

Breast ironing – This is also known as breast flattening. It is the pounding and massaging of a pubescent girl's breasts, using hard or heated objects, to try to make them stop developing. It is aimed at protecting the girl from sexual harassment and rape, to prevent early pregnancy that would tarnish the family name.

Honour-based violence – This is violence committed against a woman or girl (or sometimes a man or boy) who the family or community feel has not followed what they believe is acceptable behaviour, and so has brought dishonour or shame to the family. Honour-based violence sometimes leads to 'honour killing'.

Spirit possession and witchcraft – A child may suffer emotional abuse and physical harm if they are labelled as being 'possessed with an evil spirit'. This might be because the child has a disability, such as a learning disability, mental ill-health, epilepsy, autism, stammer or deafness. In these cases, the adults rationalise misfortune by attributing it to spiritual forces. A parent's mental ill health may also be blamed on a child being possessed.

OUTCOMES FOR LOOKED-AFTER CHILDREN

18.05 Removing a child from their family is a carefully considered decision made by the local authority to protect the child. It has significant consequences for the child and their family. These children will, mostly, have experienced traumatic events in their lives before coming into care. Studies have shown that a looked-after child is five times more likely to have a mental disorder compared with the general population of children. Around half of looked-after children have a diagnosable mental disorder.

Nevertheless, there can be positive outcomes for children in care. Stable placements can be life-changing for a child and enable them to have the childhood that they had been denied before. Many children in care say that their experiences are good and that it was the right decision for them. Many foster children feel like part of the family they live with and form lasting relationships. Also, looked-after children can have better educational outcomes than children in need who remain with their families.

Studies show it is important for professionals to support the child's birth family to address the problems that resulted in the child entering care. In time, many children can return home to their family. Even if this is not possible, their birth family is still likely to be a central part of their life and their identity. The quality of contact a child has with their birth family can have an impact on their wellbeing, so it is important to support a child to have safe, positive contact if they want to.

ADOPTION

18.06 Some mothers offer up their child for adoption because they feel unable to care for the child, but this is rare nowadays. The majority of children who need adoptive families have been removed from their birth families by order of the Family Court because their parents, and other family members, are unable to provide the care they need. These children have suffered loss and separation in their young lives. Many have had damaging experiences of neglect and abuse and subsequently develop coping mechanisms and behaviour that mean they find it more difficult to form relationships. Older children are harder to place for adoption.

Before arranging an adoption, it is important to consider: what was the child's experience of bonding and attachment; whether there is a genetic risk from the biological parents (a child with a parent who has a mental health disorder has a 10 times greater risk of having one themselves); and the family dynamics they have experienced.

An adoption order has the effect of permanently severing the legal ties between the child and the birth parents (except in the case of partner adoptions). Any court orders that existed before the making of an adoption order will become void. The birth parent is an automatic party to adoption proceedings unless he or she has given notice that they do not wish to be informed of the proceedings.

Case study – Adoption – Craig's story (see Appendix: Case studies, p 255.)

Further information

HM Government – Working Together to Safeguard Children

https://www.gov.uk/government/publications/working-together-to-safeguard-children--2

First4Adoption

https://www.first4adoption.org.uk

Coram

https://www.coramadoption.org.uk

Department for Education – Children looked after children and adoption statistics

https://www.gov.uk/government/statistics/children-looked-after-in-england-including-adoption-2019-to-2020

Department of Education – Characteristics of children in need

https://explore-education-statistics.service.gov.uk/find-statistics/characteristics-of-children-in-need/2020

NSPCC – Types of Abuse

https://www.nspcc.org.uk/what-is-child-abuse/types-of-abuse/

Department of Education – The impacts of abuse and neglect on children

https://assets.publishing.service.gov.uk/government/uploads/system/uploads/attachment_data/file/602148/Childhood_neglect_and_abuse_comparing_placement_options.pdf

Office for National Statistics – Child abuse in England and Wales

https://www.ons.gov.uk/peoplepopulationandcommunity/crimeandjustice/articles/childabuseinenglandandwales/yearendingmarch2019

The Lancet – Long-term outcomes of childhood sexual abuse

https://www.thelancet.com/journals/lanpsy/article/PIIS2215-0366(19)30286-X/fulltext

Mental Health Foundation – Mental health statistics: Domestic violence

https://www.mentalhealth.org.uk/statistics/mental-health-statistics-domestic-violence

NHS – Female genital mutilation

https://www.nhs.uk/conditions/female-genital-mutilation-fgm/

Chapter 19

Reports, assessments and the Family Court

(See also Chapter 17 The work of the Family Court.)

19.01 The Family Court will order a report where it needs further information to make an informed decision; this is usually in circumstances where there is a family dispute by private individuals over child arrangements. This might include if separated parents cannot agree how long a child should spend with each parent, which school they should attend or there may be concern as to the child's welfare. The Children and Family Court Advisory Service (Cafcass) or the Local Authority Children's Services will be asked to prepare a report for the court. In some circumstances, an expert witness or independent specialist service will also be asked to provide a report.

OVERVIEW OF REPORTS FOR THE COURT

19.02 Children Act 1989, s 7, Welfare report – The court may order a welfare report when it is considering any private law application under the Children Act 1989. The report can be provided by a Cafcass officer, or by a local authority social worker if they are already involved with the child and their family.

Children Act 1989, s 8, Private law orders – The court can ask for a report when it is considering such orders as child arrangement orders, specific issue orders, prohibited steps orders and special guardianship orders. The author of the report is instructed to provide a report on the child, with recommendations. The author also has a duty to carry out a risk assessment (Children Act 1989, s 16A) if, during the preparation of the report, they suspect the child is at risk of harm. Cafcass officers are involved in other assessment and monitoring duties for the Family Court too.

Children Act 1989, s 37, Investigation report – If, within private law proceedings, the court becomes concerned about the welfare of a child, it may consider making a care or supervision order. The local authority will be asked to initiate enquiries into the child's circumstances; this is called a Children Act 1989, s 37 investigation and report, and is a bridge between private and public law. During the investigation, the local authority must consider whether it should apply for a care or supervision order, or should provide services or assistance, for the child and their family.

Expert witness report – The court may order that an expert witness produce a report focussing on a specific matter requiring a professional opinion from someone with the necessary expertise. The court must give permission for such evidence (Children Act 1989, s 25 authorisation).

Application for Placement order or Adoption order – where the local authority has applied for a placement order, there will be a requirement for Cafcass to prepare a report as to their views about the application. Where an application is made for an adoption order, the local authority will be required to prepare a report and, if required, Cafcass can be requested to provide a report.

SERVICES PROVIDING ASSESSMENTS AND REPORTS

Cafcass

19.03 Children and Family Court Advisory and Support Service (Cafcass/Cafcass Cymru) – This is the national body for England and Wales responsible for providing qualified social workers to represent children in family court cases. Court reports are prepared by a Cafcass officer, known as a Children's Guardian in public law cases and a Family Court Adviser in the majority of private law cases. They provide reports to court in both private and public law cases and are independent of the court and other authorities, such as health, education and local authority children's services. Cafcass advises the court, in family court cases, about what is in the child's best interests. Cafcass officers have a duty to safeguard and promote the welfare of children going through the family justice system when the court is making critical decisions about their future.

Cafcass officers advise the court in the main areas of private law and public law. In private law cases, the officer will use an assessment process known as the Child Impact Assessment Framework, which focusses on the child's needs, wishes and feelings. The Framework provides several guides the Cafcass officer can use to assess the different aspects of an individual child's case. These include domestic abuse; conflict harmful to the child; child refusal or resistance to spending time with one of the parents or carers; other forms of harmful parenting such as substance misuse or mental health difficulties.

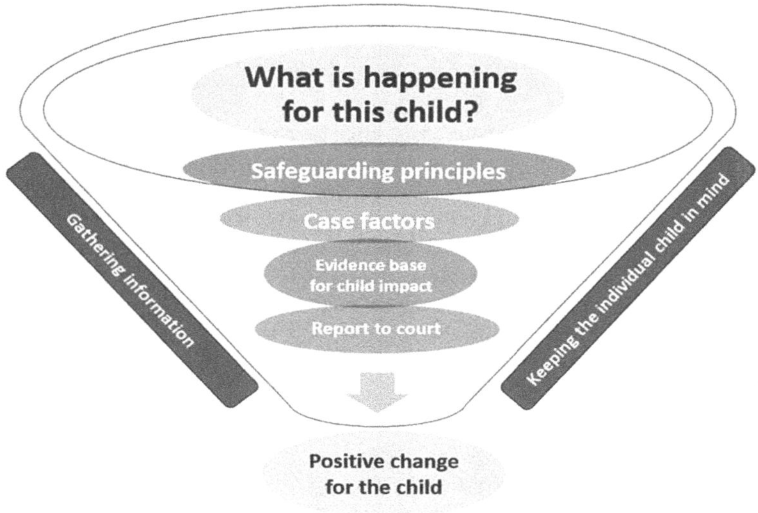

© Cafcass

The structure of the Cafcass Child Impact Assessment Framework, sets out how children may experience parental separation and how this can be assessed and understood. As the Cafcass officer gathers information, they will use their professional Judgement to decide which guides and tools from the framework are most applicable to the individual child's case. At the end of the assessment, the officer will make recommendations based on a 'child impact analysis' that takes into consideration all the information gathered and will advise the court and parents about what arrangements and interventions are in the child's best interests.

Risk assessments, Children Act 1989, s 16A – This makes it a duty for Cafcass officers to undertake a risk assessment when carrying out any function in connection with family proceedings if they have cause to suspect a child is at risk of harm. A risk assessment under the Children Act 1989, s 16A is intended to alert the court to potential harm to the child and does not require a direction from the court for such an assessment to be carried out.

The assessment includes:

- what harm has occurred and the evidence for this;
- the risk factors that give cause to suspect a child is currently at risk of harm;

- the likely impact of any harm on the child; and
- assessment of how the child could be protected from harm.

A Children Act 1989, s 16A risk assessment applies to all stages of family proceedings, where the court has the power to make an order. The assessment is in relation to the current harm to a child rather than future risk. **The outcome must be reported to the court, but is not shared with those who are parties to the case. The court can use its discretion to withhold all or part of the assessment, taking into consideration whether doing so would create a risk to the child**. A Cafcass officer can make a child protection referral to the local authority as the result of a risk assessment.

Local authority children's services

19.04 Local authority children's services have a statutory duty and responsibility to promote the welfare of children and their families and to make sure children are safeguarded and not at risk of harm. In carrying out these duties, they will at times need to make applications to the court for orders to ensure children are protected. The relevant sections of the Children Act 1989 when assessing a child, including the provision of statutory services, are:

- Section 17 – children in need;
- Section 47 – reasonable cause to suspect a child is suffering or likely to suffer significant harm;
- Section 31 – care and supervision orders;
- Section 20 – duty to accommodate a child.

Each local authority in England and Wales has its own child protection procedures and protocols for assessment, but all require the social worker to visit the family to discuss an allegation or concern. The social worker will interview the child alone, assess their developmental needs, evaluate the ability of the parents to respond to the child's needs, and consider what environmental factors may impact on the parents' capacity to respond to their child's needs and development. If a parent does not give consent for their child to be interviewed independently, and there is concern for the child, an application can be made to the court for the child to be made available for interview.

During the assessment, the social worker will liaise with other professionals and agencies involved with the child and their family, using a multi-agency approach as set out in the 2018 statutory guidance *Working Together to*

Safeguard Children. The assessment will establish whether the child is a 'child in need'. If so, a 'child in need plan' will be formulated.

Local authority assessment procedures are guided by a systematic approach to enquiries, using a conceptual model to deliver a comprehensive assessment for all children, as set out in the diagram below.

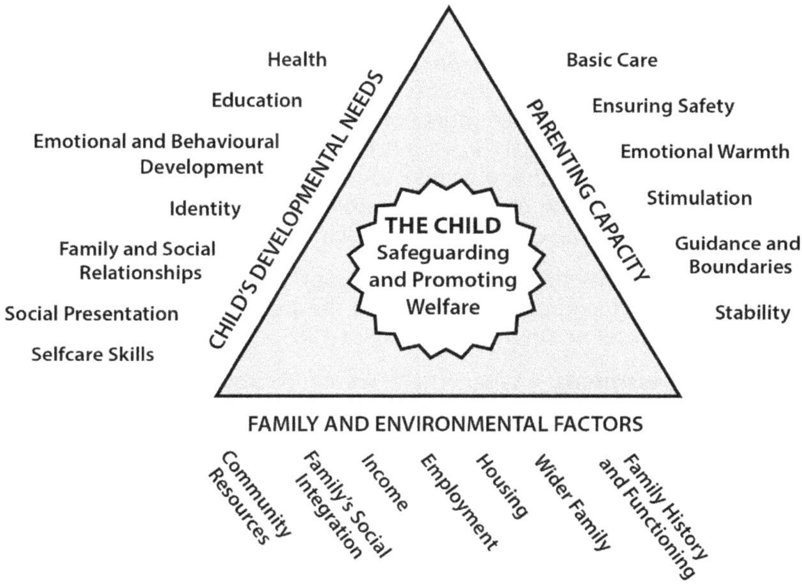

THE COMMON ASSESSMENT FRAMEWORK.

19.05 Children Act 1989, s 47 Investigation – This is undertaken when a local authority children's service becomes aware of concerns about the abuse or neglect of a child. The local authority has a legal duty to carry out enquiries within a certain time scale. This can involve making enquiries with other organisations, such as police, health and education services. There may be a need for immediate protection of the child while an assessment or enquiries are being carried out. As a result of the investigation, the child may be placed on a 'child protection plan' if they are found to be suffering, or likely to suffer, significant harm. This may lead to care proceedings.

Children Act 1989, s 37 Court reports – When, during private law proceedings, the court has a concern about the wellbeing or safety of a child, they may consider making a care or supervision order. In this situation, the court will direct the Children's Service to undertake a Section 37 investigation of the child's circumstances and consider whether further action to protect the child is required; that is whether they should apply for a care order, or provide assistance to the child and the family. If the conclusion is that the family requires the provision of services, a children's plan should be appended to the report with details of the services to be provided with timescales. This report should be completed within eight weeks unless an alternate date is ordered.

Children Act 1989, s 7 Court reports – A Section 7 report is requested in private law proceedings when the court requires information about a child's welfare and guidance on what course of action would be best for the child. Although a Cafcass officer can provide this report, where the child is known to the children's service, the allocated social worker will be asked to carry out an assessment on the child and its family. The social worker will make recommendations to the court, with an explanation for their reasons.

Both Section 37 and Section 7 reports for the court follow a similar assessment framework, which includes a comment on the 'no order principle' and the 'welfare checklist' set out in the Children Act 1989.

Parenting assessments – When there are child protection concerns the Local Authority children's services will carry out a parenting assessment to establish a parent(s) ability to look after their child ensuring their safety, health, and developmental needs. It is an important assessment that will inform the local authority and the parents if there are any gaps in the parents' ability to care for their child and meet their needs.

Wherever possible, a parenting assessment should be carried out by the Local Authority children's service before initiating court proceedings, to establish the parent(s) capacity to meet the child's needs. The court can request the Local Authority to undertake a parenting assessment in public law proceedings. The parenting assessment will form the basis of a recommendation to the court in care proceedings, or it will inform a Children's Service decision about what support the parents would require in caring for their child and the viability of such support.

The assessment can take place in the parent(s) home, family centre or at a residential family centre. It is a time-limited assessment to establish the parent(s) ability and capacity to provide 'good enough' care for their child. The assessment process can also be used as an intervention to support the parent(s) to change by developing their parenting skills.

There are a number of requirements for the parenting assessment to consider including the parent's views and attitudes towards parenting; their understanding of child development and children's needs; their resourcefulness to seek help and support and who forms their support network. During the assessment, the parent(s) will be observed with the child undertaking everyday tasks. The timescale to complete an assessment is usually 6 to 12 weeks but may take longer if a parent has a learning disability, difficulty or there are language barriers.

EXPERT WITNESSES

19.06 Experts are instructed in Family Court proceedings to provide an independent opinion, to assist the judge or magistrates, or to decide about a specific issue. The court must agree that the instruction of the expert is necessary to assist the court in the just resolution of the proceedings. Some cases are complex and expert evidence is necessary so that the right decision can be made for the child. Although Social Workers and Cafcass officers are experts in their field, an independent expert is usually instructed to provide an opinion relating to an issue that is outside the knowledge base of the social workers or Cafcass officer involved in the proceedings.

Who should assess the parent and child – Clinical psychologists and child and adolescent psychiatrists are trained in the assessment of both children and adults. Psychiatrists have additional training in the diagnosis of mental disorders and can advise on treatments that include medications. Psychologists can undertake cognitive assessments and can advise on psychological treatment.

Where there is an identified or suspected mental health disorder in a parent, additional assessment by an adult psychiatrist may be recommended to inform the court of the potential for treatment or intervention, and the likely duration and prognosis. Specialist assessments may be considered where there are issues pertinent to the case, such as adult substance misuse or forensic (criminal) issues.

Examples of the issues and identification of an expert witness:

Type of question to be answered	**Expertise required**	**Likely practitioner** (if not able to be dealt with by those already working with the parents)
Are the features displayed likely to be the effects of abuse (physical, sexual, neglect)?	Expertise in child protection clinical assessment and normal development	• General or community paediatrician

Type of question to be answered	**Expertise required**	**Likely practitioner** (if not able to be dealt with by those already working with the parents)
Is the child displaying emotional and/or behavioural problems?	Expertise in clinical assessment and child development in the context of child abuse and neglect	• Clinical psychologist • Child and adolescent psychiatrist • General or community paediatrician
Are there concerns about attachment or bonding between child and parent?	Expertise in the clinical assessment of attachment behaviour in the context of child abuse and neglect	• Social worker • Clinical psychologist • Child and adolescent Psychiatrist • General or community paediatrician
Is there significant parental mental ill-health affecting the child's wellbeing?	Expertise in the clinical assessment of adult mental illness and disorder	• General adult psychiatrist • Clinical psychologist
Is there evidence of developmental delay or learning disability in the child?	Expertise in clinical assessment and child development in the context of child abuse and neglect	• General or community paediatrician • Psychologist; clinical or educational • Child and adolescent psychiatrist

Taken from the Family Court Bench Book.

Process of assessment – The expert receives specific instructions from the court about the content of the report to be produced, and within what timeframe. This shapes how the assessment is carried out. Typically the report would include assessments of the parent(s) alone and together, of the child alone and of the child with the parent(s) – if appropriate for the child.

A psychiatric or psychological assessment is a brief snapshot in time that builds up a fuller picture over a longer period. Information is gathered from a range of sources, including, for example, the child's school, nursery and social worker. Any previous assessments or reports, a chronology, details of past attempts at intervention – and the impact of them – should also be available to the expert.

It is important that the parents and children are clear about the purpose of the assessment, and understand that it will be shared with the court in a report. The report should give a clear explanation of any opinions or recommendations. Expert witnesses may on occasion appear in court to speak about their report.

Making recommendations for treatment – Recommendations for any treatment or intervention should have an evidence base, be realistic and be available to the child/family in their local area. Previous attempts at intervention should be taken into account when considering the potential success of any suggested intervention. Timescales should be realistic, bearing in mind the child's age.

PLACEMENT AND CONTACT ARRANGEMENTS

19.07 In private law, the court deals with a child where the parents have separated and there is a dispute over arrangements for the child. Decisions will need to be made about the length of time a child should spend with each parent or other significant people in their life. In public law, where a local authority is applying to the court in care proceedings, a decision has to be made as to where the child should be placed, who they should live with and what arrangements should be made for the child to see their family.

In the case of siblings, the local authority or court may need to decide whether they should be placed together or separately. It is important to consider the needs of each child and whether these can be met sufficiently if they are placed together. A carer may be able to manage one child with significant needs, but it could be an impracticable task with two or three. A local authority considering whether to place a child away from their parent(s) or carer(s) may ask an expert witness, such as a clinical psychologist, to comment on the placement options available, their suitability and possible impact on the child.

There are many positive benefits to a child in maintaining family contacts. It can help the child maintain valuable relationships and attachments and prevent them from blaming themselves for the family breakdown. It also lessens the likelihood of the child developing unrealistic fantasies about a parent or carer with whom they no longer live and helps the child maintain their sense of culture and origin, and be informed about their family. Remaining in contact may also have a negative emotional impact on a child and cause serious upset and distress over an extended period of time. In such circumstances, it may be necessary to reduce the frequency of that contact time or to terminate it altogether.

Some upset for the child after seeing their parent, brother, sister or other family member is to be expected and is an ordinary reaction to upheaval, but this should be short-lived. Children may require therapeutic help to support them through managing this, rather than making an immediate decision to terminate it.

Further Information

Judicial College – Family Court Bench Book

https://www.judiciary.uk/wp-content/uploads/2016/10/family-court-bench-book-jan-2018.pdf

Cafcass – Child Impact Assessment Framework (CIAF)

https://www.cafcass.gov.uk/grown-ups/professionals/ciaf/

Department for Education – Working together to safeguard children

https://www.gov.uk/government/publications/working-together-to-safeguard-children--2

NSPCC – Assessing parenting capacity

https://www.nspcc.org.uk/globalassets/documents/information-service/factsheet-assessing-parenting-capacity1.pdf

The Law Society – Templates for instructing experts in family and children court proceedings

https://www.lawsociety.org.uk/topics/family-and-children/instructing-experts-in-family-and-children-court-proceedings

Chapter 20

Ten tips for the Family Court about mental disorders in adults

1 MENTAL DISORDERS ARE COMMON IN THE GENERAL POPULATION OF ADULTS SO EXPECT TO ENCOUNTER THEM

20.01 One in five adults will be affected by a mental health condition during their lifetime. Among children, about one in 20 is affected.

Among the general population of adults, the most common mental disorders are:

- stress – now the commonest reason to be signed off work;
- anxiety;
- depression;
- mixed anxiety and depression; and
- drug and alcohol misuse (or combination of illness and substance misuse).

People suffering from stress, anxiety or depression are mostly treated in primary care, by their GP, who either prescribes medication or refers them for counselling.

There is a strong correlation between common mental health problems, such as depression and anxiety, and economic disadvantage. Poorer and more disadvantaged people are disproportionately affected by mental disorders and are more likely to experience adverse consequences. This is the reason that groups such as refugees and asylum seekers, homeless people and some black and minority ethnic (BAME) communities who are socially disadvantaged, have a higher risk of anxiety and depression.

Women are more likely than men to have a common mental health problem, and are almost twice as likely to be diagnosed with depression and anxiety. A UK study of general practice records for mothers consulting their GP in the years 2005 to 2017 showed that one in four children aged 0 to 16 years is exposed to maternal mental illness. The prevalence of diagnosed and treated maternal mental illness appears to be increasing.

The Men's Health Forum reported in 2017 that 12.5 per cent of men in the UK were diagnosed with a mental disorder. Although more women than men are diagnosed with common mental health problems, the rate of male suicide is significantly greater; just over three out of four suicides (76 per cent) are by men. Studies suggest that men suffer from mental distress, but may not be receiving (or asking for) the help they need. In general, men complain of bodily (somatic) symptoms rather than saying they are mentally unwell, so they report abdominal pain, headache, joint pain and chest pain rather than feelings of depression or anxiety. Men are less likely than women to access psychological therapies.

A University of York research study reported that 10 per cent of mothers and 6 per cent of fathers in the UK have mental health problems at any given time.

The more severe mental disorders, in which people have psychotic symptoms and therefore cannot function and require specialist psychiatric treatment, including hospital admission, are less common. Only about 8 per cent of the population has a more serious mental disorder during their lifetime.

2 MANY ADULTS WITH SEVERE MENTAL DISORDERS CAN, AND DO, MAKE GOOD PARENTS

20.02 The disorders known to have the most impact on parenting are:

- depression, especially chronic and recurrent depression;
- bipolar affective disorder;
- post-natal psychosis;
- drug and alcohol addiction; and
- severe personality disorders.

When people lack insight into their mental health condition and need for treatment, they can pose a risk to themselves and others. If this is the case, they can be compulsory admitted to a psychiatric hospital under the Mental Health Act 1983. This is known as being 'sectioned'.

Those with severe mental disorders may not realise they are ill; in fact, they may feel exceptionally well, for example, when in the manic phase of bipolar affective disorder. Alternatively, the illness itself may make the person so paranoid that they do not trust anyone enough to ask for help. These are situations in which a person might be sectioned. The use of the Mental Health Act 1983 is discussed in more detail in **Chapter 21**.

Some people may inherently be more vulnerable than others to becoming mentally unwell because they have a family history of mental disorder, have been subject to severe trauma, or have a brain disorder. Others have behaviours that contribute to the disorder, such as using alcohol and/or drugs excessively.

Some people have more than one mental disorder (co-morbidity). This is more difficult for clinicians to treat and may make complete recovery more difficult. For example, someone with schizophrenia can also be depressed, and someone with depression may also have a personality disorder. People with autism spectrum disorder often have another disorder as well.

In family law work, the Family Court needs to know whether the parent accepts that they have a mental disorder – that is, they have insight into their condition. Having insight affects whether they are willing to accept help for themselves and help with parenting.

3 A CHILD IS MORE LIKELY TO DEVELOP A MENTAL DISORDER IF A PARENT HAS A MENTAL HEALTH CONDITION

20.03 Research suggests that mental illness can run in families, so there may be a genetic component, but it is not fully understood. However, it does appear that mental illness can be hereditary. This is the case with severe mental health conditions, such as schizophrenia, bipolar affective disorder and severe depression. There is less evidence to show that other mental health conditions run in families. Other causes of mental disorder can be environmental stress factors, such as neglect, abuse, isolation and economic deprivation.

The chance of a child not developing a mental illness is much greater than the possibility of developing one. This is true, even if when they have a parent or relative with a mental illness.

Relationship	Schizophrenia	Bipolar affective disorder
Lifetime chance. This is the chance of someone in the general population developing the condition during their lifetime.	1 in 100	1 in 100
If one of your biological parents has the condition	6 in 100	10 in 100
If both of your biological parents have the condition	45 in 100	40 in 100
If your brother or sister has the condition	9 in 100	13 in 100
If your identical twin has the condition	40–50 in 100	40–70 in 100
If your non-identical twin has the condition	17 in 100	20 in 100
If a second degree relative has the condition. For example, your aunt, uncle or grandparent.	3 in 100	5 in 100

4 MENTAL DISORDERS MAY PRESENT IN THE FAMILY COURT AS BOTH THE CAUSE OF FRICTION AND THE RESULT OF PROBLEMS WITHIN RELATIONSHIPS

20.04 The distress caused by problems with relationships or parenting may worsen a pre-existing mental disorder.

Depression and anxiety can be the psychological consequences of disputes between partners or parents and children. With some mental disorders, the affected person's behaviour is so disruptive that they are unable to maintain a stable relationship. Mental disorders may contribute to the parties failing in the mediation process.

When might behaviours indicate a mental disorder at a court appearance?

- **If the person's behaviour is very variable** – Consider drug or alcohol use, or withdrawal. Also, personality disorder, which is often self-evident because of the person's inconsistent behaviour at hearings.
- **If a person can't be understood, even with an interpreter** – Check the interpreter is trying to interpret the correct language or whether

there's a dialect. Ask the interpreter to translate verbatim rather than try and make sense of the speech. Write it down – if it remains incomprehensible, it may indicate thought disorder, which is linked to psychosis, particularly schizophrenia. (See the *Equal Treatment Bench Book.*)

- **A child with attention deficit hyperactivity disorder or autism spectrum disorder** – Consider whether the condition is also present in either parent.

- **If there is no appreciation of the other person's point of view** – Consider personality disorder, especially if the person also shows signs of changeable mood, self-harm or violence. Also, consider attention deficit hyperactivity disorder when there's a failure to appreciate another person's emotions.

- **If a person is extremely litigious** – Some parents may have understandable reasons to make allegations. For example, those with a child diagnosed with an autism spectrum disorder may consider that their child has not been given appropriate educational support, or parents with a child who has suffered brain damage at birth may pursue allegations of negligence.

  But if litigation is pursued beyond all hope of resolving the issue, or where the subject of the litigation is improbable, or if it's taking all the person's efforts and finances, it may indicate a mental disorder; typically delusional disorder or paranoid personality disorder.

  If a person has a fixed belief and paranoia, they may have a delusional disorder. A fixed belief might be directed at a well-known public figure or at an organisation. People with a severe paranoid personality, especially if they are also narcissistic, have a sense of self-importance and injustice that brings them into repeated conflict with organisations they perceive have injured them or their family. Pursuing such litigation may take all the person's efforts and finances, disadvantaging their family.

- **Finally, could the parent be gaining anything from exaggerating a mental illness?** In the Family Court, this is unlikely if the person wishes to continue responsibility for child care. However, in a destructive relationship breakdown, one partner may wish to demonstrate to the court how much the issues with their partner have affected them. Alternatively, a spouse or partner may exaggerate or make false allegations about the mental health and behaviour of the other parent to discredit their parenting ability.

5 REASONS WHY SOME ETHNIC GROUPS MAY BE MORE VULNERABLE TO MENTAL DISORDERS

20.05 Some ethnic groups seem more vulnerable to mental disorders, but the common factor is social disadvantage. It is likely that mental health problems go unreported and untreated because people in some ethnic minority groups are reluctant to engage with mainstream health services. It is also possible that mental health problems are over-diagnosed in people whose first language is not English.

Gypsies and Irish Travellers – An example of social disadvantage is within the white Gypsy and Irish Traveller group, formally identified for the first time in the 2011 UK census. Men and women in the Gypsy and Traveller communities have twice the white British rates of physical illness. Travellers who do not live on authorised sites face more issues than those with a permanent or semi-permanent base.

Irish – People from Ireland living in the UK, have much higher hospital admission rates for mental health problems than other ethnic groups. They have higher rates of depression and alcohol problems and are at greater risk of suicide. These higher rates are thought to be related to social disadvantage, including poor housing and social isolation.

BAME – This group includes black, Asian and minority ethnic communities, all of whom are more likely to be diagnosed with mental health problems. They are also more likely to be admitted to hospital, to experience a poor outcome from treatment, and to disengage from mainstream mental health services leading to social exclusion and a deterioration in their mental health. These differences may be explained by several factors, including poverty and racism, but also because mainstream mental health services often fail to understand or provide services that are acceptable and accessible to non-white British communities and meet their particular cultural and other needs.

African-Caribbean people living in the UK have lower rates of common mental disorders than other ethnic groups. However, they have a higher chance of being diagnosed with severe mental illness. They are three to five times more likely than any other group to be diagnosed and admitted to hospital with schizophrenia. African-Caribbean people are also more likely to enter mental health services via the courts or the police, rather than from primary health care (the main route to treatment for most people). They are more likely to be treated under a section of the Mental Health Act and to receive medication, rather than be offered talking treatments such as psychotherapy. They are over-represented in high and medium secure units, and in prisons too. This may be because they are reluctant to engage with services, and so are far more ill when they do.

The statistics on the numbers of Asian people in the UK with mental health problems are inconsistent. This may be because mental health problems are often unacknowledged as there may be cultural influences, such as stigma and shame in this ethnic group. Asian people have better rates of recovery from schizophrenia, which may be linked to a higher level of family support.

The close-knit family structure of the Chinese community provides strong support for its members. While this may be beneficial in many ways, it can generate feelings of guilt and shame around mental illness, resulting in people feeling stigmatised and unable to seek help. Stigma can lead to people presenting late for treatment.

6 CERTAIN PEOPLE CAN BE MORE VULNERABLE TO MENTAL HEALTH PROBLEMS

People who are socially isolated

20.06 **Carers** – People who care for sick, disabled or elderly family members may have little time to themselves or opportunities to meet others or engage in life-enhancing activities. Social isolation of carers can make them vulnerable to depression. There have been advances in carer support, providing breaks, respite care and involvement in support groups. In some cases carers can receive financial support too.

Older adults – Those aged 60 or above make significant contributions to society as family members, volunteers and as active participants in the workforce. While most have good mental health, around 15 per cent of adults aged 60 and over have a mental disorder. As people age, they are more likely to experience bereavements, live alone, have a chronic illness, be financially disadvantaged and experience social isolation. Many older adults are at risk of developing mental disorders, neurological disorders or substance use problems as well as other health conditions such as diabetes, hearing loss and osteoarthritis.

Mobility – For people with mobility problems, it can be a challenge to access activities, despite the adaptations now required by law. If reduced mobility causes pain, as in conditions such as arthritis, this is also a limiting factor.

Adults with a visual impairment – In adults, the prevalence of visual impairment increases rapidly with age. It is estimated that more than one in ten of the older UK population has a significant visual impairment. Sight problems are associated with falls, reduced capacity to carry out everyday activities, and being less able to continue with social commitments, all of which can have an impact on mental wellbeing.

Childhood with a visual impairment – This has a significant effect on development and learning. Among children with learning disabilities, around 6 per cent are estimated to have a visual impairment. The risk increases with the severity of the learning disability. Around half of vision-impaired children have additional special educational needs. Vision-impaired children have been found to have a lower quality of life compared to their peers, and there is evidence that they are at higher risk of psychosocial disorders compared with fully sighted children.

Those with a hearing impairment – People with a hearing impairment are twice as likely to experience mental health issues, such as depression and anxiety, compared to hearing people. This is due to isolation and the attitudes of others. The situation is made worse as people with a hearing impairment often find it harder to access support than hearing people. When they try to engage with healthcare services, they often experience communication barriers, which can make their symptoms worse.

LGBTQ+ people

20.07 People identifying as lesbian, gay, bisexual, transgender and others falling under the umbrella term LGBTQ+ are at higher risk of experiencing a range of mental health problems, such as depression, suicidal thoughts, self-harm, and alcohol and substance misuse. The higher prevalence of mental ill-health among members of this community is attributed to a range of factors including discrimination, isolation and homophobia. They also have a greater risk of experiencing hate crime compared to heterosexual people, with certain groups particularly at risk, for example, gay men, young people and those identifying as LGBTQ+ from BAME groups.

People with chronic illness or pain

20.08 Ongoing physical difficulties can make people vulnerable to mental health problems. People with chronic pain are three times more likely to develop symptoms of depression or anxiety than the general population. The impact of continuous pain and the physical limitations it can cause can lead to social isolation. Some people with a long-term physical condition are also likely to experience mental ill-health. These people have a risk of social isolation, low self-esteem, stigma and discrimination.

There are several reasons for this link:

- physical illness can cause mental illness;
- drugs prescribed to treat mental illness (antipsychotic medication) increase appetite; subsequent weight gain with obesity can lead to

type 2 diabetes, high cholesterol, joint problems because of carrying extra weight, and cardiovascular problems;

- some physical illnesses, particularly those affecting the neurological system, such as multiple sclerosis, stroke, Alzheimer's disease, Parkinson's disease and epilepsy, cause mental illness. Up to 50 per cent of people who have had a stroke suffer depression, as do a quarter of people with Parkinson's disease; and
- people who are housebound with mobility problems due to arthritis or severe lung disease for example, may lead to a restricted lifestyle and therefore become isolated, leading to mental disorder.

Be aware that:

- people with a mental disorder may not report physical illness. (If they do, it may be dismissed as due to their mental disorder)
- medications to treat mental disorders often have physical side effects
- self-medication for a mental disorder with alcohol or drugs also has physical health risks.

People in abusive relationships

20.09 Domestic violence leads to ongoing stress and isolation. Research suggests that women experiencing domestic abuse are more likely to have a mental health problem, and women with a mental health problem are more likely to suffer domestic abuse. Between 30 and 60 per cent of mentally ill women have suffered domestic violence. Domestic violence is associated with depression, anxiety, post-traumatic stress disorder and substance abuse in both men and women.

People with a learning disability

20.10 There are many reasons why those with a learning disability are more likely to have poor mental health. The biological or genetic causes of the disability may affect the brain and increase vulnerability to mental illness. People with a learning disability may also experience more negative life events, and they may have less access to protective factors, such as a close social circle and meaningful work. Other people's attitudes to them can also have a negative effect.

7 REASONS INFLUENCING RECOVERY FROM SEVERE MENTAL DISORDERS

20.11 Around 8 per cent of the adult UK population suffers from a severe mental disorder. This number does not include inpatients in psychiatric hospitals.

The prognosis of a mental disorder depends on:

- the nature of the disorder (characteristics);
- whether there is just one disorder or more than one;
- whether there is drug or alcohol misuse; or
- whether the person and their family accept the treatment; this is a significant factor.

A person with a severe mental illness, who lacks insight into their condition, will not believe they need to take medication. When unwell, the person's delusions may influence their thinking; for example, they may think they are being poisoned. Their auditory hallucinations may include voices telling them not to take medication. A person's attitude to treatment may also be influenced by whether or not a family member with a mental disorder has experienced a good recovery with treatment.

People with a better prognosis for recovery from a mental disorder are those who:

- have just one disorder;
- have a clear cause of their disorder;
- seek treatment early;
- have full insight into their condition;
- take medication as prescribed and engage with psychological therapies;
- do not self-medicate with alcohol or drugs;
- have a stable personality; or
- have support from family or community.

Medication is effective for the majority of severe mental disorders but, can be unpleasant because of side effects. These can make a person feel sleepy, have dry mouth, increase appetite (leading to weight gain), reduce sexual drive, cause the patient to shake, or be very stiff. Some treatments are given as injections, which can be painful. Others, such as the antipsychotic Clozapine and mood stabiliser lithium, require regular blood tests and monitoring.

Psychological treatments are a major factor in preventing relapse and reducing symptoms. For the patient to be able to engage with psychological treatment, they must be well enough to be able to concentrate, accept their behaviour is due to mental illness, and acknowledge it has caused problems for themselves or others. They must be willing to trust and be open in discussions with the therapist over several sessions. Psychological treatments are not an instant resolution to symptoms. Some treatments only bring improvement over some years. Medication and psychological therapies are often used in combination.

Types of psychological treatment - There are different types of psychological treatment available for mental disorders, from the most general to the most complex. Psychological treatments can be provided to individuals, but often they are conducted in groups to give opportunities for people to learn from others.

Counselling – gives patients an opportunity to talk and be guided, usually in primary care (day-to-day community healthcare).

Anxiety management – relaxation and distraction strategies, usually offered for six sessions.

Cognitive behavioural therapy (CBT) – aims to alter the person's thoughts and linked emotions, such as helping someone cope with hearing voices. Usually offered over six to 12 sessions.

Compliance therapy – usually for inpatients to help them take medication regularly. Involves psychoeducation, giving information about the illness and the benefits of medicine, and how to manage side effects. Usually, four sessions.

Relapse prevention – helps the person recognise early signs of relapse and take prompt action, and avoid their triggers for illness relapse. Usually six to 12 sessions.

Dialectic behaviour therapy (DBT) – used for personality disorders. Can take up to three years. Includes individual and group work several times a week. Aims to change the person's challenging behaviour – a difficult task. Costly, but it can be effective.

Specific treatment – for serious offenders directed towards their risky behaviour (arson or sexual offences, for example). Includes developing empathy for victims.

Recovery in less severe 'common' mental disorders

20.12 The same factors that lead to a good recovery in serious mental disorders also apply to less severe mental health conditions, known as common disorders. Whether there is just one disorder, or more than one, has a strong bearing on the likelihood of recovery from the illness.

Also relevant is how the person was coping with life, work and relationships before the illness. As with recovery from serious mental disorders, a previously stable life, well-adjusted personality, and supportive family and friends are important. Some illnesses, particularly anxiety and depression, can be recurrent.

Not all people who need services to help them recover, access them. Some find it difficult to get support. In some cultures, the stigma of mental disorder is such that the person may not seek help. Others may be concerned about health professionals' attitudes. There are also practical communication problems for some vulnerable groups, such as people who are not English speakers, those who are hearing impaired, and those who have learning disabilities.

8 PEOPLE WITH MENTAL DISORDERS ARE MORE A RISK TO THEMSELVES THAN TO OTHERS

20.13 Here we consider risk factors for those who suffer from serious mental disorders, focusing on their health, safety and vulnerability. (**Chapter 22** looks at the risks that people with a mental disorder pose to others.)

Risks to health and safety

20.14 People with a severe mental disorders, typically psychosis, bipolar affective disorder or severe depression, are at greater risk of dying early. This is because they may neglect physical conditions, such as diabetes, high blood pressure or cardiac disease, and ignore warning signs of illness, such as weight loss or pain. Symptoms of severe life-limiting illness may be mistaken by health professionals for symptoms of mental illness, particularly if the person has difficulty explaining their symptoms.

The effect of severe mental disorders on people's lifestyle can be significant. For example, some people with negative symptoms of schizophrenia lack motivation, so they may not exercise or eat healthily. Some treatments, such as antipsychotic medication and mood stabilisers, cause people to gain weight, adding to the risk of obesity.

Many of the medications used to treat mental disorder have health consequences. For instance, antipsychotic medication increases appetite, which causes weight gain and therefore raises the risk of Type 2 diabetes, high cholesterol and heart problems, and arthritis.

All patients with severe mental illness who have been hospitalised at some point have a long-term suicide rate of about 10 per cent as follows:

Anorexia nervosa – This has the highest suicide rate of all mental disorders; 20 per cent of patients diagnosed and treated by specialised anorexia services die by suicide. The greatest risk is often after treatment when the patient cannot tolerate being at a healthy weight. Death from the physical consequences of anorexia is also common.

Severe depression – The next highest suicide rate, at 10 to 15 per cent. The risk is most significant just after apparent improvement of the depression when the patient's motivation is increasing; so they have the energy to take an overdose or tie a ligature.

Bipolar affective disorder – Has a suicide rate of 10 per cent. The risk is on either side of the mood peak, when people feel their mood rising and know another potential cycle is underway, or when coming down from a high episode with insight into the consequences of their reckless behaviour while unwell.

Severe personality disorder – Has a suicide risk of 10 per cent; this risk is consistent at any time in the person's lifetime. Those with personality disorder have impulsive behaviour and impaired functioning. They will have more negative life events than others (loss of relationships, loss of work, estrangements from family), which are known to precipitate suicide attempts.

Taking drugs or alcohol – Raises the risk of suicide in all disorders, as it increases impulsivity.

Risk from vulnerability

20.15 People with mental disorders can be vulnerable because their behaviour may provoke others. Someone who is paranoid about other people may act in a way that challenges them, possibly inviting retaliation, because they misinterpret social cues. A person may have poor self-care or dress oddly and look different. The side effects of a tremor caused by medication may be frightening for some. Poor dental hygiene is not helpful for those trying to make friendships and obtain employment.

Some people with mental disorders are vulnerable to sexual exploitation; men as well as women. This might be because they are disinhibited, such as in a manic phase of bipolar disorder, or because they lack judgement, as is the case for some people with an autism spectrum disorder or learning disability. Some people with mental disorders, for example those with an emotionally unstable personality disorder, are very needy, constantly seeking attention and validation from others, which can put them in risky situations.

People with mental disorders can be exploited by being used as drug mules or get drawn into modern slavery or prostitution. People living with dementia can be vulnerable to financial exploitation, as can others who have mental health problems.

Safeguarding issues

20.16 Safeguarding issues can arise with everyone, not just people with a mental disorder, but mental disorders can be an additional element leading to safeguarding concerns. (Also see **Chapter 18**, Safeguarding children and local authority care.)

Domestic abuse – Domestic violence accounts for 25 per cent of assaults and is associated with anxiety, depression and post-traumatic stress disorder in the victim. Women who suffer domestic abuse are three times as likely to develop a mental disorder.

Cuckooing – This is the term for a vulnerable person's property being used for drug purposes – to either to grow, store or trade drugs. People with mental disorders who use drugs, or people with a learning disability, may be vulnerable to being targeted by drug gangs.

Radicalisation – This is the process by which someone is converted to support terrorism or extremist ideologies. There is no evidence that terrorist acts are more common in people with a mental disorder. However, such people with them can be at higher risk of radicalisation. They may have religious delusions and beliefs about their own abilities which bring them into contact with terrorism.

Forced marriage – Forced marriages are marriages in which one or both of the parties have not personally expressed their full and free consent to the union; this can happen to men and women. The stigma around mental illness in some communities can be a reason to remove a young person with a mental health condition from the family by forcing them into marriage. Those vulnerable to forced marriage include people with a learning disability or mental disorder, and those who are isolated or subject to domestic abuse.

9 MENTAL DISORDER IN PARENTS AND CARERS – CONSIDERATIONS FOR THE FAMILY COURT

20.17 A parent or carer may disclose they have a mental disorder to the Family Court and request liaison with their health or social care professionals. They may also come to court with suggestions for adjustments. Alternatively, a parent or carer might try to disguise their mental disorder. They may be in denial about their behaviour, for example, downplaying how much they drink, use drugs, spend on gambling, or spend time gaming on the internet. Or they may deliberately hide suicidal thoughts or plans, if admitting them would have consequences for the court's decision about their ability to care for a child.

What to note about a parent or carer's mental disorder

20.18 These are some matters for the court to consider if it is brought to their attention that a parent or carer may have a mental disorder, which could affect their ability to care for their child or children. The court may have been alerted by the contents of reports, such as those from Cafcass and the local authority, or by the parent or carer's behaviour in court. Court professionals will want to know:

- Did they seek treatment from their GP? And were they subsequently referred to the community mental health services?
- When did they seek treatment; was it early in the disorder? Did their family insist they sought treatment or was it their own idea?
- Were they given a diagnosis? Were they told they have more than one mental health condition?
- Did drugs and/or alcohol play a part in their illness?
- What treatments were offered? If it was medication, what was prescribed and what treatment did the person actually take?
- Have they been an inpatient in a psychiatric hospital? If yes, were they detained ('sectioned') for treatment? Have they ever been subject to a Community Treatment Order?
- Were they ever a patient of psychiatric forensic services? If yes, is this a person who will present risks? (See **Chapter 22** – Violent and risky behaviour and mental disorders.)
- Whatever the diagnosis and treatment, has the parent or carer recovered? Are they still taking medication? If so, what is it? Are they still in contact with the mental health services?
- Are they on the sex offenders register?

When considering the answers to these questions, think whether the parent or carer's court appearance is likely to be part of a cumulative pattern of events, and could be the trigger for a suicide attempt, self-harm, or violent behaviour. If so, could the parent or carer react in a way that would be harmful to themselves, their child, or others?

The court may find it helpful to be aware that a parent or carer who is prescribed antipsychotic medication is likely to have a serious mental illness. If they are on injectable medication, known as depots, it means the person cannot be relied on to take oral medication. If they are on a medication called clozapine, this is given for difficult-to-treat schizophrenia. Mood stabilisers, such as lithium and sodium valproate, are given for bipolar affective disorder and severe recurrent depression.

A parent or carer diagnosed with schizophrenia is likely to have been in contact with specialist mental health services and prescribed long-term medication, as with bipolar affective disorder. If the condition is stable, they may be cared for by their GP.

10 RISKY BEHAVIOURS IN THE FAMILY COURT

Private cases in the Family Court

20.19 Disputes in the Family Court can give rise to high levels of emotion between parents, and cause distress for them and their children. The parents may have debated separation, divorce or disputed care arrangements for the children. These feelings of anger could, in some individuals, lead to rage and antipathy, particularly if the parent or carer is unsuccessful in their appeal. In some extreme cases, this may precipitate a suicide attempt. The court appearance could add to the parent's cumulative risk of mental disorder, or could be a 'final straw' event.

While acute depression and distress could result in suicide when the parent fails to get what they want, it's likely that people who carry out such extreme actions are already vulnerable because of a personality disorder. Gambling disorders and financial loss are also risk factors and can increase a person's sense of hopelessness and despair. Drugs and alcohol increase the risk of suicide in people with depression or personality disorders, due to impulsive behaviour when intoxicated or in withdrawal.

Children may be upset by the outcome of the hearing, and this can be a 'final straw' event for them too. Such children may have been exposed to years of conflict and may also not have got what they wanted from the court judgment, especially if they wanted everything to be 'normal' again, with both parents at home. They too can be at risk of a dangerous reaction to the court's decision. Parents and carers can reduce the risk of distress, which may lead to self-harm and suicide in children, by being vigilant, supportive and remaining optimistic, despite family difficulties.

Public cases in the Family Court

20.20 Parents may look to transfer blame for their inadequate parenting onto others, such as their partner, social services, or the Family Court. The parents most likely to do this are those with a personality disorder, in whom transferring blame or projecting faults onto others is part of their lifelong presentation.

Some children who are taken into care will be relieved to escape the stress and violence of their daily lives. Despite this relief, it may be difficult for the child to admit to themselves that they want to escape the home. The relief can be converted into anger towards the person or people most in the firing line – social services staff, the judge or magistrates who made the decision.

Further information

Prevalence of maternal mental illness among children and adolescents in the UK

https://www.sciencedirect.com/science/article/pii/S2468266719300593

Epidemiology of suicide and the psychiatric perspective

https://www.mdpi.com/1660-4601/15/7/1425/htm

Mortality in schizophrenia and related psychoses

https://bmjopen.bmj.com/content/2/5/e001810

Suicide and psychiatric diagnosis

https://www.ncbi.nlm.nih.gov/pmc/articles/PMC1489848/

Mental Health Foundation – Black, Asian and Minority Ethnic (BAME) communities

https://www.mentalhealth.org.uk/a-to-z/b/black-asian-and-minority-ethnic-bame-communities

RAN – Extremism, radicalisation & mental health: A handbook for practitioners

https://books.google.co.uk/books?hl=en&lr=&id=Bx0gEAAAQBAJ&oi=fnd&pg=PP1&dq=RAN+–+Extremism,+radicalisation+%26+mental+health:+A+handbook+for+practitioners&ots=vozNG74Mqe&sig=Q-cwW4-TT4TQzrZP6ogJUp0JRFo#v=onepage&q&f=false

BMJ – Women who experience domestic abuse and mental illness

https://www.bmj.com/content/365/bmj.l4126

Chapter 21

Detention and the Mental Health Act 1983

21.01 The compulsory detention of adults, young people and children for assessment and treatment for a mental disorder is authorised under the Mental Health Act 1983 (MHA 1983). People may be detained under the Act by being made the subject of a 'section' when they are unable to consent to voluntary hospital admission. Being sectioned deprives a person of their liberty, the period over which, is dependent on the section of MHA 1983 by which they are detained.

Before a person can be lawfully sectioned, they will need to be assessed by a team of professionals to ensure that it is necessary. It requires recommendations by two medical doctors, one of whom must be approved under MHA 1983, s 12, and an Approved Mental Health Professional, (usually a social worker) known as an AMHP, who makes the application for the patient's admission to hospital.

The professional team must be satisfied that the following grounds are met:

- the person is suffering from a mental disorder of a nature or degree which warrants their detention in hospital for assessment (or for assessment followed by treatment) for at least a limited period; *and*
- the person ought to be so detained in the interests of their own health or safety, or with a view to the protection of others.

The process and requirements of compulsory admission to hospital are set out in MHA 1983, Parts II and III. Part II of the Act refers to patients who are detained in hospital on Civil Sections, and Part III of the Act deals with detained patients who have been involved in criminal proceedings, known as 'restricted' patients.

CIVIL SECTIONS – PART II

21.02 A person who has never had a prior admission to a psychiatric unit, or a recent admission, will usually be put on a 'section 2', the shortest period of detention. If the patient requires a further period of inpatient treatment and their continued detention is necessary to achieve this, a section 2 can be followed by an application for a 'section 3'. Patients with a known diagnosis and a chronic and relapsing mental health condition may be more appropriately admitted in the first instance on a section 3 for treatment.

Section 2 – Allows for detention in hospital for up to 28 days for assessment and treatment; about a third of sectioned patients are in this category.

Section 3 – Allows for detention in hospital for up to six months for treatment, which may be renewed for a further period; these comprise the majority of sectioned patients, accounting for about a half of sectioned patients.

Community Treatment Order (CTO) – Allows for up to six months for treatment out-of-hospital, which may be renewed for a further period; this order can only be made if the patient is first on a Section 3. The order allows for suitable patients to be treated in the community rather than in hospital. It allows the power of recall, meaning the patient can be brought back to the hospital. About 10 per cent of sectioned patients are in the community on CTO's. There is no lower age limit for a CTO, so anyone under 18 can be placed on one.

Section 7 Guardianship – This applies to a person who is 16 or over. It is used for a very small number of mentally disordered patients who do not require treatment in the hospital but need close supervision and some control in the community as a consequence of their mental disorder. Reception of a patient into Guardianship is initially for six months, then maybe renewed for a further period.

Mental health patients are usually admitted to acute (general) wards or, if very disturbed, psychiatric intensive care units. Although most beds are in the NHS Mental Health Trusts, many specialist services are in independent private hospitals, funded by the NHS.

THE NEAREST RELATIVE (NR)

21.03 'Nearest Relative' is a legal term used in MHA 1983. It has an important and specific role in the compulsory detention of patients on civil sections; (it does not have the same meaning as 'next of kin'). There is a specific hierarchy which is in order of precedence – spouse, civil partner, children, parents, or, in certain circumstances, a carer, or other relatives – the exact order of precedent is set out in the Act. Where a person under the age of 18 is subject to a care order, the local authority will be the NR, unless the person has a married spouse or civil partner.

The NR has certain rights and responsibilities. If the NR is concerned about a relative's mental health, they can request an assessment under MHA 1983, s 13. They can also make an application to the hospital for their relative to be discharged and, in some circumstances, can apply to a Mental Health Tribunal (MHT) for the relative to be taken off the section.

An approved mental health professional (AMHP) must consult with the NR before someone is detained for treatment under MHA 1983, s 3, or under Guardianship. Detention cannot go ahead if the NR disagrees with the decision. The right for the NR to be consulted can be overruled if it is not reasonable or practicable at the time of the assessment to consult them. The NR may in certain circumstances be displaced; this would be carried out by an AMHP making such an application to a county court.

The role of the NR does not apply to a mentally disordered offender, who has been detained on a section under MHA 1983, Part III.

COURT SECTIONS – PART III

21.04 Mentally disordered offenders, sometimes known as 'forensic' or 'restricted' patients, are detained in a specialist psychiatric hospital as the result of a court order; this can be for purposes of assessment for reports or for treatment. The Secretary of State can also direct that a prisoner be transferred from prison to hospital under the Act. A restricted patient is a mentally disordered offender who has committed an offence punishable by imprisonment who is detained in hospital for treatment, without limit of time. Patients on restricted sections make up 10 per cent of the total number of sectioned patients.

The main sections of MHA 1983 used are:

Section 35 – A remand to hospital for a report on a person's mental condition, this is for a period of 28 days, but it can be extended to a maximum of 12 weeks.

Section 37 – A hospital order directed by the court, which may be renewed for six months then yearly.

Section 37/41 – A hospital order with a restriction order (s 41), where there is no limit put on the length of detention.

Section 47/49 – A transfer from prison, the order expires on the earliest prison release date.

A restricted patient is directed to treatment by a criminal court. They are looked after in a hospital forensic unit; these range from high-security hospital settings to medium and low secure units, depending on the patient's risk to themselves and to the public.

The MHT has a statutory duty to discharge restricted patients if they are not satisfied that the criteria for detention have been met. The Secretary of State for Justice may authorise the discharge of a restricted patient. It is usually where a patient is ready for discharge for them to be given a Conditional Discharge, which gives the hospital the power to recall the patient back if necessary for treatment.

DETENTION OF CHILDREN AND YOUNG PEOPLE UNDER THE AGE OF 18

21.05 This area of the law is complex with a number of overlapping Acts – the Mental Health Act 1983, the Children Act 1989 (CA 1989), the Mental Capacity Act 2005, the Care Act 2014 and the Human Rights Act 1998. The following is only a brief outline and is included to illustrate and, to give an indication of, some of the issues.

There is no minimum age for detention under MHA 1983whether the Act is used depends on the purpose of the detention. If the purpose is for medical assessment and treatment in the hospital, then the Act applies. If the purpose is care and control because of the child's unmanageable behaviour, then secure accommodation using the CA 1989 may be appropriate.

The Mental Health Act 1983 – As in all cases, the use of MHA 1983should only be considered if options for informal admission are not feasible. Informal admission may be appropriate where a child, young person, or person with parental responsibility consents to admission and has the capacity or competence to do so. However, even where consent is given, admission under the Act may be necessary; where the child or young person's current mental state indicates they are a risk to themselves or others and there is a strong likelihood, they will change their mind about admission.

Any intervention due to a child or young person's mental disorder should consider the least restrictive option whereby they can receive appropriate treatment. The MHA Code of Practice, states that 'where hospital admission is necessary, the child or young person should be placed as near to their home as reasonably practicable' to avoid separation from family, community and interruption of their education and be consistent with their wellbeing. There is a duty on hospital managers to provide facilities that are age-appropriate.

The Children Act 1989 – Section 25 allows for a young person of 13–17 years to become subject of a Secure Accommodation Order (SAO) and admitted to a secure children's home; where a young person is under the age of 13 the approval of the Secretary of State is needed. The SAO applies to local authority looked after children, who have either been voluntarily accommodated under the Local Authority statutory responsibility imposed by CA 1989, s 20(3) of the Act or are subject to a Care Order

A young person aged 16 or 17 years is voluntarily accommodated under CA 1989, s 20(3) may be made the subject of a SAO. A child accommodated under CA 1989, s 20(5) cannot. They have the right to discharge themselves from accommodation, in such circumstances for children under 17 years old a care application would need to accompany an application for a SAO.

The criteria of CA 1989, s 25 must be met before a looked after child can be placed in secure accommodation. There must be a history of absconding associated with the risk of 'significant harm' or that they are likely to injure themselves or others if not in conditions of security. The duration of the order should be for the shortest time possible. A court may authorise for a child or young person to be kept in secure accommodation for a maximum period of up to three months and six months for subsequent applications. In an emergency, a child or young person can be placed in secure accommodation for up to 72 hours without a court order. The court should have regard to the child's welfare, but welfare is not paramount. The Welfare checklist under CA 1989, s 1 is not applicable. The availability of secure accommodation is outstripped by need. Numbers of children in secure care are few; just over 1 per cent of looked after children.

PARENTAL RESPONSIBILITY (PR)

21.06 All mothers and most fathers have legal rights and responsibilities, known as Parental Responsibility (PR). A father has PR if he is married to the mother or, if not married, is named on the child's birth certificate. If a child or young person is on a Care Order or an Emergency Protection Order, under the Children Act, the local authority acquires PR. Those with PR for a child have the right to make decisions about their care and upbringing, and that includes whether a child receives medical treatment.

The MHA Code of Practice states that those responsible for the care and treatment of a patient, must determine whether a person with PR has the capacity; within the meaning of the Mental Capacity Act 2005 to decide about a child or young person's treatment and whether the decision is in the 'scope of parental responsibility'.

The Code of Practice guidance doesn't give clear rules on what does and does not fall within the scope of PR; however, there are two guiding principles:

- Is this a decision that a parent would be expected to make for their child at this age? (What might be accepted by society and be proportionate for a five-year-old and is likely to be disproportionate for a 15-year-old.)
- Is there any indication that a parent might not be acting in the best interests of the child or young person?

As well as the age of the child, it's important to consider the nature or invasiveness of the intervention, including the degree of deprivation of liberty. The more significant the intervention or deprivation, the more likely it is that this falls outside the scope of parental responsibility. Specific invasive treatments, such as Electroconvulsive Therapy (ECT) or Nasogastric (NG) feeding, is likely to be beyond the scope of PR and the Mental Health Act should be applied.

LIBERTY PROTECTION SAFEGUARDS (LPS)

21.07 The Liberty Protection Safeguards are contained in the Mental Capacity (Amendment) Act 2019, are due to come into force in April 2022 to replace the Deprivation of Liberty Safeguards. Liberty Protection Safeguards apply to individuals aged 16 and over who lack capacity to consent to care and treatment – LPS can apply in settings other than hospitals so can be used in residential schools, children's homes and the family home in addition to mental health units. If, however, the young person objects to hospital admission or treatment, then the LPS cannot be applied. There are differences in the process for the use of LPS in NHS and independent hospitals.

TREATMENT, DECISION-MAKING AND YOUNG PEOPLE

21.08 The Mental Capacity Act 2005 makes the presumption of capacity in someone aged over 16 years; that is, they have the capacity to make the decision, for example, about a proposed admission to hospital and treatment, unless it is established they lack capacity.

The MHA Code of Practice states that children under 16 can be considered to be competent to give consent to admission and treatment, applying the same standards as for assessing capacity. That is, they understand information relevant to the decision, can retain the information, use or weigh the information as part of the decision-making process and communicate their decision. This is called being '*Gillick* competent,' where the child has sufficient understanding and intelligence to understand the proposed action fully and has the competence to consent. Where a young person under 16 is competent but refusing treatment, it would *not* be considered good practice to rely on parental consent, and MHA 1983 or court authorisation should be used.

If a child under 16 lacks competence, a parent can give consent to medical treatment and admission to hospital for that purpose (within the scope of parental responsibility). However, there may be factors that might undermine the parental consent, for example, if one parent strongly disagrees or a parent's interests may conflict with those of the young person or child. In some situations, the use of parental consent to enforce treatment could cause lasting damage to the parent-child relationship.

A young person with capacity, refusing treatment, when the treatment requires hospital admission for a mental disorder, should be administered under the Mental Health Act framework. A child detained under the Mental Health Act has the same rights as an adult regarding scrutiny and appeal.

THE MENTAL HEALTH TRIBUNAL IN ENGLAND AND WALES

21.09 The Mental Health Tribunal (MHT) provides a significant safeguard for patients who have been detained under MHA 1983. It is an independent judicial body whose primary purpose is to review the cases of detained and Conditionally Discharged patients and patients subject to Community Treatment Orders (CTO), known as community patients, and to direct the discharge of the section where it thinks it appropriate. In addition, where the tribunal does not lift the section, it has powers to make recommendations, for example, make a recommendation for the patient to have leave, if it will facilitate discharge; recommend a transfer to another hospital; recommend that the clinical team put in place a CTO in planning the patient's discharge. The tribunal also considers applications for discharge from guardianship.

The patient, or in some cases, their nearest relative, can make an application to the tribunal for their section to be lifted. Hospital managers have a duty to refer patients to the tribunal if the patient hasn't made an application to have a hearing within a prescribed period of time. If the patient is taken off section they may remain in hospital as a voluntary patient or discharge themselves. The patient can appeal to a tribunal at different stages in their period of detention, depending on which section they are detained on. Hearings are usually held in private, but they can be held in public at the patient's request.

The MHT consists of a panel of three members – a legal, a medical and a specialist lay member. Most hearings are completed within a half day. The patient has free representation paid for by legal aid. It is for the detaining authority, the hospital, to prove their case for the patient to remain on section, not for the patient to disprove it. The patient is usually given the decision verbally after the hearing, followed by a written decision.

The nature of the case affects the membership of the tribunal panel. For example, child and adolescent patients' cases are heard by the tribunal's CAMHS panel. At least one of the panel members, it can be any one of the three, will have specialist knowledge and training in CAMHS issues.

Restricted Patients Panels (RPP) for forensic patients have a judge with specific criminal law experience, either from the circuit court, a recorder or a salaried tribunal judge. RPP panels have different powers depending on the section. The Secretary of State can grant the patient leave or discharge the section.

FREQUENTLY ASKED QUESTIONS ABOUT THE MHT

21.10 1. Can a child be detained under the Mental Health Act?

Yes, there is no minimum age for detention in hospital under the Act. It may be used to detain a child or young person who needs to be admitted to hospital for assessment and or treatment of their mental disorder, when they cannot be admitted and or treated on an informal basis.

2. Why are there separate CAMHS Mental Health Tribunals for a young person?

Young people have a more complex legal situation. Particular issues arise in relation to children (under 16 years of age) and young people (16 or 17 years old). In addition to the MHA, other relevant legislation includes the Children Acts of 1989 and 2004, the Mental Capacity Act 2005 and the Human Rights Act 1998. So, MHT's for patients aged 18 and under, aims to have a least one panel member with CAMHS experience. That member can be a legal member, a SpLM or a medical member. Examples of CAMHS members include judges with family law experience, social workers who work with children and young people and CAMHS psychiatrists.

3. What difference does being a Looked After Child make to information at a Mental Health Tribunal?

Where a child or young person is looked after by the local authority, it will be important to establish whether they are subject to a care order (or interim care order) or are being voluntarily accommodated by the local authority. If the local authority accommodates the child or young person, voluntarily, parents or others with parental responsibility, have the same rights in relation to treatment as they would otherwise. Admission and or treatment decisions should, therefore, be discussed with the parent or person with parental responsibility (see CA 1989, s 22).

If the child or young person is subject to a care order, the local authority acquire overarching parental responsibility. Parents, and any others with parental responsibility retain PR and should be kept informed and consulted about admission and or treatment decisions. However, where the local authority is satisfied that it is necessary to do so to safeguard or promote the child or young person's welfare, they can limit the extent to which parents (or others) may exercise their parental responsibility. In areas where there is a significant issue of dispute the court in practice would be asked to decide (CA 1989, s 33(3)(b)).

4. Are the young person's parents parties at a tribunal?

No, not if it is the young person who has made the application, or if hospital managers have made a referral to the MHT. Parents (including next of kin) have no absolute right to attend, but the MHT panel can decide if it would be helpful if they do, as this may help with considering matters like accommodation and support if the patient is discharged from the section. The exception is when the parent as the nearest relative has made an application to the tribunal.

5. What happens when a young person is detained in a CAMHS unit but then becomes 18?

Most CAMHS units will try to complete a course of treatment so that the young person can be discharged before they are 18. When a young person needs to continue their inpatient treatment, then arrangements are made with the equivalent adult service. The transfer should be planned and with as much consultation and agreement from the patient as is possible. However, not all the facilities and therapies available in CAMHS services are replicated in all adult services. Psychology is limited on many adult acute wards, and there is very little specific education; it's mainly occupational therapy.

6. What is Section 17 leave, and why is it important?

Section 17 leave is granted by the patient's responsible clinician (RC), usually the consultant psychiatrist, and allows them to leave the hospital, from a short period of time for overnight stays, leading to longer periods away from the hospital before being discharged. This allows the patient and their clinical team to test out how they will cope in the community, including their compliance with medication and ensure their home is habitable before returning. Patients are usually first given escorted Section 17 leave, which means the patient is allowed off the ward with a member of staff.

7. Does there need to be a MHT to discharge a patient from the section?

The patient's RC may discharge a patient who has been compulsorily detained where they have co-operated with their treatment and no longer needs to be on the section. They may remain as a voluntary patient, or they may leave. The exception is in the case of forensic patients, subject to restricted hospital orders, where the RC does not have the power to discharge the patient without the decision of a MHT or the consent of Secretary of State.

8. Do all patients have a solicitor?

Yes, all detained patients have a right to legal representation at a tribunal hearing; this is provided free by legal aid to all patients who appeal or are referred. The patient can choose from a list provided by the hospital of lawyers who specialise in mental health law. The representative visits the patient in hospital to take instructions and help the patient challenge the statutory criteria that upholds their detention.

9. What if the patient doesn't want a solicitor?

The RC will assess the patient's capacity as to whether they can make an informed decision not to have a legal representative; the patient can represent themselves. If the patient has capacity, then they do not have to have a solicitor if they do not want one. If they do not have capacity, then a solicitor is appointed under Rule 11.7 (b) to act for them. Overall, 97 per cent of patients are represented by a legal representative.

10. Do all MHT hearings take place in the hospital with the panel present?

Until March 2020, all hearings were undertaken at the hospital where the patient resided. A few video hearings have been carried out at high secure hospitals because the patient has been very unwell; it was not safe to attend in person. The Covid-19 pandemic has caused many changes in the way mental health hearings are carried out; they are all being held remotely, usually by video and by the usual three-person panel, so the panel does not visit the hospital. Some have been dealt with as paper hearings on the reports when the patient is not contesting their detention.

Further information

Adolescent Mental Health Care and the Law; Camilla Parker 2020

https://www.mentalcapacitylawandpolicy.org.uk/resources-2/liberty-protection-safeguards-resources/

Department of Health – Mental Health Act 1983: Code of Practice

https://www.gov.uk/government/publications/code-of-practice-mental-health-act-1983

Mental Health Act Manual, Richard Jones, Sweet and Maxwell ISBN: 9780414078970

https://www.mentalhealthlaw.co.uk/Richard_Jones,_Mental_Health_Act_Manual_(23rd_edn,_Sweet_and_Maxwell_2020)

Dept of Education – Children Act 1989 guidance and regulations; Children's homes, Chapter 4

https://assets.publishing.service.gov.uk/government/uploads/system/uploads/attachment_data/file/275695/ch_guidance_final_master_for_pub_oct_2013.pdf

Mind – Information and support

https://www.mind.org.uk/news-campaigns/news/mind-comments-on-sharp-rise-in-mental-health-act-detentions/

Young Minds – Your Guide to Inpatient Care

https://youngminds.org.uk/young-person/your-guide-to-support/inpatient-care/

Chapter 22

Violent and risky behaviour and mental disorders

22.01 *It is important to recognise that it is the behaviour that is dangerous, not the person with the mental illness. Most acts of violence are committed by individuals who are not mentally ill, and most individuals with serious mental illness are not dangerous. Those with a serious mental disorder can be victimised by violent acts more often than they commit violent acts themselves. Statistics indicate that there are around 700 homicides in England and Wales a year and only about 10 per cent of these are by mentally ill patients (defined as people who have been in contact with mental health services in the 12 months prior to the homicide). Those with serious mental illness, receiving effective treatment, are no more dangerous than individuals in the general population.*

FORENSIC SERVICES

22.02 In England and Wales, forensic services provide care and treatment for mentally disordered offenders who have carried out violent crimes. They are cared for in high, medium and low security in-patient facilities as well as in forensic accommodation in the community. High security units admit individuals detained under the Mental Health Act 1983 who 'require treatment under conditions of high security on account of their dangerous, violent or criminal propensities'. Medium security units were developed in the late 1970s to bridge the gap between high security and general psychiatric care, and are designed for those patients detained under the Mental Health Act 1983 who 'pose a serious danger to the public'.

There is a higher proportion of male forensic patients than female, especially in high and medium security settings. Male patients make up 94 per cent of the patients in high security units and 82 per cent of the patients in medium security units. There are currently three high security hospitals in England, providing just over 700 beds, and around 60 medium security hospitals, providing around 3,500 beds, with nearly 35 per cent of those beds provided by the independent sector. For women, the independent sector provides the majority – 75 per cent – of medium and low security beds.

Forensic psychiatry – This is a specialism within psychiatry. The purpose of forensic psychiatric care is to improve the mental health of mentally disordered offenders while reducing their risk of reoffending. Forensic psychiatrists have specific training in the assessment and management of risk to limit further harm to the patient, their family, healthcare professionals and the public. Some forensic patients are diagnosed by prison in-reach psychiatric services because their mental disorder only became apparent after they were sentenced and imprisoned. Other mentally disordered offenders may be diverted to hospital directly from the court.

VIOLENT AND RISKY BEHAVIOUR IN ADULTS

22.03 The illnesses of violent mentally disordered patients are serious; typically schizophrenia and schizoaffective disorder alone or in combination with antisocial personality disorder. Their criminal acts are as a result of mental illness, so they act on their delusions or hallucinations. Rarely, there are obsessional conditions – for example autism spectrum disorder or obsessive-compulsive disorder – that may lead to risky behaviour such as arson. Some people obtain sexual gratification from fire-setting, known as paraphilia. Forensic patients who are sex offenders may have committed the crime because of their psychosis or personality disorder.

Patients can require treatment over many years, particularly if they have a complex mental disorder, and psychological treatment is needed. If a parent has been a forensic patient, then there is an increased risk that they will harm family members as well as others. Before being considered for discharge, patients are required to show understanding and insight into their condition, and empathy for their victim. Some patients never achieve this, despite years of psychological treatment and medication. Patients will have a carefully planned discharge when this is considered safe, and any risks are manageable in the community. Sexual offenders must have their details on the Sex Offenders Register; many occupations and residences are forbidden to them.

The Secretary of State for Justice and the Mental Health Tribunal (MHT), and sometimes, the Parole Board, have a role in the release of forensic patients. In the MHT, these patients are called 'restricted' and the judge of the panel who hears their case has experience of criminal law. (See **Chapter 21** Detention and the Mental Health Act 1983.)

Mental health disorders associated with violent, risky and antisocial behaviour

22.04 Some people with particular mental disorders can pose an increased risk to others. In most cases, the person will not be a threat to others unless there is both a mental disorder plus a trigger event present. The risk of homicide is rare.

People who are risky to others are: those who have already carried out a violent act; those who have been convicted of violence; perpetrators of domestic abuse; and those under the influence of drugs and alcohol.

The most dangerous behaviours towards other people are: radicalisation; arson and fire-setting; abduction; sexual offences; and stalking.

The more dangerous mental health conditions and their associated risks are:

Schizophrenia and **Schizoaffective disorders** (**Chapter 12**)	People with these disorders can be a risk when under the influence of their paranoid delusions – particularly command hallucinations, when the person hears a voice instructing them to act in a way that endangers themselves or others.
Postpartum psychosis (**Chapter 11**)	Some mothers with postpartum psychosis can take their baby's life because of a delusional belief.
Bipolar affective disorder (**Chapter 12**)	This disorder can make a person's behaviour risky when elated – they may feel invincible. There is also a risk of suicide when the person is depressed.
Delusional disorder (**Chapter 12**)	A delusional belief may lead the person to feel that life is not only impossible for them, but also for their partner and child.
Antisocial personality disorder (**Chapter 13**)	Someone with antisocial personality disorder can be a risk and danger at any time if they are frustrated, thwarted or feel belittled.
Fabricated illness (**Chapter 11**)	Induced illness and treatment by a carer, usually the mother, can cause significant harm to the child.

There are occasional tragic media reports of a parent seeking revenge on a partner or spouse by killing their children. This is more likely to be a vengeful act by a person with (possibly undiagnosed) personality disorder traits, than someone with a diagnosed mental disorder. In all cases, the perpetrator is at risk of suicide after murdering their children.

Other conditions associated with violent and antisocial behaviour

22.05 Paedophilia – This is the sexual preference for prepubescent children aged under 13. A person must be at least 16 years old, and at least five years older than the prepubescent child, for the attraction to be diagnosed as paedophilia. The International Classification of Diseases (ICD-11) defines it as a 'sustained, focused, and intense pattern of sexual arousal – as manifested by persistent sexual thoughts, fantasies, urges, or behaviours – involving prepubescent children.'

While not causes of paedophilia themselves, childhood abuse by adults, or comorbid psychiatric illnesses such as personality disorders and substance misuse, are risk factors for acting on child sexually abusive thoughts. The majority of paedophiles are male, but there are also female paedophiles.

In 80 per cent of offenders, sexual behaviour arises out of a relationship to a child who is a member of the family or known to the family. Vulnerable children may be more at risk of being groomed because they may be seeking affection. Fifteen per cent of people convicted for paedophilia are later reconvicted, though this is probably an underestimate of reoffending.

Offenders with a learning disability – The majority of offences carried out by people with a learning disability are minor crimes such as petty theft, or acts of criminal damage. These offences are often opportunistic and carried out without much planning, and they may be in response to suggestions from others.

Learning disabled offenders whose behaviour is abnormally aggressive and seriously irresponsible are diagnosed as also having a mental disorder. People with a learning disability who commit sexual offences, such as indecent exposure or sexual assaults of an impulsive nature, may misinterpret the nature of a relationship with another individual. Factors contributing to this misinterpretation include the person's lack of social skills and limited outlets for their sexual urges. Arson carried out by such people is often without a clear motive; it may be the result of the person acting out frustration caused by rejection. People with a learning disability are more likely to be victims of crime than perpetrators.

Stalkers – Stalking is the repeated harassing of, and threatening behaviour towards, another person. The majority of cases involve domestic partners, estranged spouses, or romantic obsessions. Stalking is considered to be such a risk that there is a specialised joint Metropolitan Police and NHS mental health unit – the Fixated Threat Assessment Centre – whose function is to manage the threat to politicians, members of the Royal Family and other public figures of people becoming fixated on them. Stalking is a behaviour seen in people with a paranoid personality disorder, sociopathic personality disorder, schizophrenia and those with autism spectrum disorder who have fixated interests.

Older offenders – People aged over 60 years account for just 1 per cent of overall recorded crime. Sexually inappropriate behaviours are a common feature in some types of dementia, especially if the frontal lobe is affected. Older adults are capable of committing the most serious sexual offences; there is no reduction in risk of reoffending based on age alone. Nearly 60 per cent of male prisoners over the age of 60 are sex offenders.

Partner homicide committed by older people occurs for different reasons compared to the younger age group. In the younger group, there are usually backgrounds of jealousy, money disputes and infidelity, and homicide is often fuelled by alcohol and/or drugs. In contrast, homicides by older people often occur in apparently close, loving relationships. The perpetrators do not generally have previous convictions, and the action could be prompted by the partner suffering from a terminal illness. The term 'mercy killing' is used if the act is seen more as assisted suicide than homicide, but it remains a crime in the UK.

Child victims of homicide – There were 68 child victims of homicide aged under 16 years in the year ending March 2019; this was the highest number since the year ending March 2004. For almost a third of child victims, the suspect was a parent or step-parent. Nearly a third of these parents had a previous conviction for violence. Child victims of homicide aged under one are most likely to be killed by their biological mother – 60 per cent of cases. Other perpetrators of homicide of children under one are the biological father, or the mother's new partner (not the father of the baby). It's very rare for a child to be murdered by a stranger.

VULNERABILITY FACTORS FOR RADICALISATION AND EXTREMISM

22.06 Most individuals who commit terrorist acts are not mentally ill. Their behaviour is shaped by a complex series of interacting psychological, social, political and personal drivers. When mental illness is present, it is more likely that the person will act alone and not be part of a terrorist group.

Autism spectrum disorder (ASD) – People with ASD may have obsessive interests, so they may not appreciate the risks extremism presents to themselves or others. Extremist groups may claim to provide an explanation for the chaos that someone with ASD may perceive their world to be. An organisation with fixed and ceremonial rituals may appeal to them.

Depression and **adjustment disorders** – People with these disorders may be vulnerable to others who offer escapism, hope, redemption and meaning to their lives. In those who feel anger as well as anguish, the vengeful ideas of terrorism may offer something to attach their pain to. Extremist acts may be seen as the only way to make the world listen. They may even wish to be reunited with their loved ones in death.

Mania – This may be a feature of other conditions such as bipolar affective disorder. Manic episodes may lead to a grandiose sense of needing, and having the capability, to create and influence world events. The irritability associated with mania may trigger anger linked to risk-taking and lack of inhibitions.

Psychosis and **schizophrenia** – Delusional ideas related to a perceived threat from a hostile enemy, and ideas of reference from news networks that the affected individual is being personally addressed, can have a direct role in shaping that person's vulnerability to radicalisation. If they also have ideas of grandeur, they may feel they have an important role to play. If their bizarre behaviour provokes others, which results in retaliation, this could confirm their belief that they are vulnerable from threats. It may seem to the person that the only people who understand these threats are other extremists.

Post-traumatic stress disorder (PTSD) – The dissociation and detachment felt by people with this disorder may contribute to the lifting of inhibitions, where the person feels emotionally numb in response to the consequences of extremist violence. There is no evidence that links PTSD due to combat with extremist violence.

Personality disorders – The factors in people with personality disorders that are relevant include poor impulse control, variable moods, a grandiose sense of entitlement (narcissism) and a paranoid cognitive style, so they perceive faults as other people's and not theirs. Those with an antisocial personality may see violence as exciting and a way to gratify themselves. Extremist groups match the person's inclination to fight authority and may provide a 'noble rationale' for resisting rules. These groups may even help the individual to attribute their own failure to an oppressive society.

People with an emotionally unstable personality disorder often have an unbalanced sense of themselves, so extremist groups can appeal as they offer security. The group may offer the person an intense and concrete new identity. They may idolise the group leader, seeing them as a safe attachment figure. Those who have frequent thoughts of suicide could find a death cause appealing.

Alcohol and drug addictions – Addictions may create vulnerability, increasing the risk of the person to themselves and removing their inhibitions. People who have a heightened need for taking risks can be drawn to using substances, and may also find extremism appealing as a risky cause. Some terrorist groups routinely use substances as disinhibitions or energisers.

VIOLENT AND RISKY BEHAVIOUR IN CHILDREN AND YOUNG PEOPLE

22.07 Young people detained in the criminal justice system in a young offender institution are three times more likely to have mental health problems than young people in the general population. They are also likely to have more than one mental health problem, a learning disability, be dependent on drugs or alcohol, and to have experienced a range of other challenges. Many of these needs go unrecognised and unmet. These difficulties may be caused by a range of factors: biological; psychological; family; community; cultural; and peer pressure.

Most young people who commit serious crimes have had disturbing and traumatic experiences during childhood, and many are in the care of their local authority. They have often experienced trauma leading to PTSD. Their traumatic experiences may include: separation and estrangement from parents; the death of a parent or main carer; sexual abuse; severe physical chastisement; domestic abuse; and substance abuse. Many have attempted suicide, although death in this group is most often as a result of a drug overdose, injury or violence.

Group behaviour – Children and young people who engage in risky behaviours can act in a group or alone. Those who are in gangs engage in risky behaviours, such as insisting their members are armed, carrying out dangerous initiation rituals, or becoming involved with drug dealing. Gang members can exert peer pressure and dare each other to carry out violent acts, especially when under the influence of drugs or alcohol. They may have been abused or neglected to the extent that they feel no empathy for other people.

Lone behaviour – Children and young people who engage in risky and dangerous behaviours on their own include: those whose home life has been unstable or lacking boundaries; those who have a fascination with guns, knives or other weapons; and those who aren't able to sense other people's emotions. Such children may have a severe conduct disorder, which is the equivalent of antisocial personality disorder in adults. Past risky behaviour is a good indicator of future risky behaviour, and violence tends to escalate over time. For example, if a child has assaulted a family member, they may pose an ongoing danger. This can include engaging in violence and abuse towards other children or animals.

Unplanned pregnancies – A review of published research showed a high prevalence of pregnancies (around a third) among detained adolescent females. A high proportion of detained adolescent males have already fathered children or been responsible for a pregnancy. The high rate of alcohol and drug misuse by these adolescents increases the likelihood of their babies having foetal alcohol syndrome disorder and/or perinatal substance dependence.

Adolescent sex offenders

22.08 Adolescents appear to commit a significant amount of all sexual offending. Typically, sexual abuse is only one form of their criminal behaviour. Different groups of adolescent sex offenders have been identified:

- The first group are adolescents who have carried out offences against children. This group are more likely to victimise males and people related to them. They tend to have social deficits and low self-esteem and have been subject to childhood sexual abuse themselves.
- The second group targets peers or adults. They are more likely to act with another offender, target female strangers and are more antisocial. They tend to report early exposure to pornography, have witnessed family violence and have criminally involved family members.

The mental disorders associated with risky and dangerous behaviour

22.09 Aggression in children and young people can be a symptom of several different underlying problems and any number of psychiatric conditions, medical problems and life circumstances.

Behaviour disorders – Conduct disorders and attention deficit hyperactivity disorder (ADHD) are the most common behaviour disorders. These disorders are characterised by impulsivity and poor decision-making, which can lead to behaviour that's interpreted as aggressive. Children with these conditions often do not consider the consequences of their actions. With conduct disorders, aggressiveness is part of the matrix of the illness and a large component of the disorder can be intentionally malicious behaviour. The treatment and prognosis for a conduct disorder are quite different to those for ADHD (see **Chapter 5**).

Developmental disorders – Children and young people who have problems with cognition (intellectual impairment) or communication (such as with autism spectrum disorder) may also display aggression. When children with these conditions become aggressive, it's often because they have difficulty dealing with their anxiety or frustration or verbalising their feelings. The aggression may also be a form of impulsivity (see **Chapter 7**).

Psychotic disorders – Young people who have bipolar affective disorder may become aggressive in their manic stages. They may lose self-control and become impulsive. At the other end of the spectrum, when they become depressed, they can be irritable and sometimes that irritability causes them to lash out. These disorders may also show themselves as aggressive. For example, a young person with schizophrenia may respond to internal stimuli which make them mistrustful or suspicious, and they may then act aggressively (see **Chapter 8**).

Injury and trauma – Sometimes there are organic reasons for aggressive outbursts, such as when a child has frontal lobe damage or certain types of epilepsy. In these cases, there may be no understandable reason for aggressive episodes.

Adolescents vulnerable to radicalisation and extremism

22.10 Young people from a variety of religious and ethnic cultures and upbringings can become subject to radicalisation. They can be at greater risk of radicalisation at this stage in their life because adolescents are exploring their identity and sense of belonging and are more easily influenced. Extremist messages or membership of a group can offer a sense of purpose, community and identity. Some of the common factors that increase vulnerability are:

- feeling isolated and lonely or wanting to belong;
- being unhappy about themselves and what others might think of them;
- feeling embarrassed or judged about their culture, gender, religion or race;
- becoming distanced from their cultural or religious background;
- questioning their place in society;
- being depressed, stressed or traumatised;
- having low self-esteem;
- being bullied or mistreated by other people or by society;
- feeling angry at other people or those in power;

- experiencing difficulties interacting socially and lacking empathy;
- not understanding the consequences of their actions; and
- feeling pressured to stand up for other people who are being oppressed.

Any of these factors make children and young people more susceptible to believing that extremists' claims are the answer to their problems. External factors also play their part, such as community tension, events affecting the country or region where they or their parents originate from, or having friends or family who have joined extremist groups. Exposure to one-sided points of view also contributes to the process of radicalisation. Extremist groups often target young people via the internet and social media. The process may involve being groomed online or in person, making the individual vulnerable to exploitation (including sexual exploitation), psychological manipulation, and exposure to violent material and other inappropriate information.

Case study – Dangerous young people – Keith's story (see Appendix: Case studies, p 353.)

Further information

ONS – Homicide in England and Wales: year ending March 2019

https://www.ons.gov.uk/peoplepopulationandcommunity/crimeandjustice/articles/homicideinenglandandwales/yearendingmarch2019

HQIP – Inquiry into suicide and homicide by people with mental Illness

https://www.hqip.org.uk/resource/national-confidential-inquiry-into-suicide-and-homicide-annual-report-2017/#.YV3IVi8w1qs

Forensic psychiatry: Fundamentals and clinical practice

Puri and Treasaden ISBN 9781444135213
https://www.routledge.com/Forensic-Psychiatry-Fundamentals-and-Clinical-Practice/Puri-Treasaden/p/book/9781444135213

Risk assessment and management instrument for forensic mental health patients

http://hcr-20.com

Social psychiatric epidemiology – Long-stay in forensic-psychiatric care in the UK

https://www.ncbi.nlm.nih.gov/pmc/articles/PMC5842247/

RAN H&SC – Extremism, radicalisation & mental health

https://ec.europa.eu/home-affairs/pages/page/ran-hsc-handbook-extremism-radicalisation-mental-health-handbook-practitioners-november_en

Department for Education and Home Office – Educate against hate

https://educateagainsthate.com/which-children-and-young-people-are-vulnerable-to-radicalisation/

Appendix

Case studies

Appendix: Case Studies

EARLY ATTACHMENT DIFFICULTIES – SARA'S STORY

This is a case heard at a mental health tribunal. Sara, aged 34, was detained on a Community Treatment Order (CTO) and had made an application for discharge from the order. A CTO means the patient lives in the community but must accept conditions, usually about attending appointments with the community mental health team. Sara had been diagnosed as suffering from several mental disorders; emotionally unstable personality disorder (EUPD), antisocial personality disorder, and had a mild learning disability, complicated by harmful use of alcohol and drug abuse.

Sara is the third of six sisters and appears to have achieved normal developmental milestones. She reported not attending school until the age of six and being expelled from several schools for fighting. Eventually, Sara became the subject of an Education, Health and Care plan (EHC plan) and assessed as having learning difficulties. She then attended a school specifically for children with mild to moderate learning difficulties, leaving at the age of 15 without qualifications; her literacy remains poor.

Sara's family was chaotic. The local authority children's services were alerted a year before Sara's birth because a sister of hers was diagnosed with hypothermia, then six months later described as 'not thriving'. Concerns were raised by the schools and the police about the children being malnourished and unkempt. Sara was eventually taken into care at age 11. She remained in contact with her family, but several foster placements broke down because of her absconding and disturbed behaviour, often due to being intoxicated with alcohol. She reports being encouraged by her father to drink alcohol at age seven and used drugs, including heroin, cocaine, ecstasy, cannabis and amphetamines, from the age 13. Sara later alleged sexual abuse by her father, saying he had prostituted her to get money for alcohol.

Sara was first referred to mental health services at the age of 17 due to repeated self-harm and was diagnosed with depression. Her behaviours became more unsafe impulsive and repetitive, with potentially severe consequences, such as when she set a fire in a hostel and a hospital; this led to a prosecution followed by ten years of hospital admissions to forensic psychiatric units. Sara was noted to be vulnerable under the influence of alcohol, becoming sexually disinhibited. She had a child at the age of 29 (five years ago) who was taken into care at birth, due to the risk from her poor mental health. The baby's father was unknown.

At the time of the tribunal hearing, Sara had been subject to a CTO for two years. Although she has had four hospital admissions since then, these have only been for a matter of weeks and have not involved incidents of fire-setting. There has been an improvement in her ability to control her impulsivity, helped by years of psychological work, psychotropic medication and intensive emotional and practical support. Sara is living in supported accommodation with five other women and 24-hour staff support. She does not work or have any current relationships. Staff need to prompt her to wash, keep her bedroom clean and tidy, and she finds it difficult to stay focused on activities unless these are her own choice. She enjoys shopping in charity shops for clothes.

At the tribunal hearing, Sara's clinical team described her as displaying superficial insight into her mental health problems. She acknowledged the role of medication and the support of staff in improving her mental state and reducing her unsettled behaviour. Still, she struggled to reflect on her problems at a deeper level, and although she has expressed remorse for self-harming and aggressive behaviours, she seems unable to control these. Most of the time, she is reasonably stable and taking medication, which includes mood stabilisers and the antipsychotic, clozapine; this medication is recognised treatment for severe EUPD. The tribunal panel also heard about the risks to Sara's health and safety. Two years previously, when her mood was low, there were concerns about her attempting to jump in front of trains and numerous self-inflicted injuries including a black eye and burns. The tribunal panel decided that the power of recall to the hospital (which is possible with the CTO) was needed to manage these risks effectively.

Interestingly, although it was Sara's application for the CTO to be lifted, she accepted the decision of the panel for it to remain in place. It is possible that she recognised that the legal structure of the CTO and the supported accommodation offered her security and protection and was potentially nurturing. For the first time, she is considering whether she could do voluntary work in a charity shop – Sara joked that she 'would get first divvy on the clothes'.

Questions to consider

What would be expected before a decision was made to take Sara's baby into care at birth?

A parenting assessment would be expected. In summary, this would include an examination of Sara's mental disorder and her ability to meet her baby's physical and emotional needs.

In Sara's case, what could have been the risks of her mental health to the baby?

There were concerns about Sara's impulsive behaviour, self-harm and suicide attempts, and the difficulty she has forming and maintaining relationships. If the only issues were her lack of literacy and a learning disability, these alone would have not inevitably resulted in the baby being taken into care, especially if Sara were able to rely on and accept support from family and professionals. However, her mental disorder and her troubled upbringing plus the learning disability all contributed to the decision to take the baby into care.

Have mental health services helped Sara progress and overcome her early difficulties?

There is strong evidence that Sara has progressed. Her very risky behaviour, resulting in years of forensic inpatient care, has remitted. Recent hospital admissions have been short. She has been able to maintain herself in the community with support. She has not absconded from the accommodation, and neither have her hospital admissions or behaviour jeopardised her accommodation. She has gained insight in that she accepts the need for such support and that legal measures are required (the CTO). The tribunal panel considered Sara's intention to engage in voluntary work, which she enjoys, was a strength and was a positive plan for her future.

(Back to **Chapter 1**.)

ENMESHED FAMILY – BEA'S STORY

Bea was 16 at the time of the mental health tribunal hearing. She was detained on Section 3 (a treatment order) of the Mental Health Act 1983 in a specialist adolescent psychiatric unit. She had applied to the tribunal to come off section and be discharged to her parent's care.

Bea required continuous supervision as she repeatedly tried to tie ligatures around her neck and self-harmed by cutting herself with objects she contrived to obtain – pieces of CD and a plastic pen, for example. At times, she refused food and fluids so had to be fed by nasogastric tube under restraint.

This was Bea's fifth admission to a psychiatric unit. Each time, she and her parents had complained so much about the care she received that any therapeutic relationship had broken down and she was moved to another unit. There was now no adolescent unit that had not been tried and no other provision that could manage her behaviours. She had been on this unit for six weeks and was 120 miles from the family home.

Bea had little contact with the other young people on the unit. Typically, she did not participate in groups or activities when they were held but did them alone afterwards. For example, when the activity was painting, Bea did some supervised crochet work at the side of the room, but then used the paints and created her own pictures when others had left.

Bea phoned her parents at least five times each day with complaints about her care. These ranged from feeling ignored by staff, to nasogastric feeding times being late, to missing the family dog and querying why it could not come on a visit. Her commonest complaint was about the attitude of the staff who were supervising her: 'they're just care assistants' or 'they don't watch me closely all the time'. When she self-harmed, she blamed the staff for not preventing her access to the objects used. Bea's parents would then phone the ward to pass on her complaints and become demanding when they felt these were not taken seriously enough each time.

Over the six weeks on this new unit, the clinical team were trying to establish clear lines of communication with the parents which did not involve Bea, such as a weekly meeting with the consultant (a level of input not given to any other patient's parents). They wished to limit Bea's time on the phone, but not deprive her completely. Efforts by the occupational therapist and psychologist to interest Bea in previously gratifying activities (she had been a keen athlete and artist) were underway. The suggestion that family therapy would help the parents separate from Bea and allow her to focus on her recovery had been met by disbelief from the parents, who asked: 'Surely it's the unit that is at fault, not us?' Bea refused to participate.

At the tribunal hearing, it became apparent that Bea read her parents' emails and texts when they visited, as she referred to some email correspondence between her social worker and father. Bea appeared dismissive of her mother who said Bea demanded to read the emails and texts and she couldn't refuse; her father said he thought Bea should read everything written about her.

Bea's father remained visibly annoyed for most of the hearing, sighing in an obvious manner when Bea's consultant psychiatrist was describing the behavioural contract designed to help Bea. Her mother brought a huge file of paperwork to illustrate how the different hospitals and units had failed to meet Bea's needs. Both parents and Bea maintained there must be another unit closer to home that could properly help.

Questions to consider

What mental disorders could Bea's behaviour be demonstrating?

Bea is showing a dramatic change in behaviour from a previously, apparently, successful young person to someone withdrawn from any 'normal' life. She is detained in hospital, choosing not to socialise with peers and not able to make trusting and supportive relationships with staff.

Mental disorders that result in such dramatic behaviours include severe depression and eating disorders; these can affect a previously successful young person. Autism can also present with social difficulties and withdrawal but seem unlikely if Bea's previous level of functioning is confirmed. Although the diagnosis of a personality disorder is generally not made until much later in adolescence, Bea's angry withdrawal, described by the team as 'passive-aggressive' when she does not join in but pointedly does the activities later, is considered significant.

The panel was convinced by the hospital's clinical team's case that Bea should remain detained on section, as she was suffering from a mental disorder with a diagnosis of emotional and behavioural disorder and eating disorder. The treating consultant psychiatrist also indicated an additional diagnosis of pervasive arousal withdrawal syndrome (PAWS), an extreme state of depression.

What could the parents' behaviour be demonstrating about the family dynamics?

In the tribunal panel's deliberations after the evidence, it was agreed that there were two 'elephants in the room'. Firstly, what had happened to change this previously 'normal' child to one who was presenting such problematic and self-destructive behaviours?

Bea's 'invisible' elder sister was only mentioned in passing in the social circumstances report. She was at university, living away from home with her boyfriend. The tribunal members would have liked the clinical team to have obtained her opinion of the family dynamics and family history; the issue of sexual abuse was not excluded in any of the reports.

The second 'elephant' was whether the parents were willing to have Bea return home, which was her wish and the reason for her application for the section to be lifted. Despite being asked in several different ways by the panel, they were unable to give a clear view on this, other than to complain about Bea's care and demand a change of unit. The panel repeatedly explained that their role was not to decide the care package or in the context of this hearing, recommend a transfer to another unit. The parents had not requested for Bea to have any home leave from any of the units, just that she should be made better by 'appropriate treatment'.

What are the treatment options for Bea's family?

The clinical team said 'appropriate treatment 'would include individual psychological work and family therapy. The consultant told the tribunal panel that they had accepted Bea on the understanding from the funding authorities that there were no other NHS or private units suitable. There are a limited number of such specialist units so young people may be placed a long way from their home area. The father was indignant when told by the panel that they could not recommend a transfer to another unit; he stormed out, and his wife followed when called.

What is the prognosis for Bea?

The current unit was optimistic with their plan for clarifying lines of communication with the family and the proposed therapies: the weekly meeting for information exchange with the parents was to be separate from therapy by a skilled family therapist on the unit.

(Back to **Chapter 2**.)

CONDUCT DISORDER – TRUDI'S STORY

Trudi was 15 years old when she was referred to the Child and Adolescent Mental Health Service (CAMHS) outpatients for assessment. She had allegedly been sexually abused by her stepfather. Her biological mother had refused to believe her daughter, but a police investigation was instigated. In the meantime, Trudi was in a short-term foster placement, where she was showing difficult behaviour, aggression towards the foster parents' own children, and refusing to go to school. When she did go to school, she was aggressive to younger children and verbally abusive to teachers. This was all recent behaviour. She had previously been a keen student who had a passion for her local drama club and playing hockey and enjoyed spending time with her friends.

At her first sessions with a female CAMHS therapist, Trudi presented as indifferent to her situation. She was very difficult to engage in therapy, remaining silent or shrugging in response to questions or suggestions. She would only say that she missed her three-year-old stepbrother (whose father was Trudi's stepfather) very much, and said that was why she was not attending school. She would not discuss how she was feeling. The therapist was concerned that Trudi was depressed and disguising this by her indifference.

Weekly therapy continued. The investigation into Trudi's allegation proceeded, and abuse was proven true. The mother cut off all contact with Trudi, and she was heard by the social worker to blame her for the stepfather's subsequent custodial sentence, and she refused to have her home.

Trudi told the therapist that when her stepfather abused her, she felt powerful as it was their secret from her mother and stated that was why at first she had not told anyone. She had only spoken out when her mother had refused to give her money to attend a concert with friends, and she wanted to gain the upper hand over her. Despite her reluctance to keep to rules in the foster home and at school, Trudi did attend reasonably on time for her therapy sessions.

As therapy continued, Trudi began copying the therapist's clothing, hairstyle and accessories. This was explored and gently challenged, but Trudi did not acknowledge it. She began to self-harm and to go missing from the foster placement, repeatedly presenting at A&E saying she had self-harmed or was about to. The foster parents were unable to cope, and Trudi was transferred to a residential placement. There, her self-harm became life-threatening, and she was admitted to a local CAMHS psychiatric inpatient unit and was sectioned under the Mental Health Act 1983.

Trudi was diagnosed with a conduct disorder and subsequently moved to another adolescent unit specialising in young people who self-harm. Her original therapist was invited to attend a review to establish Trudi's initial presentation and strengths. It emerged that a second female therapist, from the CAMHS inpatient unit, had been targeted by Trudi, who when on leave from the unit had followed her home, making such threats that the police became involved.

Trudi by this time was in seclusion (isolation) due to the severity of her self-harming, which included tying ligatures with clothing and cutting herself with objects. Any mention of her mother by the clinical team worsened her behaviour, but Trudi refused to discuss her emotions.

The saddest aspect for the therapist was that Trudi was now regarded as a safeguarding risk to her stepbrother, now aged five, because of her self-harming behaviour and impulsivity. She had therefore lost all contact with her family.

Questions to consider

Is Trudi's report about abuse making her feel powerful a usual reaction?

No, usually children who are being abused experience fear, sadness, anger, guilt, self-blame and confusion. They can feel humiliated or self-conscious, and will often not feel equipped or able to talk about what has happened. Sometimes, a child may be confused if they experienced positive physical pleasure, arousal, or emotional intimacy from the abuse. The abuser may convince the child that he or she enjoyed it and wanted it to happen.

So, Trudi's feeling of power is either misdirected anger towards her mother who she may feel is not protecting her, a denial of Trudi's own powerlessness in this situation or evidence of the psychological manipulation of her abuser.

Has her mother's disbelief worsened Trudi's conduct disorder?

More than 8 out of 10 children who are sexually abused know their abuser; they are usually family members, friends, neighbours or babysitters. For Trudi's mother to accept Trudi's allegation, she must take her word rather than that of her partner and father of her son. Believing Trudi would mean that her own judgement as a mother is at fault for choosing him. To Trudi's mother, the disclosure of the abuse when Trudi had been thwarted from attending a concert may have seemed vindictive or fantasy.

When the abuser is prosecuted, the child can face the loss of all their family support, as happened to Trudi. They may consider they have nothing to gain by good behaviour. The behaviour leading to a diagnosis of conduct disorder is not a conscious choice.

Does the breakdown of her foster placement inevitably mean the worst prognosis for Trudi?

The prognosis is worse if a child cannot be managed at a placement; the more failures, usually means the worse the prognosis. The changes in Trudi's conduct, with aggression, impulsivity and self-harm, could indicate depression in addition to an emerging emotionally unstable personality disorder. Trudi's earlier academic potential suggests a more stable personality structure, which appeared evident before the abuse.

Is Trudi's fixation on the female therapists a feature of a conduct disorder?

A child or young person with a conduct disorder, (also known as a disinhibited social engagement disorder and or oppositional defiant disorder) would typically have problems forming relationships; Trudi did not have features of these disorders before the age of five.

However, Trudi has lost all female role models. Her mother has rejected her by not believing her. She has either alienated herself or been abandoned from previous friends and school teachers, sports or drama coaches by school refusal or difficult behaviour there. Thinking back to the abuse may fill Trudi with disgust that all these people were in her life while this was going on, and she may be blaming them.

Her copying of the therapist's style of dress may be viewed as an attempt to avoid abandonment by another female figure. Also, there is no 'safe adult' for her within her family, so the therapist becomes this figure. The therapist is also in the position of being the 'ideal' figure that Trudi's mother was not, and which Trudi wishes to aspire to herself.

It is common for young people who have been abused to shift their notion of the therapist to being supportive to being rejected in line with shifts in their emotional states. The persecution of the second therapist is an extreme reaction to Trudi fearing rejection by the therapist.

(Back to **Chapter 5**.)

ANXIETY DISORDER – MICHAEL'S STORY

Michael is seven and has an older brother. He has always been a 'nervy' child, according to his mother. He has been refusing to go to school and found the transition from infant to junior school difficult. He says that he will be killed at school. He is also scared to go to bed alone.

Michael's mother describes herself as sensitive and ladylike in comparison to her own sister, so she initially saw Michael's fear as evidence of him being sensitive and artistic like herself. She also has a phobia of thunderstorms and being struck by lightning which restricts her activities. Michael's father is impatient with Michael, thinking him a 'cissy' in comparison to his rumbustious older brother.

Through play therapy, Michael has disclosed that he watched an X-rated violent film with his older brother in which a boy was stalked and killed. He is convinced that this could happen to him.

Questions to consider

Why has Michael's anxiety peaked in this way?

He is described as an anxious child, with a possible genetic predisposition. The mother appears to see Michael as an extension of herself as she identifies with his sensitiveness. Therefore there are perpetuating factors of almost 'approval' from his mother for anxious-avoidant behaviour. The violent film seems to have been a precipitating factor. Phobias can start in this way, from a traumatic event, or from an event that could be shrugged off in a less anxious child.

What treatments are likely to help in the situation?

Family therapy, to explore and challenge both parent's beliefs and expectations, can be used alongside a cognitive approach with Michael. He is likely to respond well to therapy that shows him the low chance of being killed, and how films are designed to scare people, but usually in a way they can manage and even enjoy.

Are there any adjustments that can help Michael return to school?

It is clear that moving from infant to junior school had an adverse impact on Michael's confidence. A behavioural programme to improve his sleep, and then plan a gradual return to school, with the school's help, would help Michael manage his anxiety.

(Back to **Chapter 6**.)

CHILDHOOD DEPRESSION – ROHAN'S STORY

Rohan is a 14-year-old boy who has been referred to a general paediatric clinic by his school because teaching staff have become increasingly concerned about his weight loss.

On examination, Rohan is an average height for his age, but he's very underweight. On questioning, he denies feelings suggestive of an eating disorder and states that he is 'just not hungry'. The paediatric team note that he appears withdrawn refuses to make eye contact and sits in the clinic room with his hoodie jumper pulled up throughout the consultation. They decide to admit him for dietetic treatment and ask for specialist Child and Adolescent Mental Health Services (CAMHS) input.

The CAMHS team explore events prior to referral. Rohan was previously a bright, academic student who enjoyed playing football. Eighteen months earlier, his older brother Thom got involved with a local gang and had become so aggressive towards his mother that Thom had been moved from his home to an emergency foster placement. About a year ago, Rohan answered the door one evening to find Thom on the doorstep, severely beaten. He had been kidnapped by a rival gang, who had beaten and burnt him. Over the next weeks, the rival gang would often heckle and threaten Rohan when he was out of the house. Despite police advice, the family were reluctant to move as they run a local shop.

The change in Rohan's behaviour has been since this event. His school noted that he had become withdrawn and difficult to engage in class. His mother reports that he often refuses to get up and go to school. On questioning, Rohan admits he finds it difficult to get to sleep and usually does not drop off before 3am, and therefore sleeps in to compensate. His mother reports cooking all his favourite meals only to have them refused, and Rohan returns from school with his packed lunch still in his bag. The team find Rohan's father difficult to engage and he resents the suggestion that his son may have a mental health problem. He tells his son to 'pull himself together'.

Following CAMHS input and some weight increase, Rohan is discharged home from the paediatric ward with a meal plan and CAMHS follow up. But he is re-admitted approximately one month later after refusing to follow the plan and losing further weight.

Questions to consider

Does this pattern indicate a clear cause?

Yes, it does seem to. Rohan is indicating by his behaviour that the situation at home is the problem; both within the home and externally in the community.

What treatment could help?

The CAMHS team could try family therapy, but if this was not effective and his weight continued to decrease, his admission to a specialist psychiatric adolescent unit may be necessary. A final resort would be foster care as an alternative to Rohan returning home.

Is there a role for the school?

Rohan was performing well, and it's vital for him to re-engage with education. There is a limited window of opportunity before he falls so behind in class and becomes so isolated that complete school refusal could result. The school could offer support through its pastoral and safeguarding services.

(Back to **Chapter 6**.)

ANOREXIA NERVOSA – LUCY'S STORY

This was a case heard by the mental health tribunal. Lucy was 15 and had a diagnosis of anorexia nervosa and autistic spectrum disorder. Her eating problems had begun three years previously at the age of 12 when she began a strict diet. After three months, Lucy had lost so much weight; her mother took her to her GP. Lucy was referred to the outpatient Child and Adolescent Mental Health Service (CAMHS) for treatment. But when she lost even more weight, she was admitted to an adolescent psychiatric unit as an informal patient. The unit made a referral to the local authority children's service when she was 13 due to concerns that her parents did not understand her mental health needs. Lucy had never been a looked-after child or subject to a child protection plan, but a child in need plan was in place.

Lucy was the eldest of four children, with two sisters, aged 13 and 11, and a brother aged seven. Her father worked in finance, and her mother gave up her job as a university admissions administrator when Lucy was born. During Lucy's hospital admission, she struggled to cope with eating and required nasogastric feeding. Only Lucy and her mother attended family therapy sessions. After a long admission, Lucy was discharged home at a healthy weight and with a meal plan.

One month after returning home, Lucy went on a skiing holiday with her family. She started to restrict food during this holiday, losing 15kg over four months. At home, she shouted at her sisters when they were eating chips and hit her brother when he was eating an apple, saying he would 'get fat'. Her weight loss affected her physical health, and she was then admitted as an emergency to a paediatric ward as her blood pressure and heart rate were very low. When more medically stable, she was transferred to an eating disorder unit on Section 3 of the Mental Health Act 1983. By this time, Lucy had spent more than two years in hospital since her first admission. She had applied to the mental health tribunal for the section to be lifted and to return back home.

At the time of the tribunal hearing, Lucy was 90 per cent of her healthy weight. This was considered safe and a sufficient weight gain by her clinical team; Lucy had been unable to tolerate a further increase in her weight. Although she was compliant and polite on the ward, she did not engage in any ward activities. When not in education classes, she spent all her time standing outside her room, which was thought by the clinical team to be a covert form of exercise. Lucy was sure she could manage her meal plan at home. She did not want to return to school but wanted one-to-one education at home. She agreed that she had autism and said the diagnosis 'had helped me to understand myself a bit more'.

Lucy was in the early stages of a needs assessment with the special education needs team, called an education, health and care plan (EHC plan): the draft plan, which is part of the process, had not yet been given to Lucy's parents.

Her weekend home visits had not always gone well. Just the week before the tribunal, Lucy had screamed at her mother about food planning and her mother had to lock herself in the toilet. Lucy's siblings were not welcoming during her home visits.

Questions to consider

Was the additional diagnosis of autism spectrum disorder significant?

Young people diagnosed with anorexia nervosa are obsessive about food and calorie intake, weight and exercise. However, Lucy's rigidity of thinking and her literal and concrete interpretation of language had been noted during both inpatient admissions, so an autism assessment was carried out, and she was found to be on the autistic spectrum. The clinical team noted that Lucy's father was described as aloof and unemotional and spent long hours at work away from the family. Lucy's mother was preoccupied with her own vegan diet.

What were the accommodation options for Lucy?

When Lucy had been admitted to the current unit, her mother had stated she could not have Lucy at home. The clinical team had, therefore explored options of specific accommodation for young people with mental health disorders. This meant that on discharge, Lucy would have to become a looked-after child with the local authority children's service, under the Children Act 1989, s 20.

However, at the tribunal hearing, Lucy's mother insisted she would try having Lucy returning to live at home, despite the difficulties experienced on her previous weekend home visit. At the tribunal, Lucy requested to be discharged home immediately.

What were the options for the mental health tribunal panel?

The panel could discharge the section or allow it to continue. The tribunal panel upheld the appeal and discharged the section as Lucy's solicitor had the support of her mother for the care plan. Lucy was, therefore discharged home from the unit on a community treatment order (CTO). The conditions of the CTO were to attend all professional appointments and to have her weight measured. If these conditions were not kept and Lucy's health deteriorated, then she could be recalled to hospital.

What happened after Lucy was discharged from hospital?

Lucy struggled to follow the meal plan and lost weight rapidly. This lead to arguments and violence towards her mother. Lucy had to be physically restrained at home by her father. She was recalled to hospital using the CTO, for treatment and weight restoration. It was clear that Lucy could not be managed at home. The new plan was to present Lucy's case to the complex needs panel for tripartite funding for specialised accommodation, with Lucy becoming a looked-after child with the local authority.

What is Lucy's prognosis?

Lucy has had two diagnoses which interact. Her autism spectrum symptoms, particularly rigidity of thinking and her anorexic symptoms means her ideas are resistant to treatment. She cannot tolerate a weight higher than 90 per cent of her healthy weight, and patients discharged with a lower weight often do not do well.

There appears to be a family history of an undiagnosed eating disorder with her mother and autism spectrum disorder in her father. It is possible that Lucy will not recover. She had not recovered, so far, despite intensive treatment. Her behaviour has had a damaging consequence for her family, and she too has suffered as her siblings have effectively excluded her.

Although people with anorexia have rigid views about their own food and weight, Lucy's extended to other people – she was violent to her siblings when they ate. This is unusual. People with anorexia usually promote others' eating, even to the point of becoming skilled cooks and 'feeders'. Such concrete thinking as Lucy's is difficult to challenge and reduce.

(Back to **Chapter 6**.)

GAMING ADDICTION – EDDIE'S STORY

Eddie is 12 years old and spends 20 hours a day online; he is sleep-deprived and has no other interests. He will only eat if food is placed next to him but has gained two stone in weight in six months. When asked by his parents to stop gaming, have a bath, go to bed or go to school, he becomes angry. When physically removed from his gaming station by his parents, Eddie is physically violent to them.

Eddie is referred to the local Child and Adolescent Mental Health Services (CAMHS) unit. When seen at home by a therapist, Eddie has been incontinent of urine in his clothes as he is reluctant to leave his game to go to the toilet. He tells the therapist he wears dark coloured clothes deliberately so no-one can see when he's wet himself. Eddie is unable to say to the therapist how life would be if he didn't game. He sees no reason to change his behaviour.

The parents were guided by the therapist to set firm boundaries for Eddie and to stick to them. Individual sessions tried to explore his worries about school and social contact with others. An assessment, including his earlier development and school performance, indicated he had autism spectrum disorder.

However, Eddie's parents were unable to reinforce the boundaries. He became increasingly violent, especially to his mother when efforts were made to restrict his behaviour. Following an assault by Eddie, she required hospital treatment and a safeguarding alert was raised. A Mental Health Act (MHA) assessment was carried out, and Eddie was admitted to a CAMHS psychiatric unit. When his care plan did not allow access to the internet, to prevent him from gaming, he became violent to staff.

Questions to consider

How typical is Eddie of children with a gaming disorder?

Eddie's behaviour is extreme for the general population of children, but not unusual for a presentation to a specialist gaming clinic. Regarding weight, children can become either obese from little or no exercise and food is being provided, as in Eddie's case, or very thin as they prefer to play games than eat.

What may be the cause of Eddie's gaming disorder?

It is not clear-cut; for such a severe presentation, the likely underlying disorders are obsessive-compulsive disorder (OCD) or autism. There were no reported severe obsessive symptoms or rituals in Eddie's earlier childhood, so OCD was not a consideration. For Eddie, the diagnosis of autism may be more likely. His presentation to services at age 12 follows the transition to secondary school. This is a difficult time for children with autism to manage. In fact, some children are only diagnosed with autism when they struggle in secondary education.

What treatment can help Eddie's gaming disorder?

His prognosis is uncertain. Eddie's social disability and other obsessive behaviours are now more apparent when he is no longer gaming. His parents had hidden his symptoms and the level of violence he had subjected them to for several years, fearing the stigma of mental illness in their community. His violence was worse when faced with social challenges, so the whole family were almost 'housebound' by the time of the MHA assessment. It is unclear if Eddie can return home.

(Back to **Chapter 6**.)

POST-TRAUMATIC STRESS DISORDER – SAMIRA'S STORY

Samira is a six-year-old girl who arrived from Syria two months ago. She was accompanied to the UK by her mother and two younger brothers. Her mother is grief-stricken as the family fled after witnessing Samira's father and older brothers being brutally murdered.

Samira is waking the family at night by screaming and crying, apparently in her sleep. When asked in the morning, she will not speak about any dreams. She begins to wet herself during the day.

Samira's mother is encouraged to enrol Samira at a local primary school to help her integrate into the community. Not long after, the class take a trip to the seaside nearby. The following day, the children are asked to draw a picture of the seaside. Samira's teacher is horrified to see Samira's drawing of blue waves, yellow sand and what appear to be dead bodies covered in red blotches on the sand.

Questions to consider

What can be done to help Samira?

Samira is referred to her local Child and Adolescent Mental Health Service (CAMHS). The therapist notes that Samira's distress was revealed usefully in a 'play' situation. She receives sessions to help her express her distress and manage it. Her mother is included in family sessions using an interpreter.

How does this help?

Samira's sleep improves, and she's dry during the day. She continues at school, which she enjoys and being a quick learner, helps her two younger brothers learn to speak English.

What other support could help?

The family are referred to a local charity who help Samira's mother, where she joins English classes and, with links to other refugees, starts to build a new life.

(Back to **Chapter 6**.)

AUTISM SPECTRUM DISORDER – YUSHFA'S STORY

Yushfa is a seven-year-old girl who has been referred by her school to her local community paediatric team due to concerns that she is having difficulty with her speech and behaviour. The referral states that Yushfa speaks with an American accent, even though no one in her family is American, and she has never been to America. Yushfa is reported to be very academic and loves to read, but she often lashes out at other children when she does not get her own way, having to wait her turn to play a game, for instance.

Yushfa's father attends the clinic and reveals that Yushfa's mother is unwell with severe depression due to several miscarriages. This means that while he is at work, Yushfa is left to amuse herself, which involves her watching a lot of American children's television programmes. He reports that Yushfa often repeats phrases she hears on the television. Due to her love of reading, her father buys her many books, and when he is home from work, they spend time reading together.

On examination, Yushfa is polite and compliant. She answers all the paediatrician's questions in an American accent and enthusiastically reads a storybook out loud. When asked to participate in a game of snakes and ladders, Yushfa becomes very distressed when she has to go down a snake back to the beginning of the game. She bangs her head against the wall and tries to hit her father. A referral is made to the children and adolescent mental health service (CAMHS).

Questions to consider

What behaviour is Yushfa displaying?

Echolalia is the term for copying another person's speech. Yushfa is copying the speech on the TV programmes she watches. She becomes very distressed, self-harms and is aggressive when forced to follow the rules; the term 'meltdown' is often used to describe this behaviour.

What are the likely consequences to Yushfa of this behaviour?

She could be isolated at school as other children will not play with her due to her 'American accent' which could lead to bullying, and her aggressive behaviour could lead to possible exclusion from school.

What are the next steps for the clinical team?

The paediatric team refer Yushfa for an autism assessment, and a diagnosis of autism is confirmed. The CAMHS team also assess her for the comorbidity of depression and or an anxiety disorder.

Why is Yushfa at risk of an additional diagnosis?

Children, adolescents and adults with autism are highly likely to suffer another mental disorder such as anxiety, depression and attention deficit disorder. Yushfa's mother has a serious mental disorder which makes her vulnerable also to an additional disorder.

What are the positive facts in Yushfa's case?

After a diagnosis of autism is made, Yushfa receives specialist help at school. Both parents find the diagnosis helpful; they can see a way forward using Yushfa's strengths, such as her academic prowess. Her parents are willing to support their daughter and are taught behavioural strategies to help at home, which include identifying and reducing trigger factors to avoid meltdowns.

(Back to **Chapter 7**.)

FOETAL ALCOHOL SPECTRUM DISORDER – PHILLIP AND JEROME'S STORY

Phillip and Jerome were five-year-old twins when their mother told their headteacher at school that she could no longer cope with them; she was agitated, shaking and in tears. She had been asked to go into school to bring them home as they were so disruptive in class. She said that she could not cope and that if she took them home now, she would hit them 'again' or run away and leave them alone at home.

The Local Authority Children's Social Services were asked to assess urgently. The boys' history and case file at the GP surgery showed there was a concern when they were six months of age due to failure to thrive. Their mother had two convictions for drink driving. The pregnancy had not been planned but was welcomed, and the mother told staff at the antenatal clinic she had stopped drinking. Phillip and Jerome had been born six weeks before their due date because the mother went into premature labour. There had been a concern at the mother's ability to care for the boys, but the maternal grandmother mother moved in for some months to help.

Phillip and Jerome were both small for their age, difficult to feed and settle to sleep and slow to talk. The challenges with Phillip and Jerome increased as they became older, and their behaviour was noticeably more aggressive and impulsive towards each other and other children. The mother found herself isolated as her social network of other parents began to fall away, as the boys were so difficult to control. The husband was not always at home to support her as his job meant he worked away for several weeks at a time.

Their mother was reluctant to acknowledge the twin's behavioural difficulties. It seemed that the situation reached a crisis point over a few days. Phillip had not been sleeping, had to be forced to attend school, and then on the morning their mother was asked to remove them, bit Jerome and then his mother when she tried to intervene. None of the professionals involved with the family had identified foetal alcohol spectrum disorder (FASD) in the boys.

Questions to consider

Were there any hints to indicate FASD?

Mother's conviction for drink driving could have triggered a more detailed investigation into her alcohol consumption during pregnancy. As the pregnancy was not planned, it's unlikely she was abstinent early in pregnancy.

A full assessment of Phillip and Jerome helped clarify their needs. A diagnosis of FSAD was made due to the combination of the difficulties that both boys displayed and the mother being frank about her alcohol consumption. Phillip was found to be short-sighted, and Jerome to have a hearing impairment, and correction of these by aids helped them concentrate and engage. Attention to Phillip's sleep meant his sleep pattern improved to seven consecutive hours. Extra assistance at school for their learning and concentration difficulties has helped, but the weekends are very difficult times for their mother as a sole parent.

The father was unaware of his wife's drinking during pregnancy and had thought that the boys' problems were due to being born prematurely; he is reluctant to consider marital therapy. The mother feels that the diagnosis of FASD is damaging and stigmatising for the boys. At this early stage – soon after diagnosis – she is reluctant to socialise with other parents and their children, thinking that other parents will know about her drinking during pregnancy.

The Local Authority Children's Social Services remain involved – there is concern that a potential marriage break up will mean Phillip and Jerome cannot be managed at their home.

(Back to **Chapter 7**.)

GENDER DYSPHORIA – JAY'S STORY

Jay was 12 years old when referred to a Child and Adolescent Mental Health Services (CAMHS) unit, specifically to request a further referral to a specialist gender service for young people. Jay self-identified as female. The referral was requested by Jay, who threatened to kill herself if it wasn't made.

Jay was born six weeks prematurely as a boy and was regarded as a delicate child. His sister is five years older. There were concerns about Jay's isolation and preference for individual play at nursery. At primary school, Jay would play with other children only when encouraged. Average academically, he managed primary school, but the transfer to secondary school was traumatic. Jay could not cope with the larger, noisier environment. He was bullied by other children and became phobic about school. His stepfather tried to intervene, but the local authority was about to become involved due to Jay's school refusal. The situation reached a crisis point when Jay was found self-harming by his mother, leading to the referral.

Jay asked the CAMHS clinician to refer to 'him' as 'she'. She was sure that she had been born into a boy's body by mistake. Jay said from the age of nine she had been wearing her sister's clothes secretly. She was very distressed at the adolescent changes in her body. The self-harm had been triggered by her fear when she'd had an erection. She told the therapist she'd wanted to cut off her penis, but she cut her arm instead. Since refusing school, Jay was wearing make-up and female clothing during the day while only her mother was at home.

Both parents attended the CAMHS appointment. They were very distressed. Jay's stepfather thought that at some point, Jay would be able to grow out of this and return to school. Jay's mother supported all of Jay's wishes.

Questions to consider

What is a helpful first stage when a young person presents to services?

Despite the self-harm, Jay was not admitted immediately to an adolescent psychiatric inpatient unit. The clinician, instead, conducted a thorough psychiatric assessment that stretched over three sessions to identify how best to help and treat Jay.

What does the assessment of a young person with gender dysphoria involve?

The clinician explained to Jay and her parents that the decision to proceed to a referral to the gender clinic was a major one, and the medication necessary to halt puberty could have serious side effects. The clinician was not persuaded that Jay had possessed a long-term wish for gender change; usually, children associate much earlier with their preferred gender.

What were Jay's vulnerability factors predisposing to gender dysphoria?

The outcome of the assessment was that Jay was diagnosed with an underlying autistic spectrum disorder (ASD) and depression. The early lack of social play and difficulties with a new environment, such a secondary school, are a time when ASD presents in older children. Further exploration revealed that Jay's biological father had a bipolar affective disorder, which increased Jay's risk of depression, as did her ASD.

What treatment was helpful for Jay?

Jay was persuaded to attend the day service and explore whether her unhappiness with her body was related to her ASD, making her feel different compared to others, rather than a genuine wish for gender change. Her depression was treated with medication and psychological therapy.

What are the risks of proceeding immediately to a referral to the gender clinic?

Gender dysphoria can be a contentious issue due to the possibility of children being prescribed puberty-blocking drugs with serious side effects. In addition, young people with this condition are at risk of suicide and self-harm if they choose their affirmed gender prematurely. It was wondered what Jay's sexual preference in adolescence would be.

What was the outcome for Jay?

Jay is still considering whether to proceed with the referral to a specialist gender service. She continues to self-identify as female, but the diagnosis of ASD has helped Jay make sense of the difference she feels in herself. She says she does not feel the need to dress permanently in female clothes or wear make-up. There has been no further self-harm, and her mood is brighter. She is participating in education at the day unit while decisions are made about her future education and funding.

(Back to **Chapter 7**.)

SCHIZOPHRENIA, EARLY-ONSET – TOM'S STORY

Tom is a 13-year-old boy who lives with his parents, who are both lawyers, and his nine-year-old twin sisters, one of whom has cerebral palsy having been born prematurely.

Over the past year, Tom's parents have noticed a change in his behaviour. They report that he has become increasingly paranoid about unusual things. He first became concerned that his school teacher was spying on him during the school day, even when he was not in the same class, and this has progressed to Tom being convinced that the teacher is following him home and has set up secret cameras within the house. Tom has started covering up random windows or parts of the wall with paper.

Tom's parents report that he used to be extremely clean and tidy but is now neglecting his self-care. He refuses to shower due to fear of being spied upon, and no longer wants to attend his local swimming club.

The triggering event which led Tom's parents toseek help was when he dismantled his sister's motorised wheelchair as he was convinced there was a camera hidden inside. Tom was unable to explain why he thought this and became so distressed that the family were afraid he might harm himself or even kill himself as he could not cope.

Tom was seen by his local Child and Adolescent Mental Health Services (CAMHS) team and admitted to an adolescent psychiatric unit as an inpatient. The initial diagnosis was of a severe depressive illness; there was no evidence of Tom using cannabis. Despite starting antidepressant treatment, Tom's symptoms persisted and his self-neglect increased.

Questions to consider

Why was Tom's first diagnosis of severe depression?

Some of Tom's symptoms do resemble those in depressed children. Children and young people with severe depression can have paranoid symptoms such as thinking they are being spied on. In depression, these ideas are 'mood-congruent' which means the paranoid belief matches their mood. In Tom's case, his belief he was being spied upon was an upsetting, depressing and disabling one. Losing interest in activities and self-care then followed. The clinical team tested Tom to check he did not have drugs such as cannabis in his system, so eliminating the possibility of drug-induced psychosis.

Why was he admitted to an adolescent psychiatric unit?

Tom was so distressed by his beliefs about the hidden camera that his parents thought he might kill himself. His behaviour to try and prevent being spied upon may put himself and others at risk. He does not seem to feel safe anywhere – either at home or at school. This was a serious situation that necessitated inpatient treatment.

Why was there a change of diagnosis?

The appropriate treatment for depression (antidepressant medication) did not help. The clinical team reviewed Tom's development of symptoms over time, and it became more evident that the paranoid ideas came first, then anxiety and depression because of his absolute beliefs which were distressing. His self-neglect meant he did not wash or change clothes, even for bed. This behaviour seemed to be indicative of negative symptoms of schizophrenia, so Tom's diagnosis was changed to schizophrenia.

What happened next?

Tom was detained in hospital on a section of the mental health act as he was unable to consent to stay in hospital or to take medication. The clinical team prescribed risperidone which is an antipsychotic medication. As a result, he became less distressed and was willing to think that his beliefs about his teacher weren't correct. He showed pleasure when he Skyped his twin sisters. The medication made him gain some weight, and he is sedated, which is a side effect of his medication. The family are being supported by family therapy.

(Back to **Chapter 8**.)

ANXIETY DISORDER – MELANIE'S STORY

Melanie is 27 years old. She attends her GP accompanied by her mother. Her mother tells the GP that if she had not brought Melanie, she would not have attended. They both report that Melanie is so anxious she is unable to get out of bed in the morning. She has crying episodes when she finds it difficult to breathe. At times, she feels hopeless and too anxious to think ahead to another day. She is not eating, saying that she feels sick and is afraid of eating in case she chokes. When her friends phone the house (as she is refusing to answer her mobile phone or respond to texts), she refuses to speak to them.

Melanie agrees to speak to the GP alone. It appears that she had high levels of anxiety when at school, and her exam nerves were such that she did not fulfil her academic potential. She decided to do a practical qualification to avoid the stress of exams and completed catering college successfully, obtaining a job in a restaurant.

At the age of 22, she met Alan, who was the restaurant manager, and they rented a flat together. After three years, they married. Melanie became pregnant and was contented to remain in their flat while Alan took a job with a hotel chain requiring him to travel. When their son John was nine months old, Melanie was devastated when he informed her that he had accepted a job in another part of the country, and he wanted to move there without her, but have access to John.

Melanie struggled to remain in work where everyone knew she'd 'been ditched'. She moved to another restaurant and organised child care and a flatmate so she could pay the rent. She felt fragile but coping over the next six months, with monthly visits from Alan, and felt she was doing well as a mother. But then a friend told her than on Alan's Facebook page was evidence that he had been a father for some time in his new relationship. It was clear to Melanie, and her friends, that he'd been in this other relationship for some time before telling her their relationship was over. She became fearful that Alan would wish to take John from her, but with no actual evidence that this was the intent.

This had led to acute anxiety, and when her flatmate had contacted her mother, Melanie was in a state of distress, unable to care for herself or John. She said that her heart was beating so fast she feared a heart attack.

Questions to consider

What treatments are likely to help in the situation?

The GP did blood tests to rule out a physical cause for her anxiety, such as an overactive thyroid. Melanie was prescribed a short course of sedative medication plus propranolol which reduced her heart rate and made her less afraid of having a heart attack.

She was offered CBT to help her manage her symptoms – initially, this was by an app and then one to one sessions. She accepted that to be rejected in this way would be damaging for anyone, but that she had become dependent upon Alan as a way to manage her anxiety. Group therapy helped her look at future ways of coping.

One trigger for her becoming panicky, despite the improvement, was the fear that after the divorce was finalised, Alan would want access visits to John.

What adjustments in Family Court can help Melanie if Alan does wish for contact?

Melanie's fear is that John's contact with his father may mean an alteration in her relationship with him. Alan does have a right to contact. John has a right to have a relationship with both parents.

She may have a relapse of anxiety if they are unable to negotiate contact. If not legally represented, Melanie could be assisted by having someone to accompany her in court, can be encouraged to give a written statement and have breaks during any discussion.

(Back to **Chapter 11**.)

POSTPARTUM PSYCHOSIS – SACHINI'S STORY

Sachini was a qualified doctor, though not currently practising. Her first child was greatly anticipated within her and her husband's extended family. She had no previous history of mental illness, but a maternal aunt had bipolar affective disorder. Sachini gave birth by caesarean section due to a rise in her blood pressure at week 38 of the pregnancy and made a good physical recovery. The baby inhaled some amniotic fluid and was kept in the special care baby unit for two days.

The second morning after the baby's birth, Sachini seemed over-excited; she had not slept much for several days. She asked to see the hospital chaplain, which puzzled her husband as she'd never been particularly religious. She said it was to think about the baby's baptism. Sachini, and her husband's large extended family, arrived and said they would look after her, so she and the baby were allowed home.

On the baby's seventh day (second day at home) the visiting midwife was concerned at Sachini's elated mood. She also thought Sachini had appeared to drop the baby deliberately from a height into his cot. The family were adamant that Sachini was coping, although she was sleeping only two hours a night and staying awake gazing at her sleeping baby. When the midwife asked Sachini about this, her response was that her baby had special powers and she was 'testing' him in a number of ways. She was watching him sleep, convinced he was doing good in the world and thought perhaps he could be immortal.

The midwife was very concerned that Sachini dropped the baby into his cot and her beliefs that the baby had special powers. She asked for an urgent home visit by the perinatal psychiatrist. During the assessment, Sachini told the doctor she had deliberately not fed the baby for many hours to test whether he could manage without food. She did not think her behaviour was unusual. The doctor told the husband and the family that they were very concerned. They were shocked at Sachini's disturbing thoughts and actions but determined to look after her and the baby at home.

Questions to consider

Can Sachini be looked after safely at home?

As her family were supportive, the perinatal psychiatrist, community psychiatric nurse and the midwife set up a plan to support her at home. Their working diagnosis was of a manic episode of psychosis. Sachini was prescribed antipsychotic medication, and healthcare professionals visited daily. She assured the professionals that she was coping and claimed the issue was 'only a shortage of sleep'. She continued to be elated and was neglecting herself. She was irritable with all family members who were looking after the baby, accusing them of deliberately keeping 'the star child' from her. (The family did not reveal this at the time to the professionals.)

The medical team was concerned that Sachini was not taking her medication, though the family assured them that she was being given it. Voluntary admission to psychiatric hospital was refused by Sachini who said there was nothing wrong with her. Her husband maintained that he and the family could cope. The situation reached a crisis when Sachini screamed at her husband that he did not deserve the baby, and had to be physically prevented from leaving the family home with the baby in the early hours, both dressed in only nightclothes.

What is a likely diagnosis?

A diagnosis of bipolar affective disorder was made. This was based on Sachini's grandiose mood, lack of sleep, irritability, her belief that her child was special, her attempts to test her beliefs and her paranoid beliefs towards her family. She did not have insight, in that she did not believe her behaviour was unusual.

What is the appropriate treatment?

A Mental Health Act assessment was carried out, and Sachini was admitted to a local psychiatric hospital for two days, then transferred to a mother and baby mental health unit. Sachini said she had been hiding medication at home as she thought the family and clinical team were poisoning her to harm the baby. Once in the unit with her baby and under supervision, she responded to medication and was discharged after eight weeks. She had been somewhat aloof from the other mothers, explaining she did not think her condition was like theirs.

The family had different views about Sachini's illness and behaviour. Her husband's parents were concerned about the stigma of mental illness, in their family and whether this would happen again in a future pregnancy. Sachini and her mother blamed the caesarean section rather than accepting she had been mentally unwell. They thought she had been delirious post-operatively. Sachini agreed to take the medication only for six months to recover from 'the delirium' fully.

What are the positive factors in Sachini recovery?

Sachini bipolar disorder responded quickly to treatment. She was swiftly admitted to a mother and baby unit so remained with her baby and was able to bond with him as well as be monitored so that she could look after his needs safely. Social services monitored her for three months, then closed the case as there were no immediate concerns.

What issues are of concern?

The family did not inform the professionals of the full extent of Sachini's beliefs when they were looking after her at home. Mothers with postnatal psychosis can successfully hide their beliefs, and this can lead to a dangerous situation. Sachini could have further tested out her beliefs about her baby being special, resulting in his death.

Sachini does not seem to have had insight into her illness and the impact on her baby and family. She did not engage fully with the treatment and separated herself from other mothers.

The denial and stigma felt by her husband, Sachini and their extended family, meant the team were unable to get her and her husband fully involved in psychological treatments, which would have helped.

The different views within the wider family are likely to cause problems in future. The perception of stigma may prevent the husband and Sachini asking for help in the event of a relapse. If Sachini takes the medication for only six months, she may suffer a relapse. There is a fifty per cent chance of the condition reoccurring in any future pregnancy and a thirty per cent chance of psychosis at another time.

(Back to **Chapter 11**.)

FABRICATED OR INDUCED ILLNESS – AYESHA'S STORY

Ayesha is a three-year-old girl who is usually fit and healthy. She is brought into the hospital emergency department having repeated seizures which only respond for a short period to the usual medical protocol. On arrival, she is found to be profoundly hypoglycaemic (very low blood sugar) and requires multiple doses of concentrated sugar solution. Her mother is distraught and cannot provide a reason for her daughter's symptoms. She denies any injuries or medication in the house, which may have caused the seizures.

Ayesha is admitted for a week and makes a full recovery. She has no further episodes. There is no identifiable cause for her hypoglycaemia, but it is thought that it was the cause of her seizures. She is discharged home with emergency treatment for hypoglycaemia, should this occur again.

Three weeks later, Ayesha returns to hospital by ambulance having hypoglycaemic seizures again. She is stabilised but, due to a prolonged seizure period, she requires breathing support and has to be taken to paediatric intensive care for further support. The intensive care team are suspicious of Ayesha's presentation, which has no obvious medical cause and sends blood samples for specific tests. These identify that Ayesha had been injected with insulin. Ayesha's mother denies having insulin in the house, but a police investigation reveals a close relative uses insulin and it is readily available.

Tragically, Ayesha's prolonged seizure caused permanent brain damage and she is now unable to walk, talk or feed herself. She has been removed from her mother's care and placed in foster care.

Ayesha's mother was charged with child cruelty. At her trial, her defence lawyer pleaded that she was mentally unwell. However, this did not persuade the court and she was found guilty and given a prison sentence.

Questions to consider

When did the abuse of Ayesha first present?

The first detected episode was at the age of three. However, it is possible that her mother's abusive behaviour was long term and had increased in severity.

What could be the motivation of Ayesha's mother's behaviour?

This has been very difficult to determine. She too may have been abused. She may suffer from an emotionally unstable personality disorder or depression. She is a single parent with access to insulin; however she consistently denied harming Ayesha or wishing to harm her.

(Back to **Chapter 11**.)

SOMATIC SYMPTOM DISORDER – AURELIA'S STORY

Aurelia was referred for a psychological assessment when she was 25 years old. The referral came from her GP, who said the practice were 'absolutely exhausted' by her repeated presentations as an emergency. She has a diagnosis of irritable bowel syndrome, but her repeated attendances were for many other symptoms.

The referring GP had listed as an example, the calls and attendances to the practice and to A&E over a period of a month; there were 29 phone calls and eight appointments with the GP, three with the practice nurse and four attendances to the A&E walk-in service. There had been two calls for the out of hours GP service to visit at the weekend, and one outpatient appointment for a colonoscopy, arranged by the A&E department.

Aurelia attended the psychology assessment reluctantly; her GP had said that if she did not, they would have to consider removing her from their list. At the appointment, she was near tears. She explained that no-one understood her pain, that no-one took her seriously, and that she could die. She had overheard the receptionist joking with one of the GPs that she was a 'frequent flyer' and felt insulted. Aurelia acknowledged she was depressed and agreed to attend four sessions with the psychologist.

Aurelia had been the elder child of a single mother, who herself had depression and severe migraines. She had looked after her two younger siblings when her mother was unwell, missing time off school to do so. She said she had suffered badly from pre-menstrual abdominal pain, but that her mother had been unsympathetic about her condition. Aurelia became pregnant at the age of 17 but had a termination at her mother's insistence. Aurelia's boyfriend at the time was the same age, and his parents insisted he remain at school.

Aurelia left school and started working in a hairdresser's, intending to study at college. Over the next year, she began to suffer more abdominal pain, back pain and headaches. These were investigated, but no cause was found. She missed much time from college and resat the year. At 19, she met Derek, and they moved in together. Derek was aged 27. Aurelia said this was the best time of her life; she gave up college and work, and they spent two years together until he was arrested for aggravated burglary. At his court appearance, she found out that Derek was married with a two-year-old son.

Aurelia's relationship with her mother had not recovered since she was 17. She moved into temporary housing and tried to resume college, but found this impossible as she was now older than the other students. Her health worsened, and she explained that for the past two years, she had been in continuous daily pain.

Questions to consider

What could be the predisposing factors to Aurelia's symptoms?

Aurelia's mother has depression and was also troubled by physical symptoms, which required Aurelia to take on a carer's role. Aurelia may also be suffering bereavement from the termination of her pregnancy. Her long-term relationship with Derek was ended in a traumatic way, and her self-esteem suffered. In another person, such circumstances could cause depression, but with Aurelia, her distress manifested itself in a peak in her somatic symptoms. She appears to be socially isolated without family support.

What treatment could help Aurelia?

The psychologist and Aurelia worked together for four sessions when she was able to recognise the link between her physical symptoms and life events. However, she remained adamant that her life was at risk if she did not receive medical help, and she had become fixated on a number of gastric investigations.

The psychologist attended a meeting at the GP practice. It was agreed that Aurelia would be offered two half-hour appointments a week for the next four months with the same GP, and one with the practice nurse. Aurelia was told at each appointment that she wouldn't be referred for unnecessary tests. She was also prescribed a sedating antidepressant, which she agreed to try to help her sleep. Aurelia at first said this was insufficient support, but she agreed to try the arrangement.

What was the outcome for Aurelia?

The regular appointments reduced Aurelia inappropriate visits and calls. She kept a mood and anxiety diary, which she discussed with the psychologist who had agreed on three more sessions. Although she would not admit any of her symptoms had eased, her help-seeking behaviour and anxiety reduced in the short term.

(Back to **Chapter 11**.)

PERSONALITY DISORDERS – KAREN AND DAVID'S STORIES

Karen and David are brother and sister who were brought up in the same family home. Their home life was chaotic with the father being an alcoholic and the mother suffering domestic abuse that the children witnessed. Mother regularly left the family home taking David and Karen, with her, along with their younger brother, but they always returned.

Emotionally unstable personality disorder – Karen's story

Karen is 28 years old and attending a psychiatric assessment. During Karen's early school years, she was supported by her grandmother, who favoured her over the other children. Their shared physical appearance of red hair and green eyes had been comforting to both. Her grandmother died when Karen was 13 and this event was devastating for her. She still becomes upset when describing this event 15 years later.

Karen was not aware of grieving at the time of her grandmother's death. Before her grandmother's death, she had been self-harming by cutting and she reports this used to bring relief. She says that from age 13 she lost interest in school and spent more time with a gang who truanted. She had been on the outskirts of this group whilst her grandmother was alive. She has always found it more difficult to relate to other girls and felt more at ease spending time with boys. She alternated between a tomboyish lifestyle or being in a sexual relationship. These relationships were intense for her at the time but typically lasted only a few weeks because she became bored. She recalls that the excitement of a new relationship was the most exciting thing in her life; she preferred that to taking drugs. She moved on to relationships with older men. The relationships became more erratic, some of her partners used drugs or alcohol, and some were violent.

Karen became pregnant at age 19 but had a termination as she felt unable to care for a baby. This seemed to provoke an episode of depression and her first suicide attempt. An unsettled lifestyle, living with her partners' or living back at home and without a job, resulted in repeated low moods and further suicide attempts, with many crisis admissions to hospital.

Karen would say she wanted a settled life and a job with animals. She agreed to attend appointments with the community mental health team (CMHT), but always missed the appointments offered, and so did not qualify for the lengthy waiting list for psychological therapy. She would then appear unannounced either at the CMHT office or in A&E, at a time of crisis demanding to be seen.

During one crisis admission to hospital, Karen was told about a newly set-up patient support group for young women with personality disorders. This was an 'open group', meeting twice a week, and people could come along without a referral. Failure to attend did not result in discharge from the group as it was accepted that people with personality disorders lead chaotic lifestyles. Karen attended the support group, and for the first time, was able to hear from others, with similar life stories, and relate these to her own situation. The experience of loss, but denial of this loss (for Karen it was her grandmother) was common among this group. Although it's early days, Karen reports that she went to the group recently when feeling low, rather than self-harming.

Antisocial personality disorder – David's story

David is 23 years old and serving a prison sentence. He is currently on the hospital wing, due to repeated suicide attempts by hanging and is being seen by the prison liaison psychiatrist.

During David's early school years, he struggled with his disruptive behaviour, finding it difficult to concentrate. His poor school reports angered his father who would punish him with a beating.

From the age of 11 David started drinking alcohol with other boys. His school attendance was poor, approximately 60 per cent, until he stopped attending school completely at the age of 15. Acquisitive crimes to buy drugs and alcohol, plus fighting, brought him to court. The time he spent in a young offenders' institution hardened his dislike for authority. He was well known in his neighbourhood for aggression.

To improve his physique – and become more feared – David started body-building and abused steroids. He had a number of relationships, but all faltered due to his violence and unreliability. He married Mandy in a 'whirlwind romance' after meeting her on holiday. This broke down after their first child was born nine months later. Mandy was unable to tolerate his temper and feared for their daughter.

Following this, David self-medicated with alcohol. During a drunken brawl with a nightclub bouncer, he assaulted two policemen. During his lengthy custodial sentence, he was told that Mandy had met another man and was pregnant. She had applied to the Family Court for an Arrangements Order to give her sole custody of her daughter, saying she was not David's child after all.

As he was in prison, David was unable to continue with his drug use, particularly steroids. He had noted that increased use made him more prone to outbursts. Having received the letter from Mandy, he thought there was no point trying to look good to win her back; this contributed to his low mood and suicidal thoughts.

The prison liaison psychiatrist prescribed antidepressants but did not think more intensive psychiatric treatment was necessary at this point. The issues in David's life were as the result of his personality disorder and he would not, in the psychiatrist's opinion, respond to psychological therapy.

Questions about and Karen and David's stories

What impact did their early lives have on the development of their personalities?

The features of their personality that they both exhibit is a consequence of their traumatic childhood. For example – their impulsivity and inability to sustain relationships, inability to self-soothe and feelings of emptiness. Both use self-harming behaviours as a maladaptive way of coping, either by drug and or alcohol misuse or by cutting.

Why have they come to the attention of the health service and prison service?

The different institutions they came into contact with – Karen's admissions to hospital and David's time in a young offender institution and prison – are typical. Males with personality disorder turn aggression outwards while females internalise it, leading to self-harm.

Help-seeking is also different. Men generally don't seek help, whereas some women become over-dependent and request hospital admission, either directly or through their actions.

Society and the justice system also view these expressions of personality disorder differently – men are more likely to be imprisoned; women more likely to be hospitalised.

(Back to **Chapter 13**.)

AUTISM SPECTRUM DISORDER LATE DIAGNOSIS – HEATHER AND MANUEL'S STORIES

Autism spectrum disorder late diagnosis – Heather's story

Heather is 28. She works as a radiology technician. As a child, her family recognised a level of stress in certain situations that her siblings did not have. When she returned home from school, they would encourage her 'to have a good cry' to relieve tension. She made one good friend at infant school, and that person remains her best friend today.

Heather is recognised as a joker in her family, as she says quirky things that are always slightly off-topic. At secondary school, she found the change of teachers and classrooms so difficult to manage that she carried all her books and kit in a backpack at all times. Although somewhat isolated at school, she was not bullied. She always made an excuse not to go on any school trips to avoid being in a new environment. She would return home from school exhausted, sleeping for three to four hours and much of the weekend. No physical cause was found for this sleepiness.

Heather studied radiology at a college close to home, so she could live at home. Her pattern of sleeping during most of her time away from her studies continued. Her radiology supervisor, who had a son with autism, had noted in Heather's first term that she had stimming hand movements when stressed, which she tried to hide. She also noticed Heather's speech style – lagging in conversations and missing the point, causing others to laugh, not always kindly. She asked to meet with Heather and her mother and gently suggested that Heather should ask for an autism assessment.

Heather was helped by the diagnosis, which confirmed that she was on the autism spectrum; this was also a help in her subsequent NHS employment. Adjustments have been made and she is now able to pace her work, having a quiet day after a busy one. Heather has no problems with the bright lights and humming machines in the environment she knows. Her quirky humour is now regarded by workmates as 'that's Heather'. Patients coming for breast scans, which is part of Heather's job, seem to relax more with her rather off-beat comments.

Heather was recently asked by her organisation whether she would be willing to talk at an autism awareness session. She is considering doing so.

Questions to consider

What could be the reasons Heather was not considered to have ASD in childhood?

There is no information about many of the features that are common in childhood – lack of eye contact, no social interaction or reciprocal play, delayed or unusual speech patterns. However, it can be inferred that she attended normal school and was academically successful. It's also possible that when Heather was school age, her normal behaviour observed at school did not lead to any exploration of difficulties at home and, being female, a diagnosis may not have been considered even if enquiries were made of her parents.

Positive factors are that Heather has sustained a friendship over many years and that her family were able to help her with coping strategies of stress release and rest and recovery time following social interactions.

Can it be helpful for a person diagnosed with ASD in adulthood to find a diagnosis beneficial?

People with ASD have difficulty recognising and understanding their own feelings and those of others. They also find difficulty in developing and maintaining friendships and mixing in social groups.

According to the National Autistic Society, for many people, a diagnosis can help the person, their family, colleagues, friends and employers understand why they experience certain difficulties. It entitles a person to reasonable adjustments by their employer, and appropriate services and benefits.

For others, who have gone through life without an autism diagnosis – feeling that somehow they don't quite fit in – a formal diagnosis may be a relief.

Autism spectrum disorder late diagnosis – Manuel's story

A late diagnosis of autism spectrum disorder, alone or with other mental health disorders, is not rare.

Manuel is a 32-year-old man with a diagnosis of a psychotic disorder. Manuel first came into contact with mental health services aged 21. At that time, he felt he couldn't communicate with others in college and couldn't make friends. He had been studying for Level 2 qualifications in English and maths. He did not recall whether he was prescribed medication at the time and thought he was only given counselling.

Manuel had lived with his mother until she died when he was 30 years old. Manuel then moved to the North West of England where he bought a flat. According to Manuel, he went to the North West because he wanted to 'get away from the suffering' he experienced after the loss of his mother. He described 'supernatural experiences', involving an 'entity' that did not leave him alone. He was admitted to a psychiatric hospital. Manuel did not think that had helped him but said that the 'entity' then left him when he was at the hospital because he had prayed to God, who took it away.

After being discharged from hospital, he moved back to his home area in the South of England where he was now renting a bedsit in a shared house and was going to sell his flat. Manuel was then admitted again to hospital on Section 3 of the Mental Health Act following a relapse. He had gone to a church, and during a service had shouted at the priest and congregation to take away the 'entity'.

Dr S, the consultant now in charge of Manuel's treatment, was struck by the robotic manner of Manuel's speech, his literal interpretation of conversation and inability to express emotion, which had previously been thought to be due to his psychotic illness. Dr S spent time with Manuel, reviewed his history and then spoke with his brothers.

In response to questions about the 'entity', Manuel said this was a spiritual matter that would need to be dealt with by a pastor if it came back. 'It's crazy, I know', he said. He added that the 'entity' could be from space, and he thought it was trying to irritate him. Manuel said he was worried about his brain being damaged, perhaps by devils, but he did not think he was ill. Manuel did not accept that medication had helped him. He remembers having depot injection of antipsychotic medication but said he is now 'finished' with depot as he doesn't think he needs it anymore.

Manuel told Dr S that he had thought about suicide many times. When asked how he spends his time, he said investing in bitcoin and going to a local Christian centre. He tends to stay in his rented room a lot, and he sees each of his brothers weekly.

Manuel's brothers told Dr S said that Manuel had never been able to make friends. He had many obsessions during childhood, varying from collecting toy trains, to comics and then football magazines. He had been 'slow' at school and spent most of his time with his mother. He never really spoke about anything other than his obsessions – currently, it was online investments. His brothers said he could never see the point of a joke. Both brothers were married and told Dr S that their wives regarded Manuel as 'weird'. He would only eat food served to him in a certain way, as his mother had been willing to do. All this behaviour had not been a problem for his mother who had always protected him, and who had said she was glad of his company.

This information helped Dr S build a treatment plan. The clinical team would assess Manuel using an ASD assessment tool, but the working diagnosis was now ASD and psychosis. The priority was establishing a rapport and creating a trusting relationship so they could work with Manuel. They wanted to help him gain insight into his condition, using information specifically designed for people with ASD and working around his inflexibility.

The social worker expressed her concerns to Manuel's brothers about his vulnerability – his online investments, his potential vulnerability with religious groups, and the money he will receive from selling his flat.

Questions to consider

What impact did Manuel's ASD have on the diagnosis he was given by mental health services?

Manuel's difficulty in expressing his symptoms and his isolated lifestyle could seem to be symptoms of psychosis, such as thought disorder and either negative symptoms or evidence of paranoia, such as his preferences about food. His obsessions may be thought to indicate fixations or delusions.

People with ASD do have a high rate of additional disorders such as anxiety, depression, obsessional compulsive disorders and psychosis. Importantly, the diagnosis of ASD may avoid over treatment of an additional diagnosis. For instance, antipsychotic medication given to Manual in the belief that his ideas about food are delusional will have little effect on his beliefs but can produce side effects such as sedation and weight gain.

What impact did Manuel's additional diagnosis have on his family?

Manuel's vulnerability – and potentially unwise decisions – were discussed with his family as a long-term issue, not just related to a relapse of psychosis but also because of his ASD. This hopefully will ensure a more stable future for Manuel.

(Back to **Chapter 14**.)

POST-TRAUMATIC STRESS DISORDER – NATALIE'S STORY

Natalie was 27 years old when she was injured by glass shards whilst waiting at a bus stop. The car that was involved in the incident hit the bus stop where she was waiting. It was driven by a young man who had not yet passed his driving test and who had borrowed his mother's car to give a lift to his three friends. All had been drinking. None of the young men were seriously injured and all ran away from the scene. Natalie was very lucky to escape with just cuts and bruises. She went back to work the week after. She was regarded by her work colleagues as a hero.

She had a panic attack in her friend's car two weeks later. She recovered and thought she was still suffering shock after her injuries. However, two nights later, she had a nightmare, and from then on became increasingly anxious. Colleagues at work commented that she was jumpy and startling at sudden noise such as doors slamming and not concentrating. Her irritability caused difficulties with her boyfriend and he ended the relationship. Natalie could only sleep with help from alcohol, her work performance dropped, and she did not earn a commission. She avoided situations where she would have to travel in cars. She made excuses not to see friends. By this stage, most workmates had forgotten about her injury and thought she was unhappy about the loss of her relationship.

Natalie's panic attacks became more severe. She was dismissed from her job. This precipitated an overdose, and she was taken to A&E where she was assessed by a liaison psychiatrist. The assessment revealed many features of PTSD, and Natalie explained that she and her mother had been subjected to domestic abuse during her childhood. Her father had a gambling habit and would take out his anger at losses on Natalie's mother, especially when he had been drinking. Natalie and her mother had spent time in a women's refuge before her father was prosecuted. Natalie had thought she had overcome this.

Questions to consider

Is Natalie suffering PTSD?

Natalie has symptoms: anxiety, flashbacks, mood changes, irritability, and suicidal actions. She is avoiding situations and people. She may have become dependent on alcohol. This all indicates PTSD.

What can be done to help Natalie?

Natalie was offered CBT which she agreed to do. She had a short course of antidepressants, which helped her sleep. She joined Alcoholics

Anonymous (AA). Encouraged by her therapist, she explained to friends about her history.

Are there any factors that predisposed Natalie to suffer from PTSD?

Domestic abuse, a mental disorder in the family; gambling, alcohol abuse, possible low self-esteem may have all contributed. Natalie's own harmful use of alcohol has probably lowered her mood as has social isolation. She said to the therapist that the one possible thing to come out of this was that she had examined her own relationship history and found she was developing a pattern with choosing, or being chosen, by potentially abusive men.

(Back to **Chapter 15**.)

DEMENTIA – GRACE'S STORY

Grace was 62 years old when her husband took her to her GP, saying she'd become more anxious lately. Grace had been regarded as 'highly strung' and 'nervy' by her family for years. For instance, before a family event – even something pleasant such as a birthday party – she would take a Valium tablet. She had devoted her life to her husband and family and was a loving mother. She enjoyed looking after her grandchildren, Tom aged six and George aged eight, and was pleased to be of help. Her daughter was now a single parent following her divorce. She was a nurse, working antisocial hours, including weekends.

The GP did blood tests to investigate whether Grace's thyroid gland was overactive (a common cause of anxiety), but the results were normal. The anxiety was regarded by the GP as 'just Grace', and no additional medication or treatment was suggested.

Her daughter then noticed that Grace was more forgetful over the next few months. Since Grace's husband relied on her, birthdays were missed, and Christmas was more chaotic than usual as Grace had forgotten several items for lunch.

She had never learned to drive as she was too anxious, so she travelled by bus. Her family were contacted by a shopkeeper when Grace had left her purse in the shop. When Grace took the wrong bus on another day and was hysterical at getting lost, her daughter took her back to the GP.

Investigations and referral by the GP to a psychiatrist for older adults showed Grace had early-onset dementia, probably Alzheimer's disease. There was a family history in that her own mother had become 'very forgetful' around the same age.

Grace was prescribed rivastigmine, but her decline continued. For a time, her anxiety peaked when she was disorientated or when she thought her husband was late home. When she lost an item, which she thought had been stolen, she became uncharacteristically verbally abusive. She seemed to be living in the 1970s, at the time when her own children had been young, and her husband was at work. She began to confuse the generations, believing her grandchildren were her children and her daughter was her long-dead sister.

Attendance at a day care centre is currently giving Grace some respite, though Grace's daughter acknowledges that her mother does not seem to benefit from it. Her closest friends were a neighbour and sister, both dead for some years. Grace's daughter is sad for her own sons who have 'lost' their grandmother.

Questions to consider

Whilst Grace had been caring for her grandchildren, how might symptoms of dementia be noted?

Grace may have become increasingly anxious, so much more of a worrier. Possibly over-worried about small things such as whether they are coping at school, have eaten, or are going to bed on time. She may even have become so worried about their health that she took them on unnecessary trips to the doctors, or asked their school teachers.

As symptoms progress, she would have become more forgetful. Her grandchildren's meals, washing, homework may have suffered. She may have become muddled about whether she has done the shopping. Perhaps even muddled about the days. Coping with her finances may have become difficult.

What could be the possible effect on the grandchildren if Grace became their main carer?

The effect on Grace's developing dementia on her grandchildren could be considerable. Their main adult figure starts to behave oddly (children can be over tolerant, and they may have never even considered telling someone). Both would be at risk of unintentional neglect due to a possible chaotic lifestyle, (lose weight and look neglected). Not understanding what is happening to their gran, and feeling anxious themselves, they could be psychologically damaged; this could affect their education and their behaviour at school. They may even have reversed roles; become her carers and so have inappropriate responsibilities. They may try to hide the chaos, so friendships suffer as gran becomes an embarrassment.

(Back to **Chapter 16**.)

ADOPTION – CRAIG'S STORY

Craig was adopted by Dr and Mrs D at the age of four with his younger sister Hannah who was two. Dr D was a medical academic. Craig did well at school but at home would not go to bed, would not eat meals with the family at a table, and stole any toys given to his sister. Other stealing from home was blatant.

Dr and Mrs D paid for Craig to attend a private prep school as they felt Craig was bored and under-stimulated at his primary school and that small classes would be helpful. Although Craig progressed at school, he was bullying towards his sister Hannah and her friends. As he did not seem to have made friends at school, Dr and Mrs D thought this bullying was jealousy and loneliness – so they bought him a pet rabbit. This had to be given away when Craig held it by the neck – his explanation was that he was trying to see how long it was. His parents consoled themselves that Craig did seem to enjoy the academic part of school life and they paid for private secondary schooling.

At around age 16, Craig suffered a first depressive episode, which his parents thought interfered with his exam results. The school asked him to leave, so Craig attended a local college to study for A levels. At this time, his verbal aggression at home and lack of self-care (poor personal care and untidiness of his room) worsened, causing conflict between Dr and Mrs D. Dr D thought Craig was using drugs and should live away from home and support himself if he was 'going down this line'. Mrs D, as always, said Craig had good points and was going through a phase. They funded some private psychology for him, which seemed to help.

By the time Craig was 19 and referred to NHS adult services, he'd had one episode diagnosed as depression and one as mania. He occasionally used ecstasy, which the assessing psychiatrist thought was insufficient to cause such mood swings. Craig was monitored in an outpatient clinic. This was not easy as he did not want to attend, but his mother persuaded him. After another depressive episode, he agreed to take antidepressants and the mood stabiliser lithium. He resumed college, where he had a relationship with another student who was a regular drug user. For Hannah, this was the final straw, and she told her parents that she was going to live with a school friend.

Craig's subsequent experimentation with cocaine resulted in a serious manic relapse. He was violent to his parents. When a Mental Health Act assessment was arranged, he jumped out of a first-floor window to escape the police who were assisting mental health services. After a spell as an inpatient, Craig was stabilised on medication, but there was much friction at home and Dr D agreed to fund a rented flat for Craig to live independently.

Mrs D asked to meet with Craig's psychiatrist alone; Craig agreed. Mrs D told the psychiatrist she felt so guilty that she was unable to help Craig and was neglecting Hannah. They were older parents at the time of the adoption, and Mrs D felt very lucky to have been accepted as an adoptive parent. She thought the couple's obvious advantages – wealth, professional occupations – had played a part. She had always been the keener parent regarding the adoption. She told the psychiatrist that she and her husband had not been made aware of Craig and Hannah's parentage at the time of the adoption. Their biological mother had bipolar affective disorder and their father had drug problems. Craig and Hannah had been severely neglected.

Dr D resented having to fund what he saw as a 'louche lifestyle' for Craig. He had always been an irritable man. Early retirement brought on by ill-health had not helped his anger and he had been physically abusive to Mrs D. Mrs D told the psychiatrist her loyalties were torn between her daughter, her sick husband and Craig, whom she had protected all his life. The psychiatrist was told by social services colleagues that this lack of information about biological parentage was not unusual in the 1970s and 1980s. The intention was to give children 'a clean start'.

Over the following two years, Craig's mental state was variable. He frequently spoke of suicide to his mother, who continued to persuade Dr D to fund the flat, until he became unwell and died after a short time in a hospice. Craig did not visit him or attend the funeral. This was the final straw for Mrs D. After much anguish and deliberation, she sold the family home and moved to a flat on the south coast. She gave Craig and Hannah an equal sum of money from the house sale.

Hannah applied for university in the same coastal town. The relationship between her and Mrs D became warmer. Craig spent his money and, having committed a number of acquisitive crimes related to drug use, was imprisoned. He has spent time in the prison hospital due to suicide attempts.

Mrs D made a circle of friends and enjoyed activities she felt Dr D would have disapproved of – rescuing stray dogs and working in charity shops. She says that most of the time she feels happy, but she worries each day about Craig and wishes the circumstances had been different.

Questions to consider

What were the early indications that Craig had a conduct disorder?

Craig showed oppositional behaviour from a young age; stealing from such a young age is unusual. There was aggressive behaviour to other children, evidenced by bullying at school and of his sister. He also showed a harmful attitude to animals.

What are mental disorders did Craig present?

Craig showed symptoms of depression, and later, mania; this is typical of bipolar affective disorder. He had also suffered a drug-induced psychosis. His lack of remorse, difficulty with relationships, impulsive and risky actions, plus the early conduct disorder, indicate sociopathic personality disorder. He demonstrates ongoing drug use with criminal activities to fund his habit so probable drug dependence.

What was Dr and Mrs D's parenting style?

Their wish to present as competent parents may have prevented them from seeking appropriate help sooner for themselves and for Craig. Dr D's wishes took priority over Mrs D's. When Dr D was physically abusive to Mrs D, she did not seek help.

Mrs D reflected that compared to other parents, she and Dr D might have tried harder than those with biological children. She found the 'tough love' advice very difficult, and she said she had wished to rescue Craig and Hannah. She blamed herself for feeling torn loyalties for many years, to the disadvantage of Hannah.

(Back to **Chapter 18.**)

DANGEROUS YOUNG PEOPLE – KEITH'S STORY

Keith was 19 years old when he had a psychiatric assessment in a Young Offender Institution. He was transferred to a psychiatric forensic unit with a provisional diagnosis of psychosis. His urine drug screen showed positive for cannabis on transfer.

Keith had been arrested and charged with attacking a stranger at a railway station. The attack was unprovoked. Keith would only say that the man was looking strangely at him. The police investigation showed he had a sustained interest in the Illuminati with frequent social media postings, indicating he considered himself a leader. He told the assessing psychiatrists that he'd met a group of Illuminati via social media. He showed a large tattoo on his leg that he said was only allowed by commanders in his group.

He reported sexual abuse by his mother and was subsequently taken into care. His school reports showed he had high academic promise, particularly with maths and science. The school were aware of the sexual abuse and Keith received counselling at school in addition to psychological treatment with CAMHS from the ages of 14 to 16. He had stopped attending school at 17

In the forensic unit Keith's psychotic beliefs in the Illuminati changed with medication. He explained that it was just an interest like other people liked war games. He found it difficult to explain his attack on the stranger and he showed little remorse. His relationship with staff and patients was varied. He rarely made contact with other patients, whom he regarded as ignorant, preferring to speak with staff, particularly female staff. He would frequently talk about being a victim. He was attacked by a fellow patient who overheard a derogatory comment Keith had made to staff about them.

A diagnosis of drug-induced psychotic disorder was made, and an additional diagnosis of antisocial personality disorder was discussed. The views of the nursing team were divided about the psychotic diagnosis. He was considered to portray himself too readily as a victim, and his use of psychodynamic terms such as transference and projection alienated him from some staff and patients.

Keith developed a sexual relationship with a nursing assistant which required her to be moved to another unit. She herself was considered vulnerable as she had suffered a bereavement. Keith had initially provided support and encouraged her to view her 'lowly' role as beneath her. She had managed to keep the relationship secret and had not discussed any concerns in the staff support group.

Questions to consider

What does the case show about Keith's relationships with others?

Keith's sexual abuse as a child has affected his life in many ways. He failed to fulfil his academic potential. He appears unable to form relationships with people of his own age and had a relationship with a vulnerable staff member which must have involved some coercion on his part.

What risks does Keith present?

Keith did present with psychotic beliefs that he acted upon. He shows no remorse for the attack, which was unprovoked and on a stranger. His justification that his interest is similar to online war games minimises the consequence of his actions.

His narcissistic beliefs of superiority over other patients are not borne out by facts but do make him vulnerable to others. His beliefs of superiority centred on the Illuminati and could also be a defence against the trauma he suffered and his low self-esteem. If challenged on the reality of his beliefs, he could be a risk to others. Keith may be able to coerce vulnerable people, as evidenced by his relationship with the staff member. If he retains his psychotic beliefs, he could coerce others to act.

Was Keith himself radicalised?

This remains unclear, though he does have many of the vulnerability factors for radicalisation: distanced from family, questioning his place in society, traumatised, mistreated by other people or by society, difficulties in interacting socially and lacking empathy and not understanding the consequences of his actions.

Keith refuses to discuss his contacts or social media use. The clinical team had referred his case to PREVENT; the government's counter-terrorism unit. There is no evidence of the Illuminati operating as a known terrorism organisation, as described by Keith.

What can the clinical team do to reduce Keith's risk?

The clinical team asked for a second opinion on Keith's presentation. This opinion was that Keith has a psychotic disorder, as he is rationalising his beliefs rather than admitting they are false. An additional diagnosis of antisocial personality disorder was made. Keith was considered a serious risk to others both physically and psychologically. Advice on managing his relationship with staff was given. He is to be transferred to a forensic unit specialising in treating patients with personality disorders.

(Back to **Chapter 22**.)

Index

[References are to paragraph numbers except for case studies which are indicated by their page numbers in **bold**]

www.ingramcontent.com/pod-product-compliance
Ingram Content Group UK Ltd.
Pitfield, Milton Keynes, MK11 3LW, UK
UKHW021036150926
475561UK00003B/136

9 781526 521897